MW00903546

Storyboard Notebook

www.visualstoryartist.com

VISUAL STORY ARTIST

This book belongs to:

____

____

____

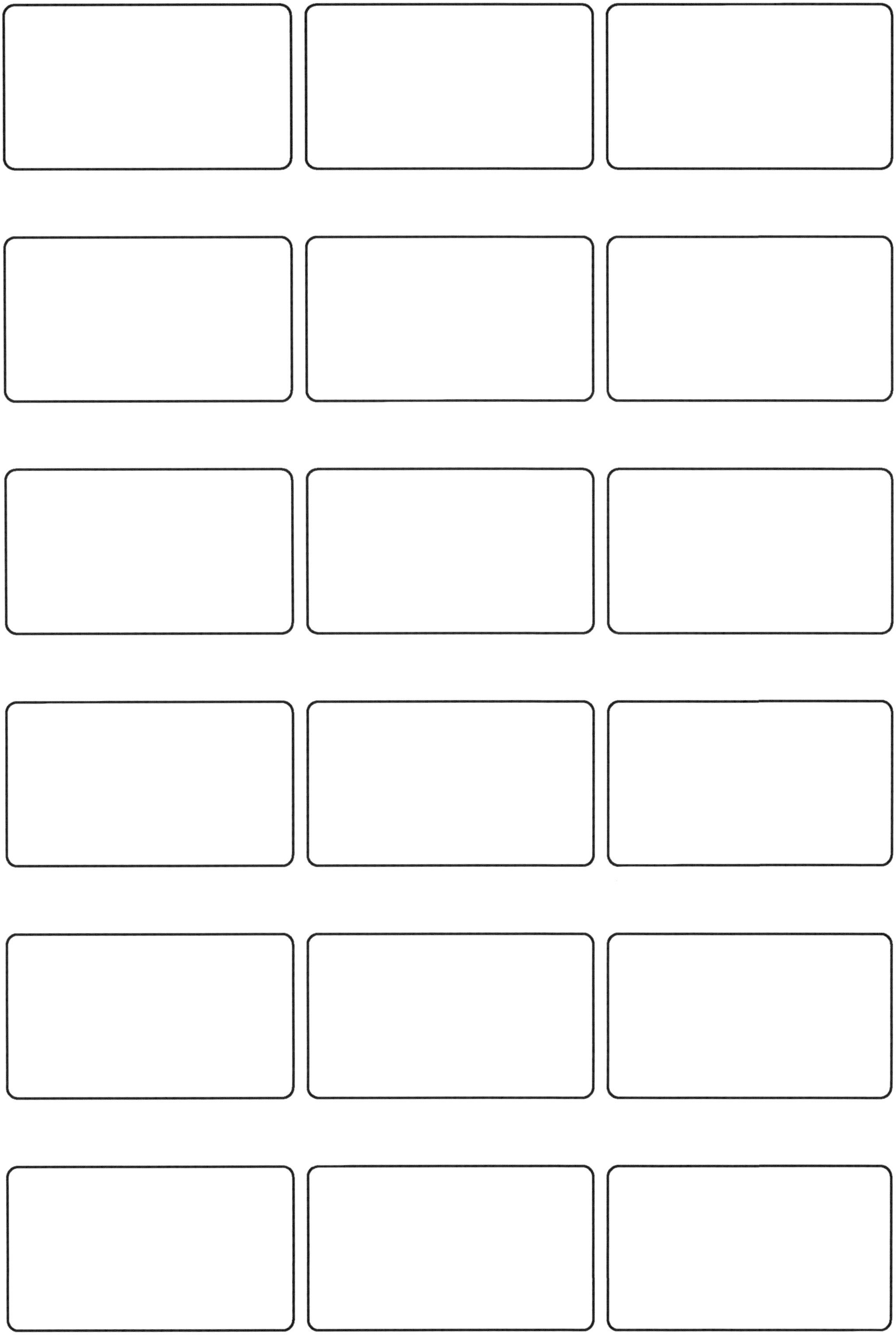

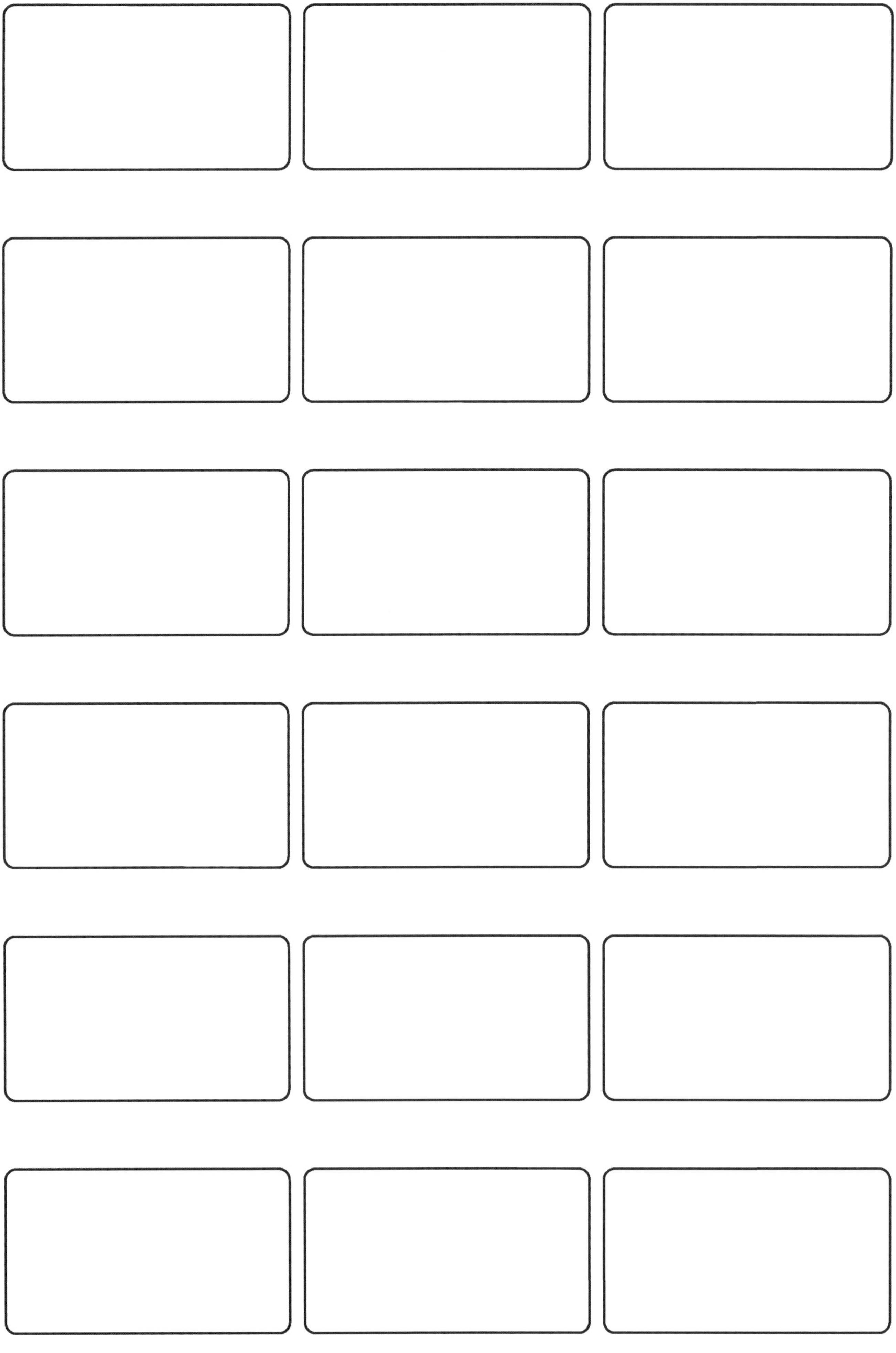

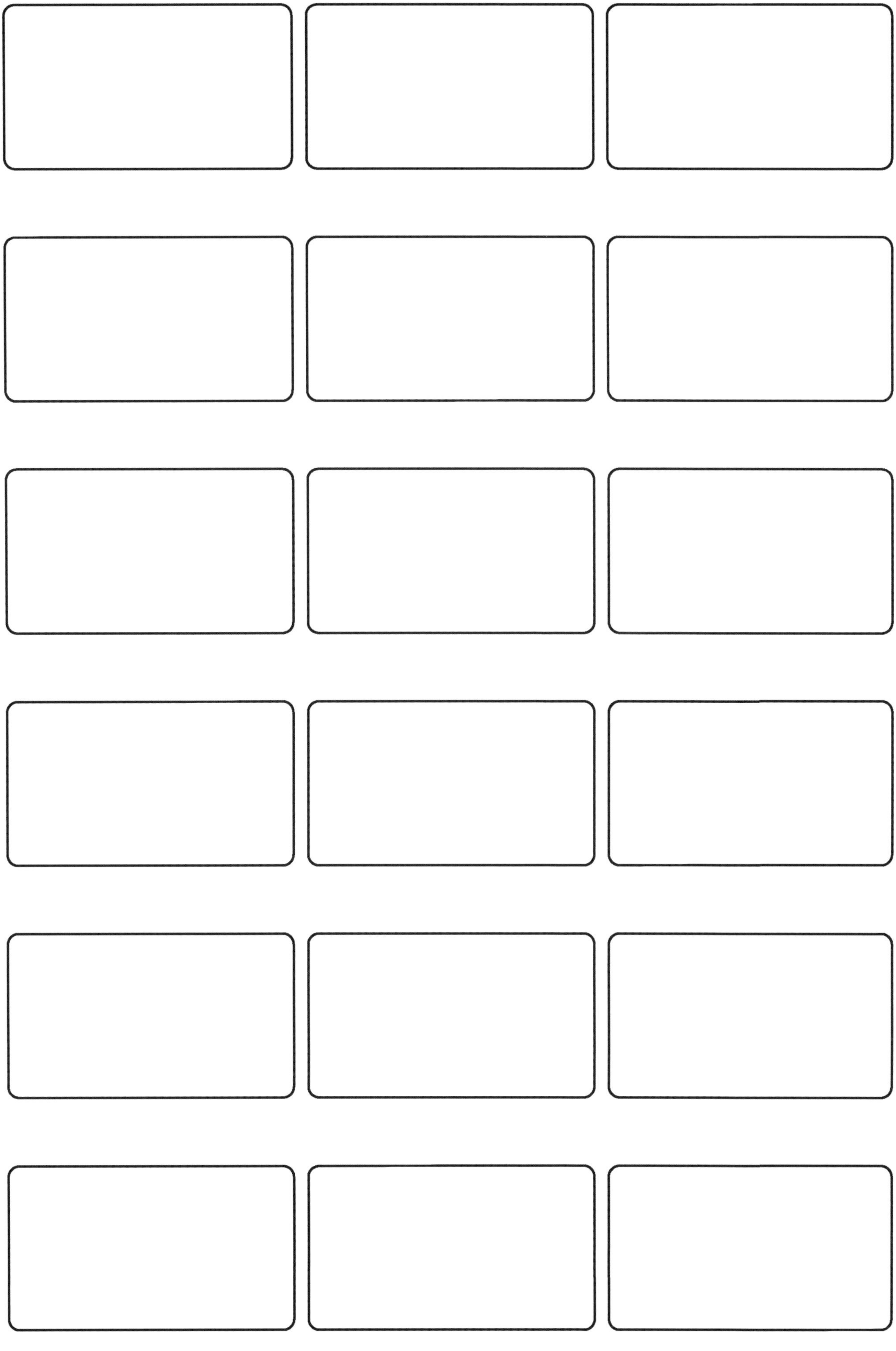

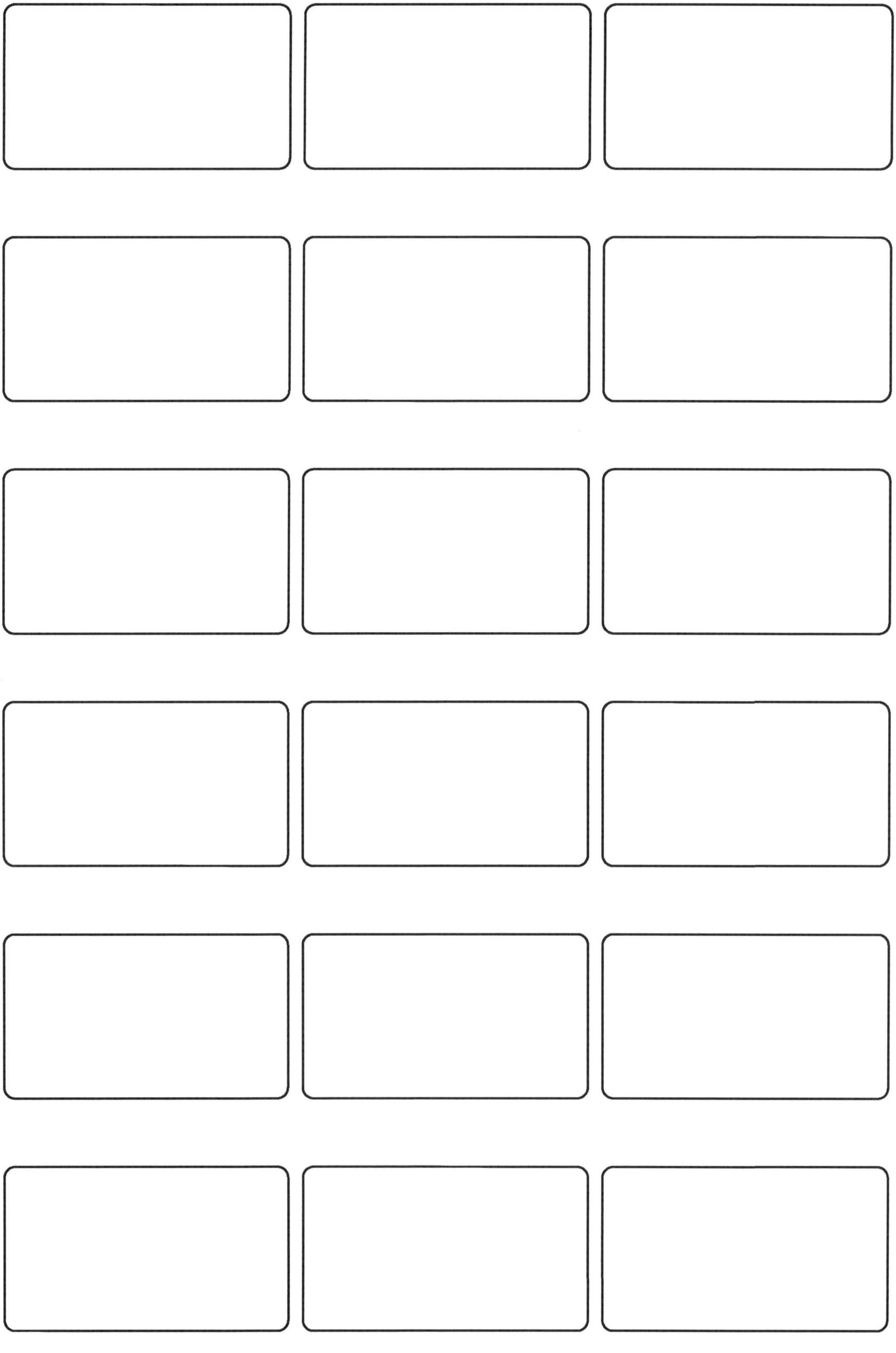

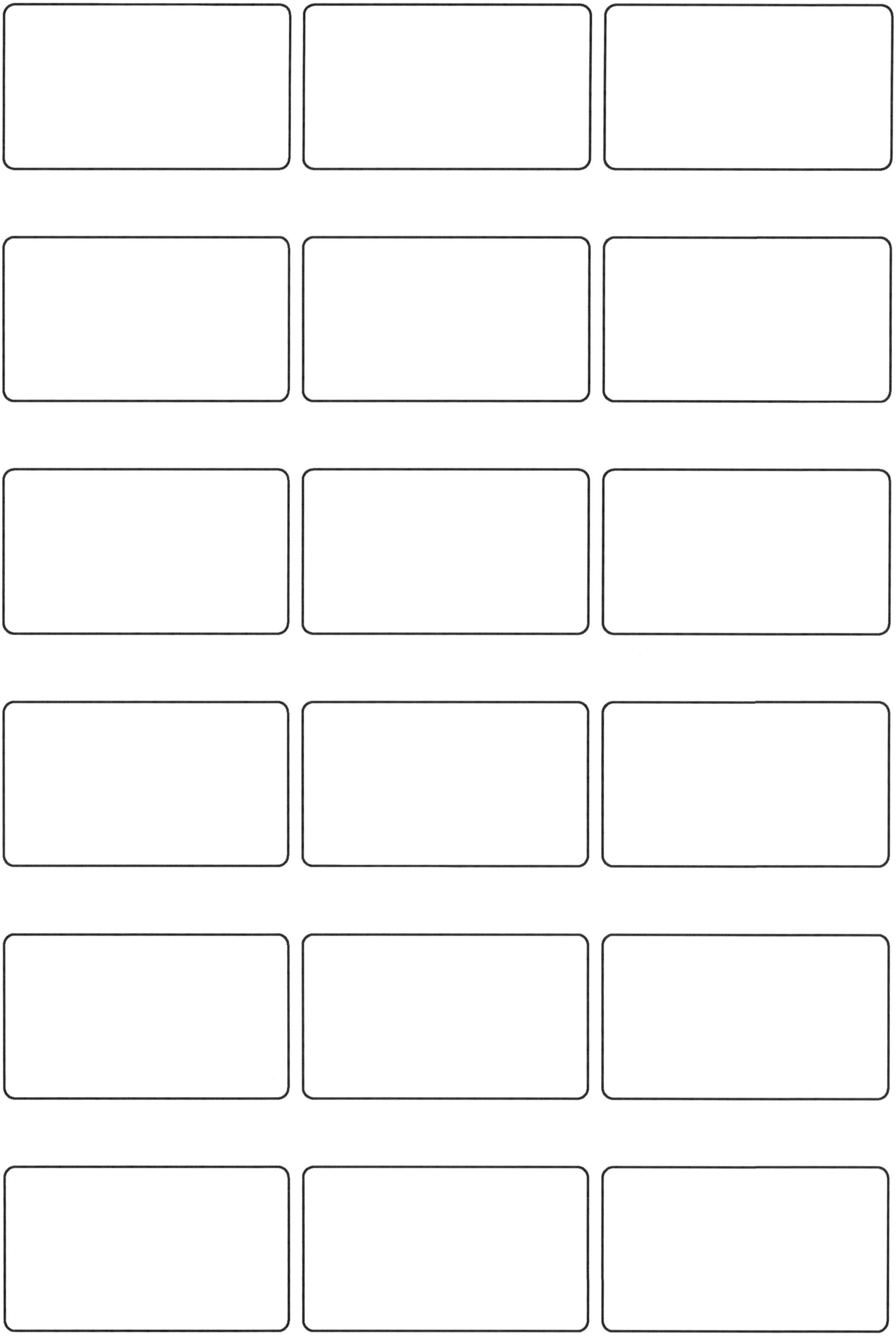

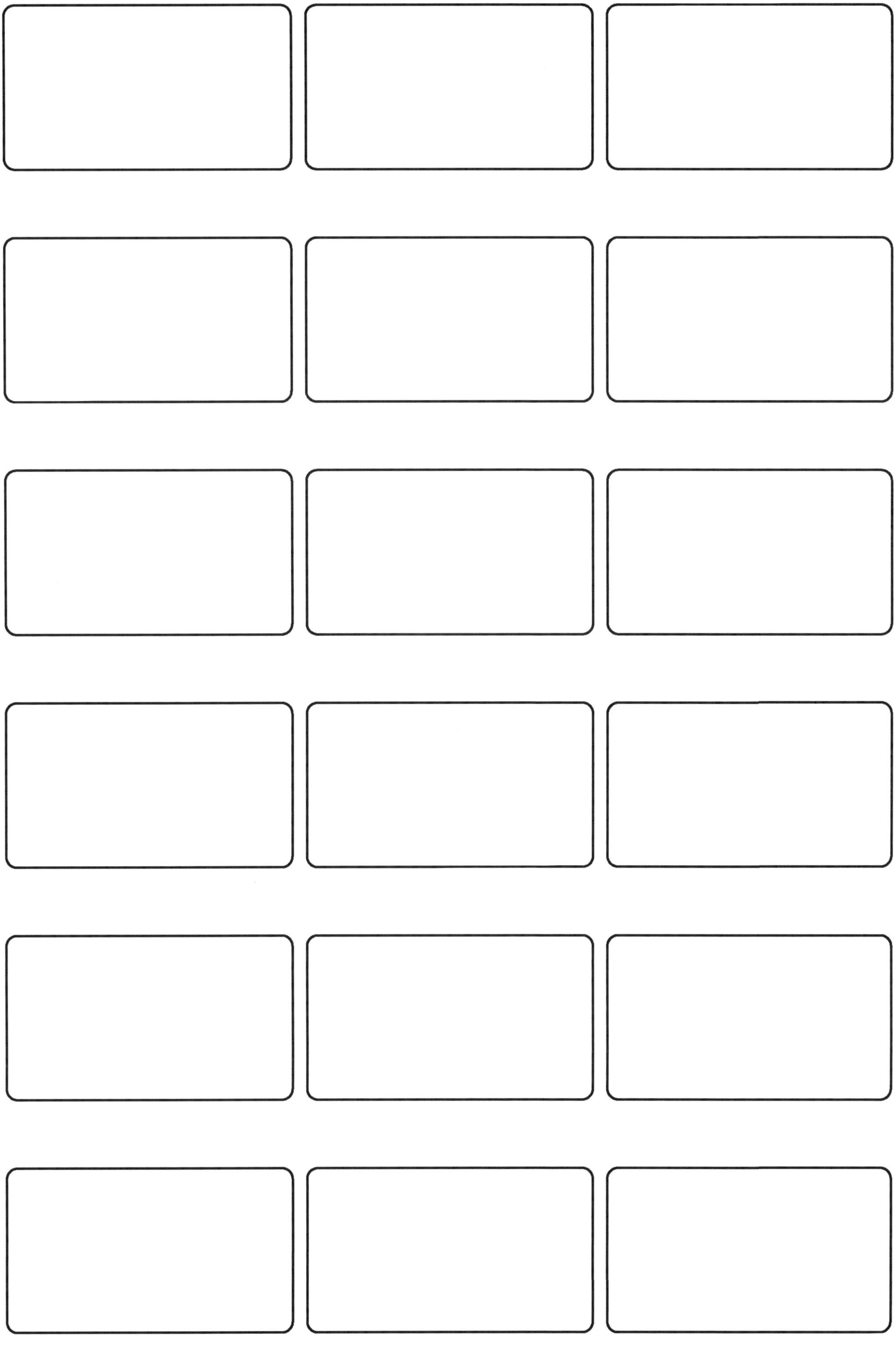

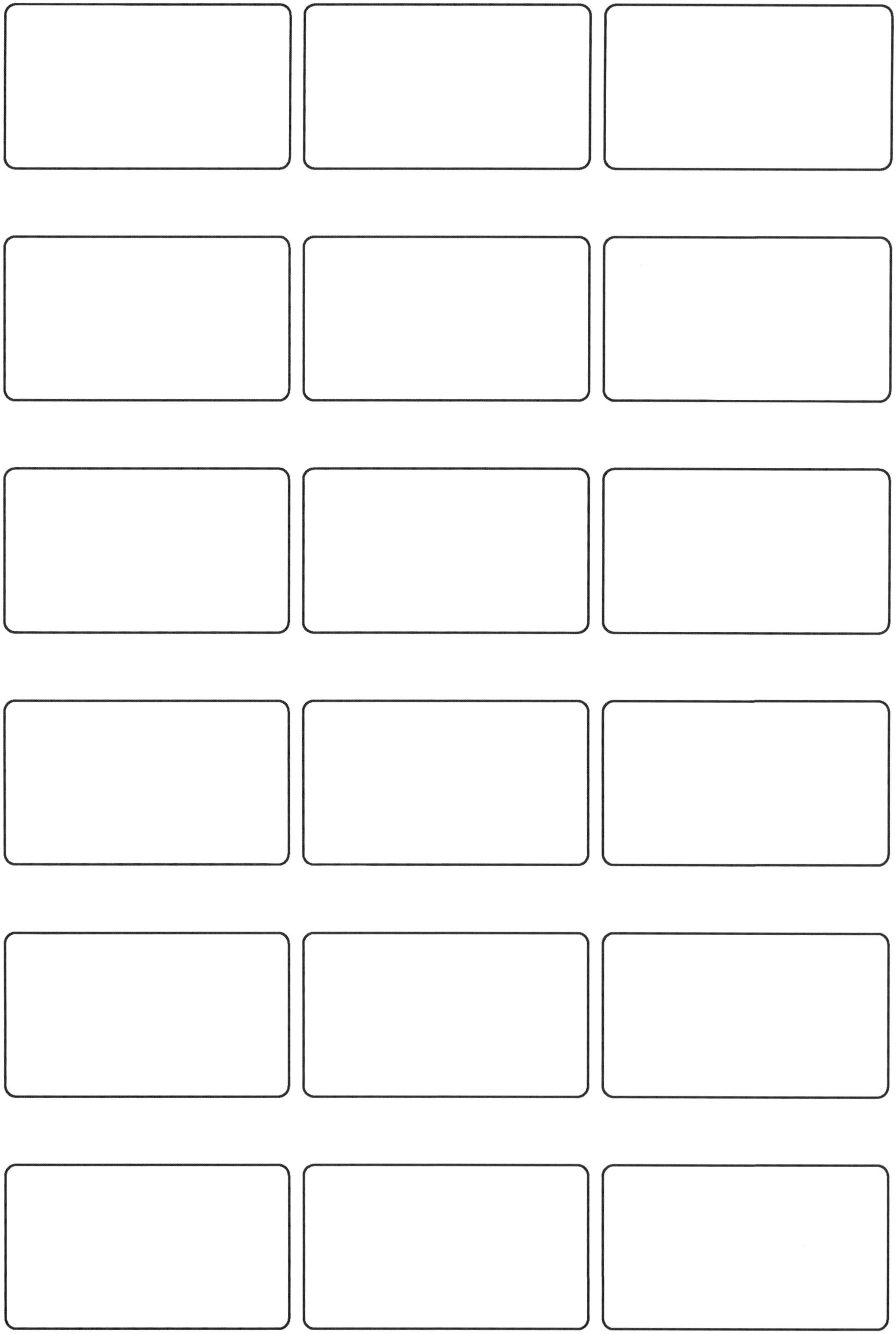

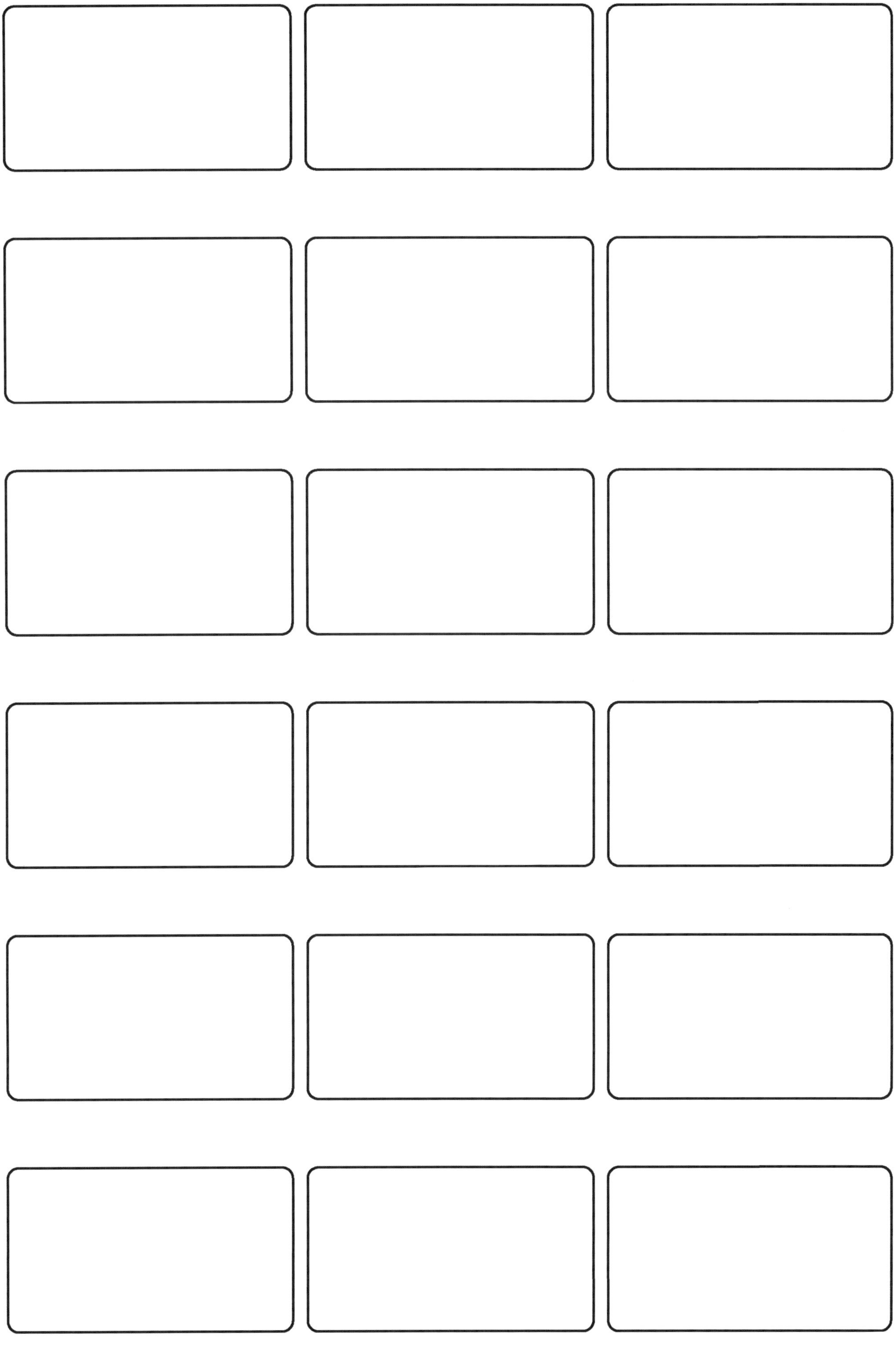

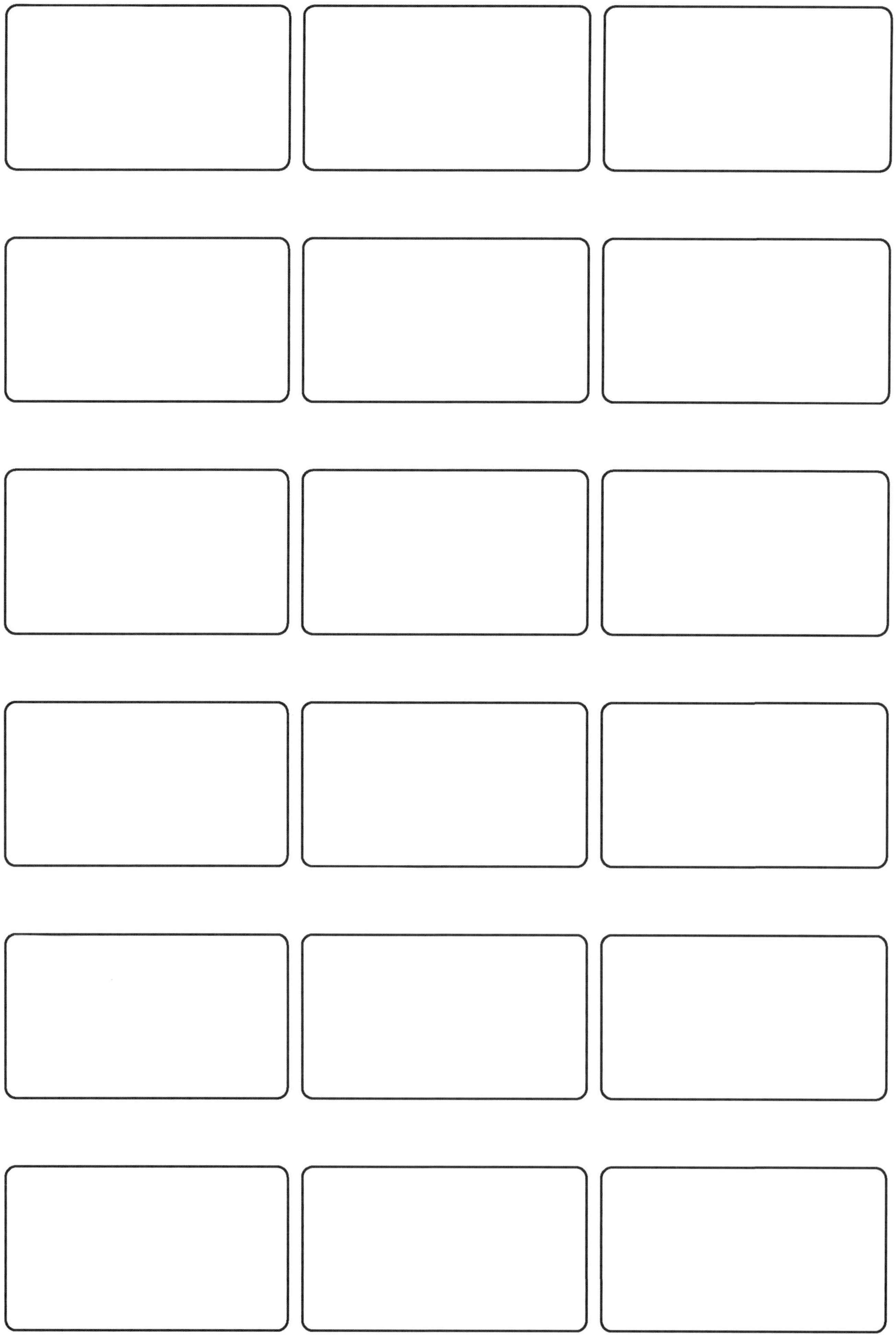

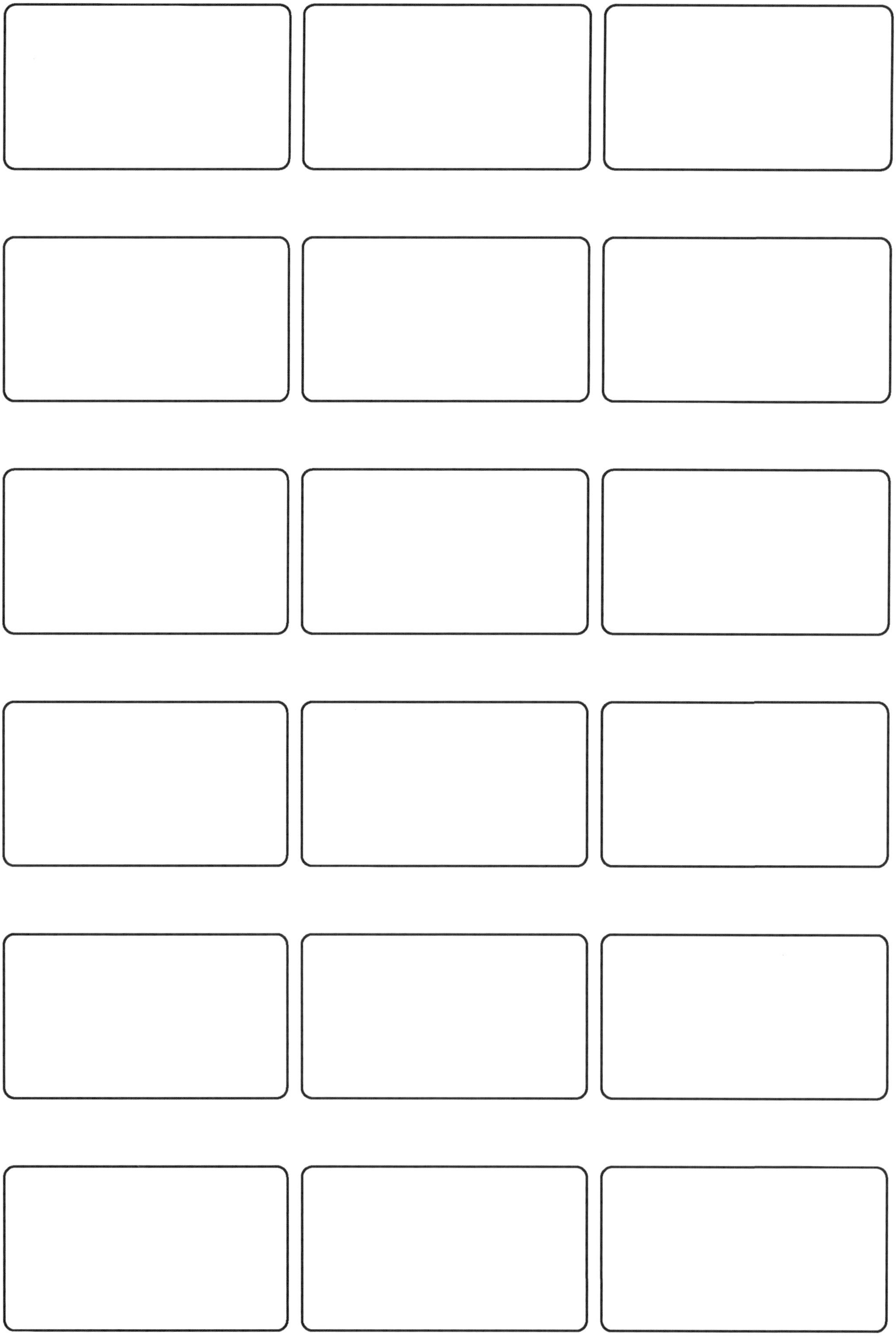

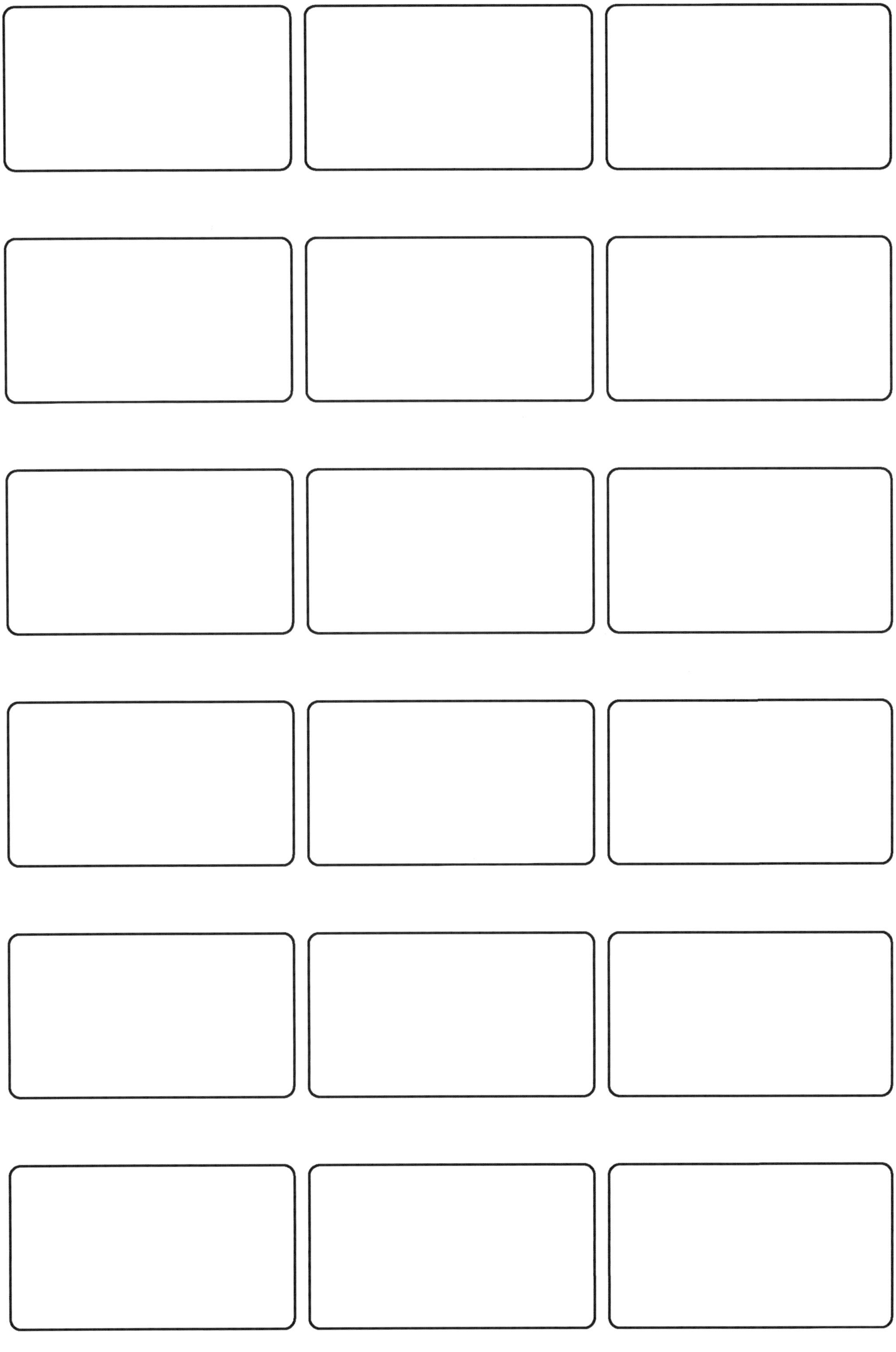

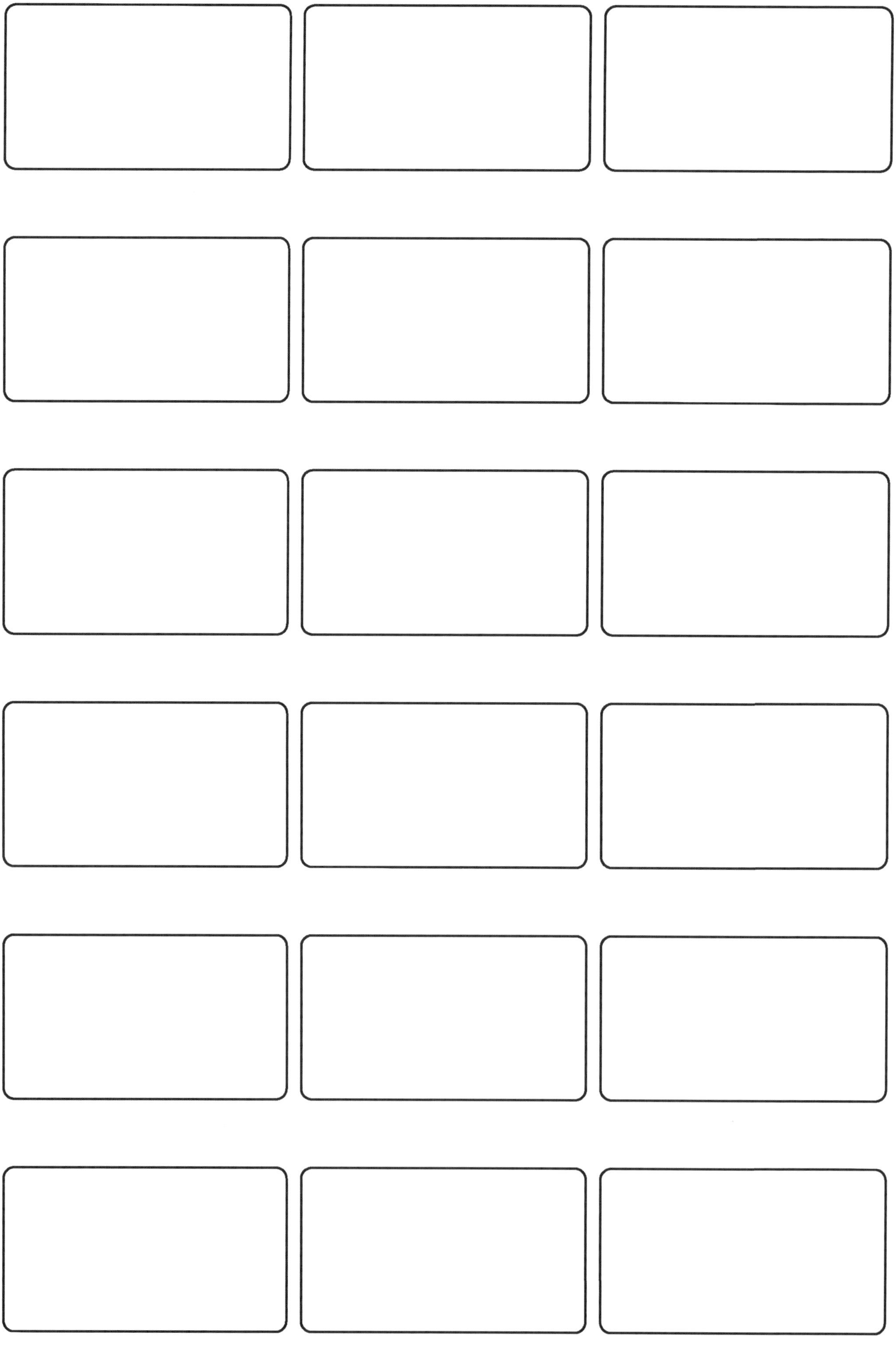

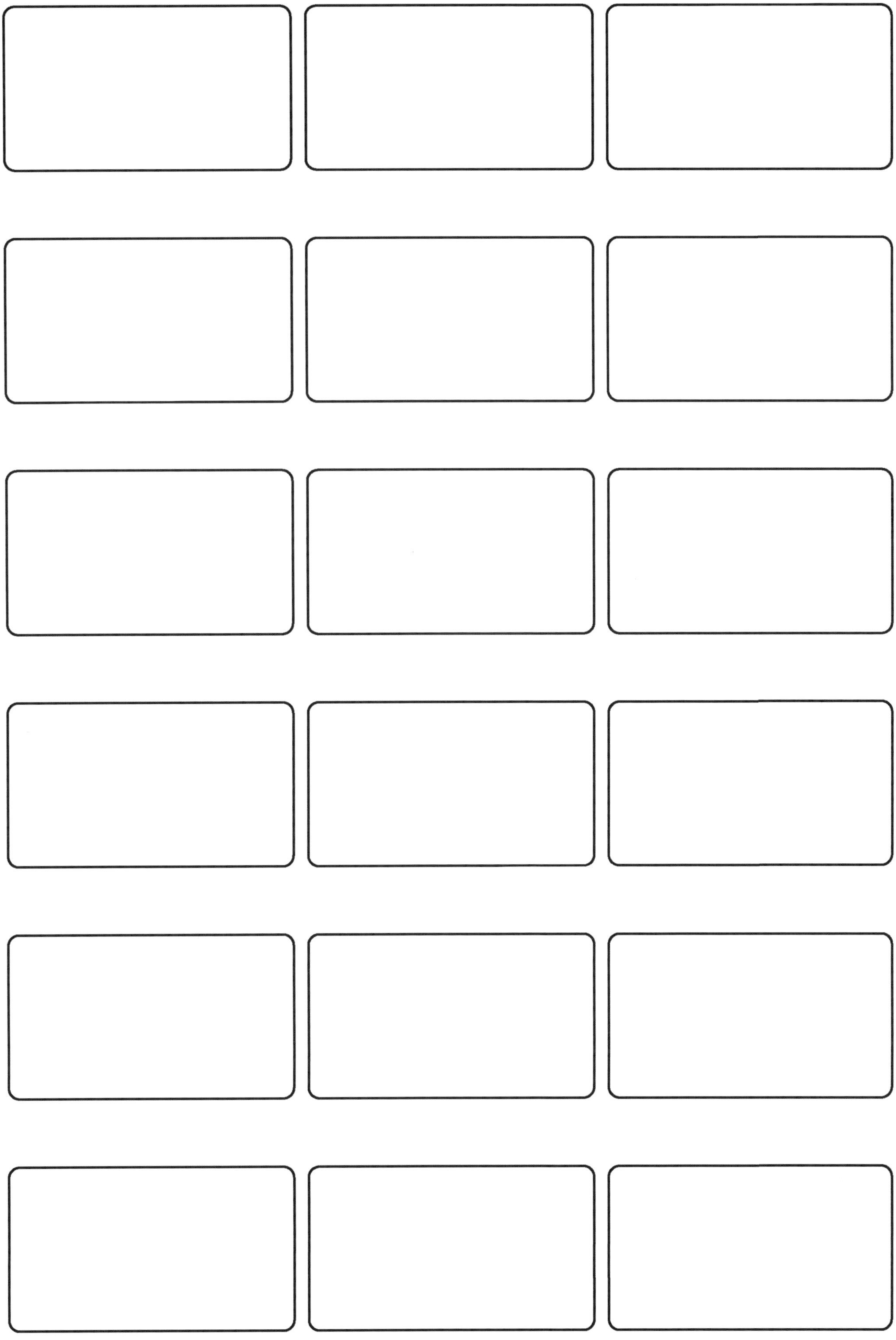

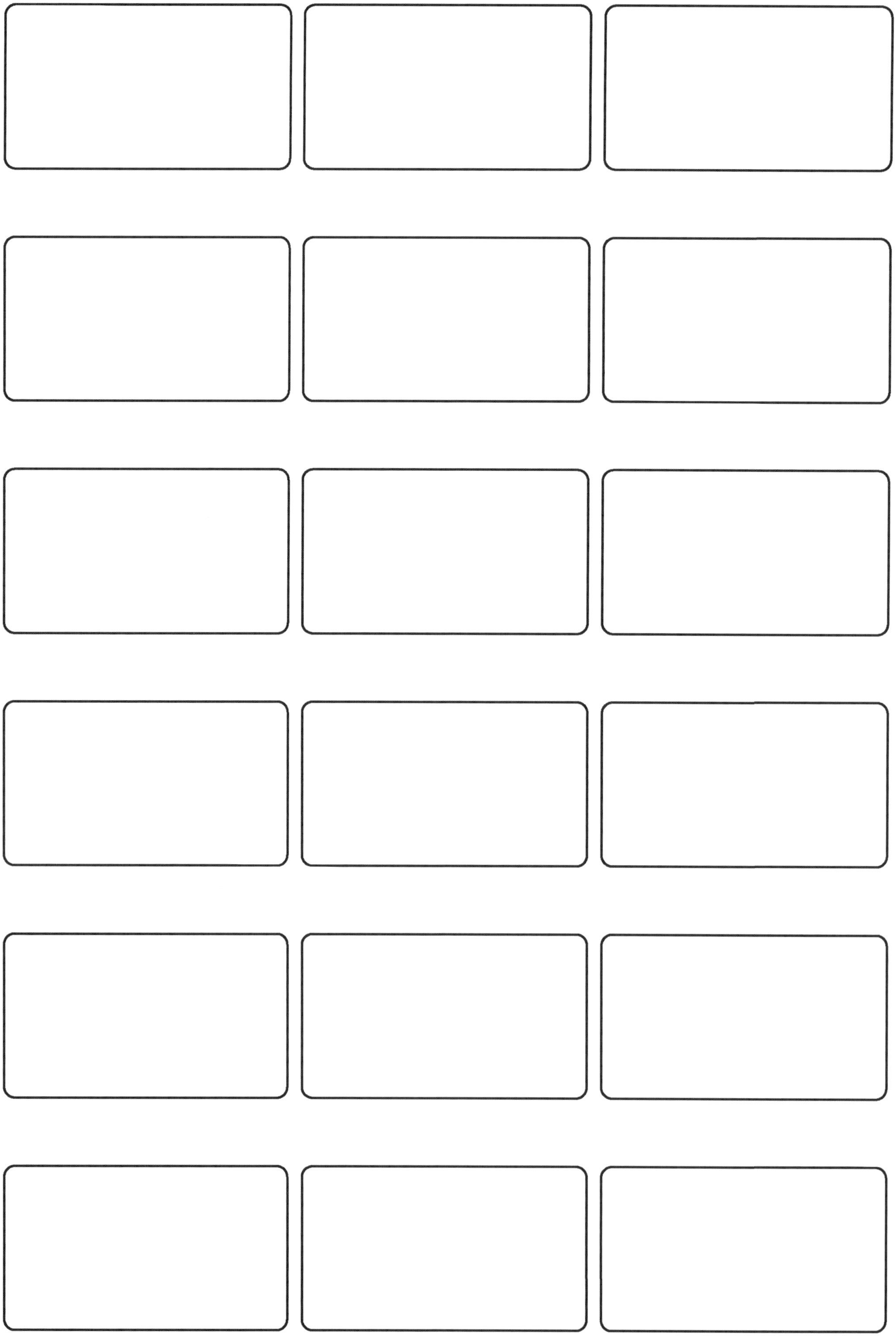

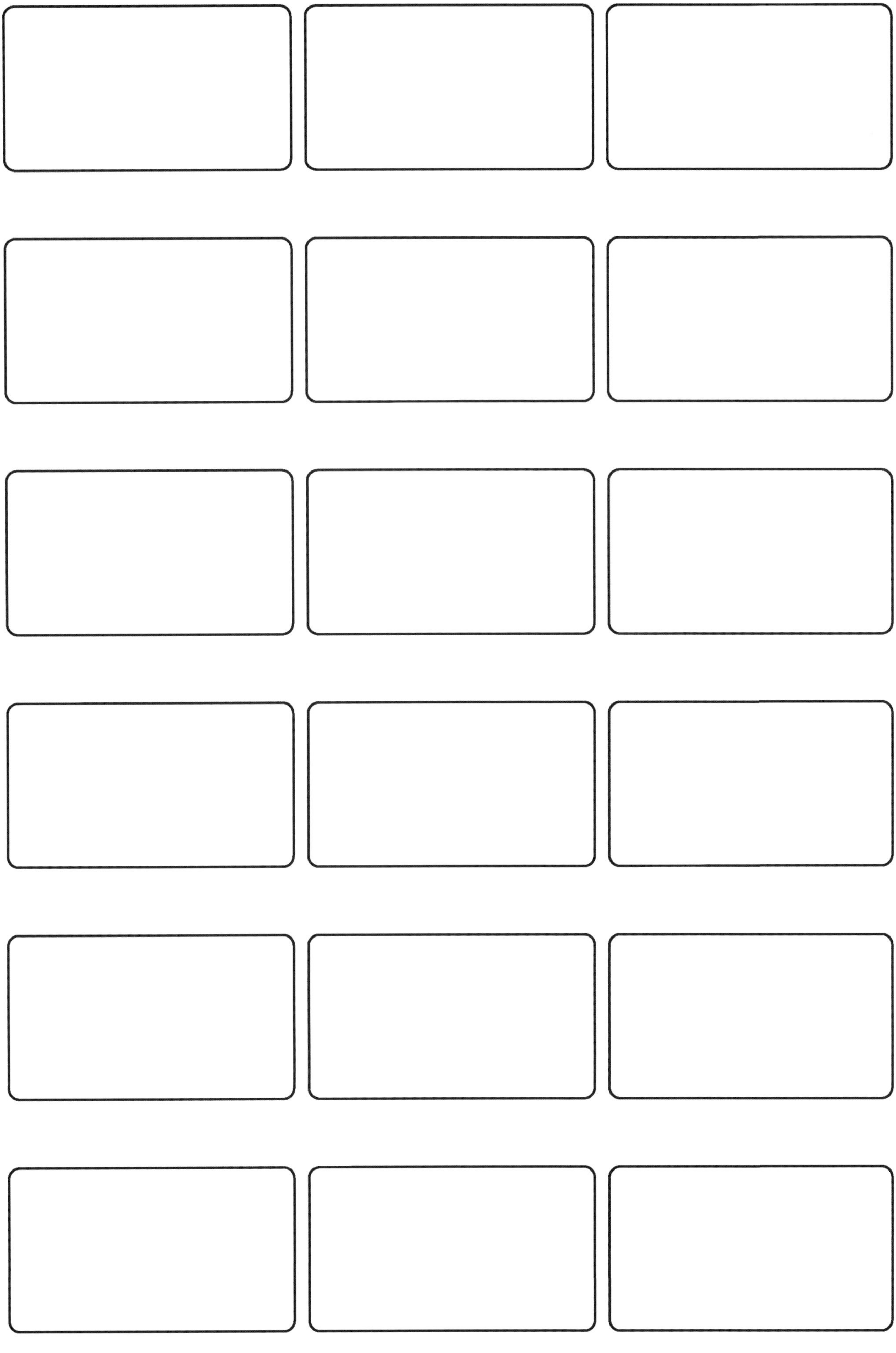

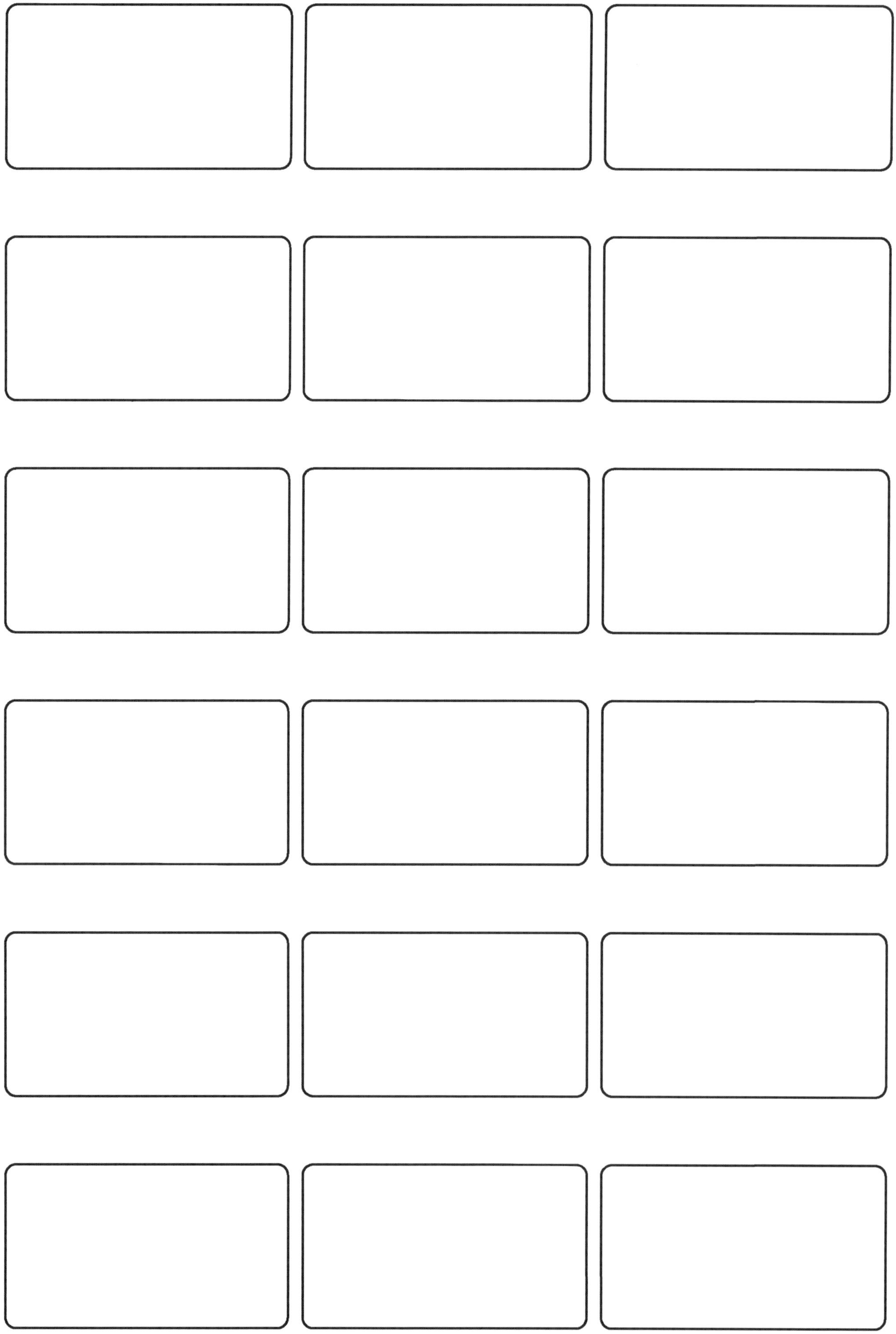

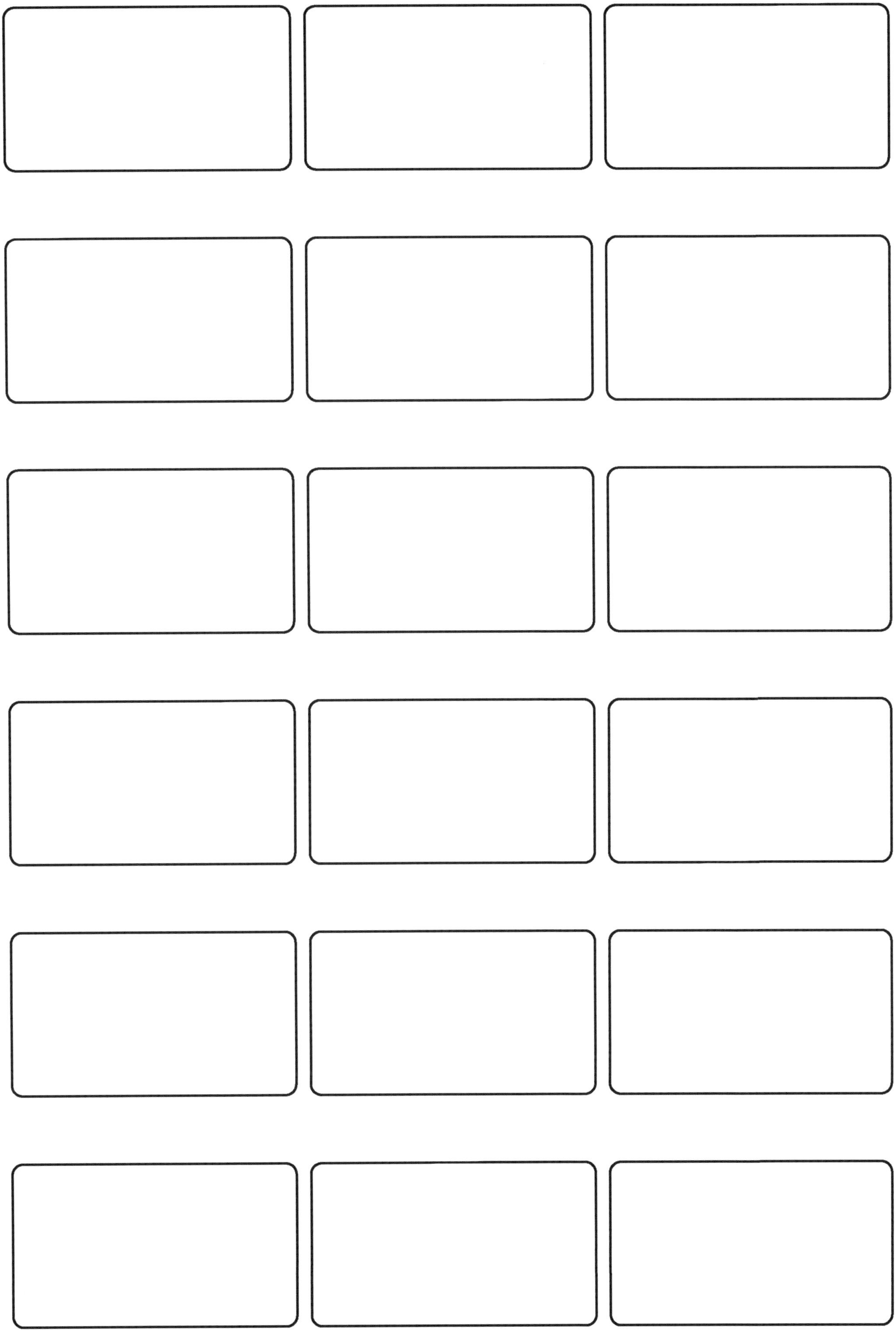

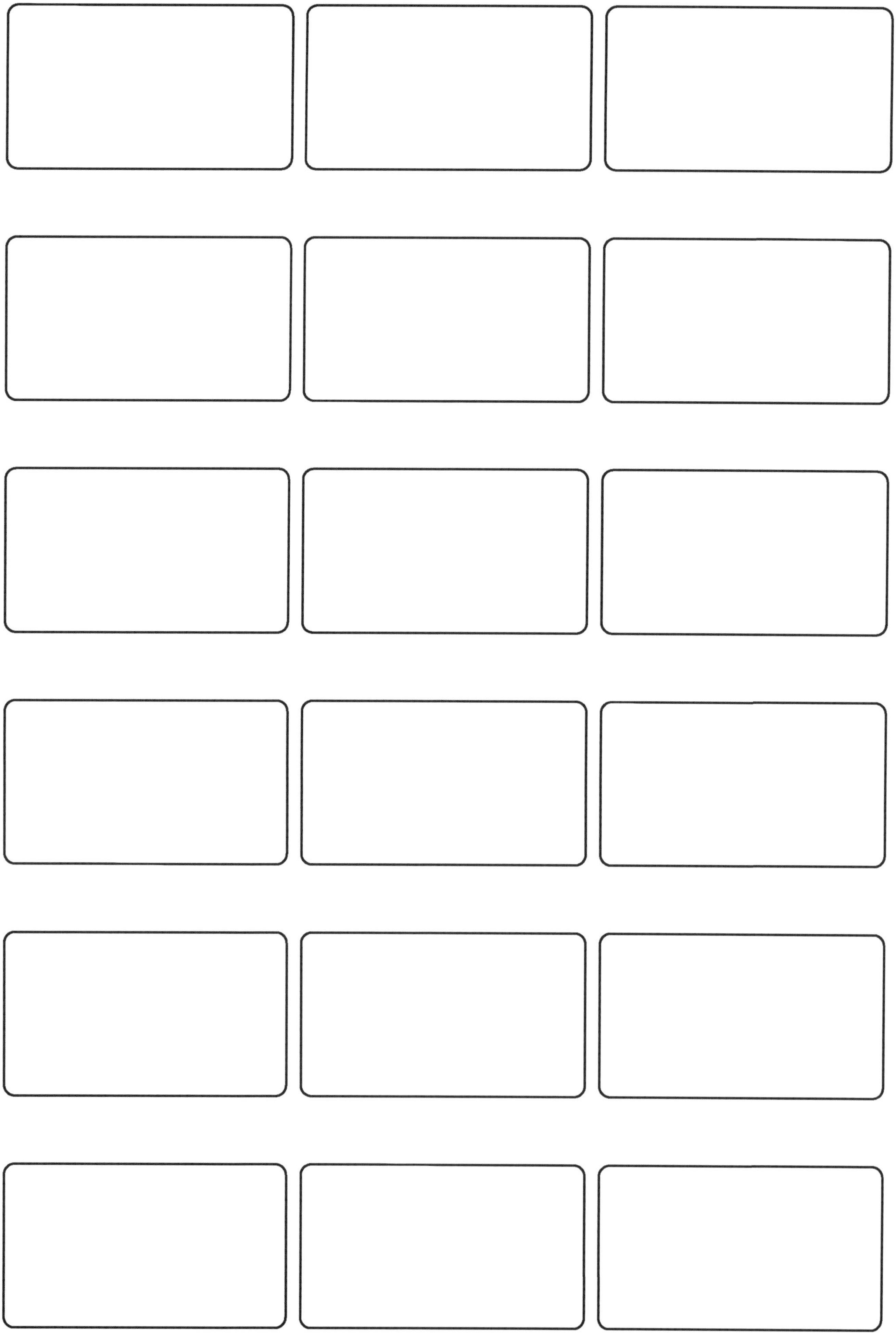

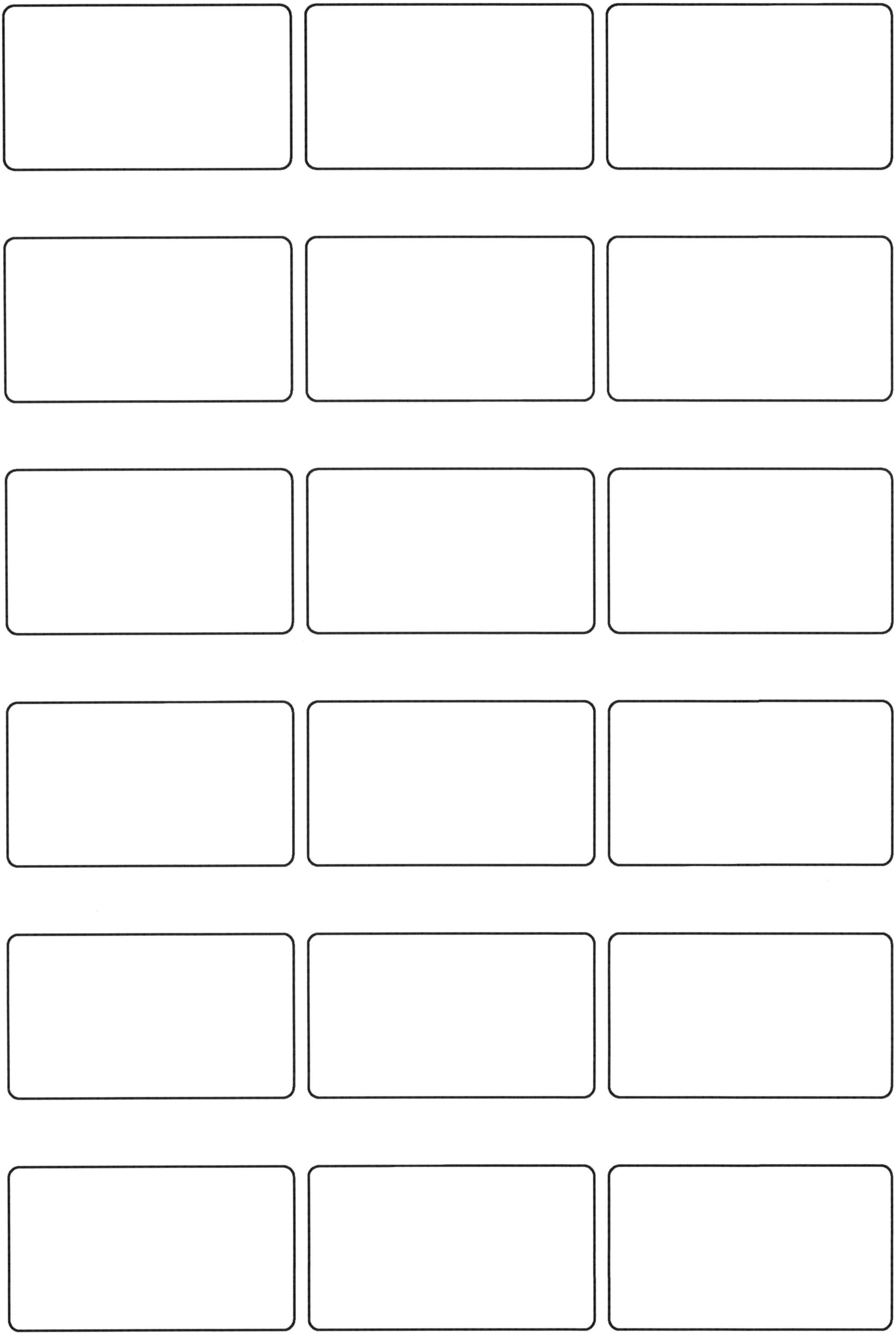

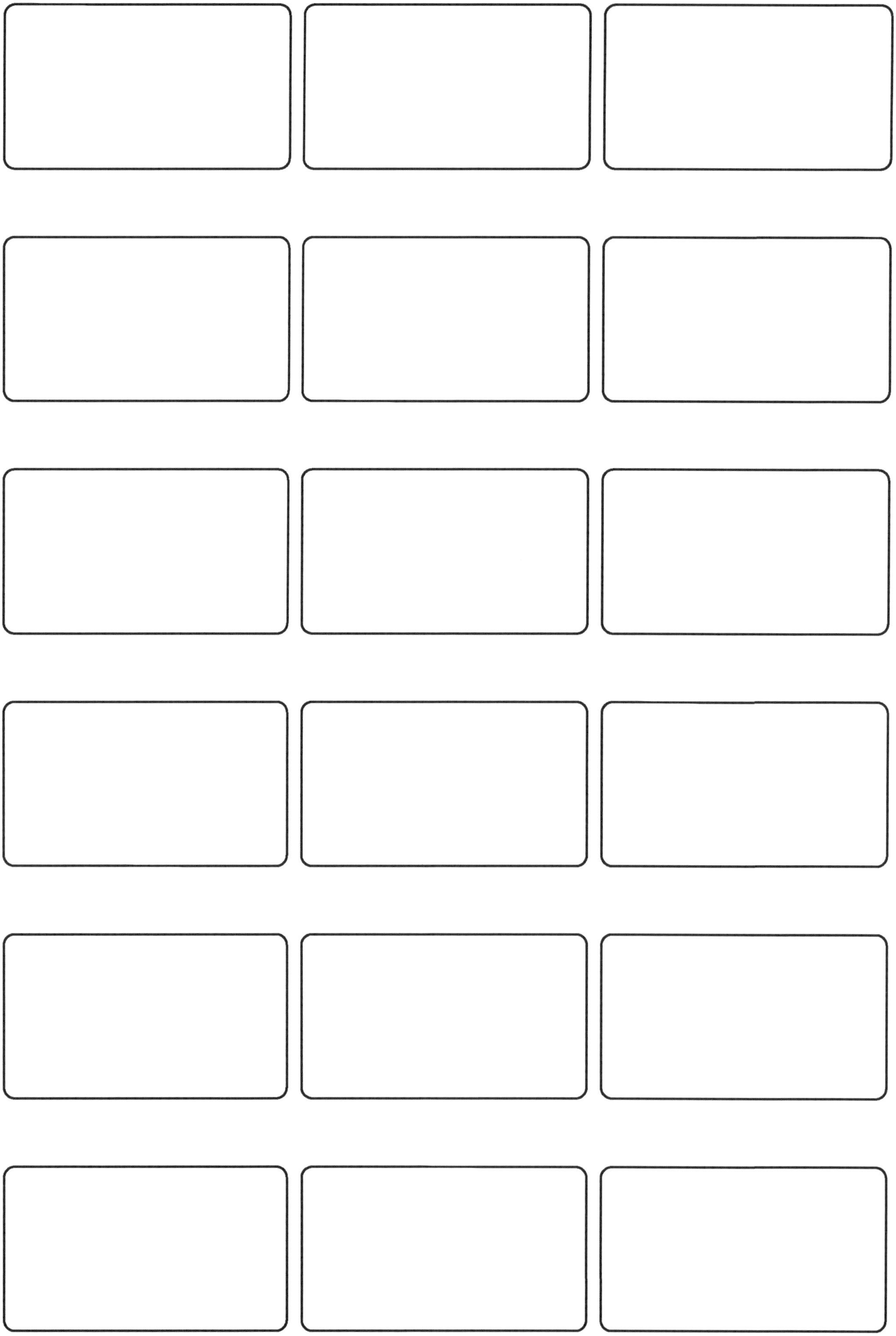

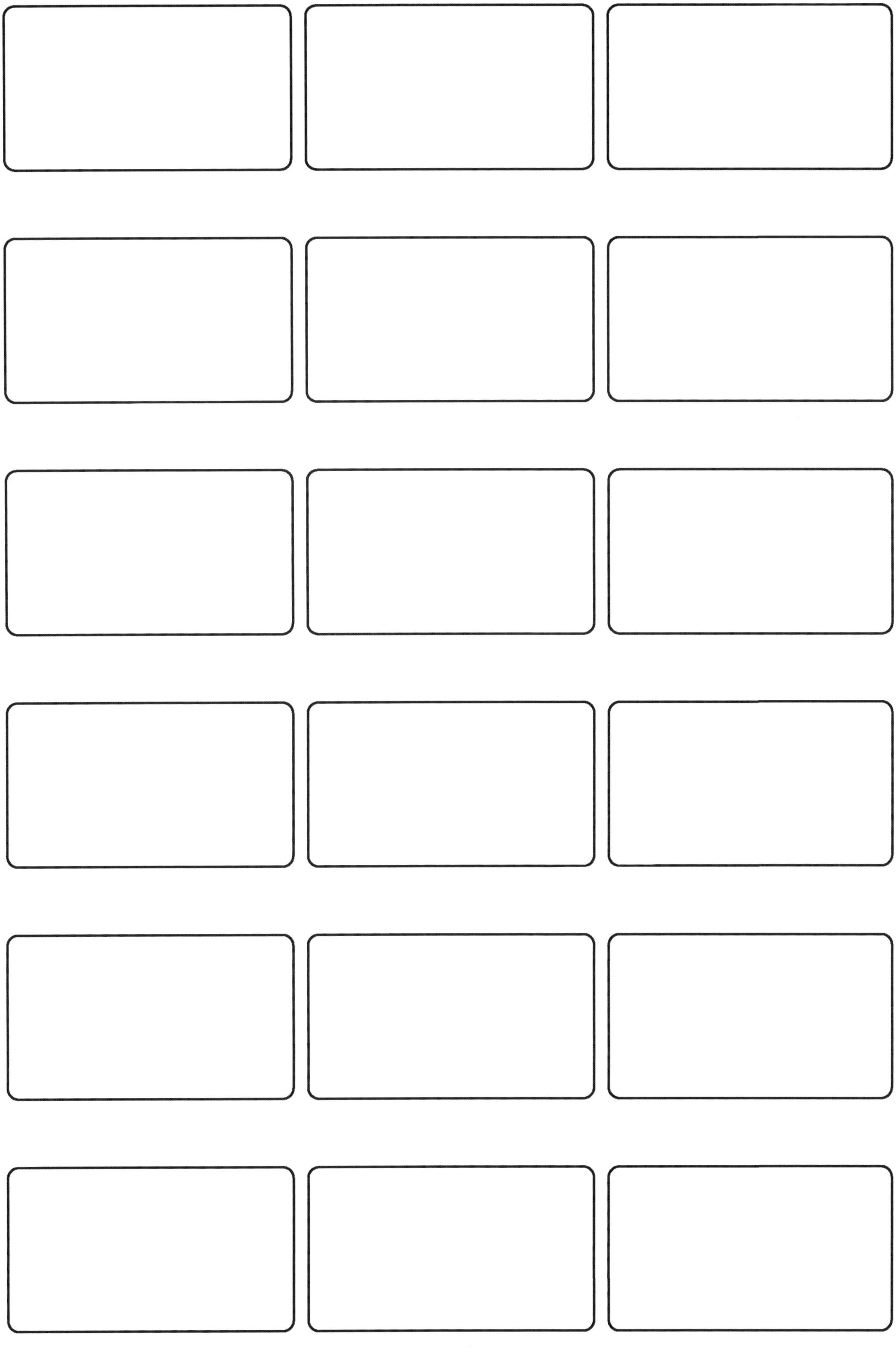

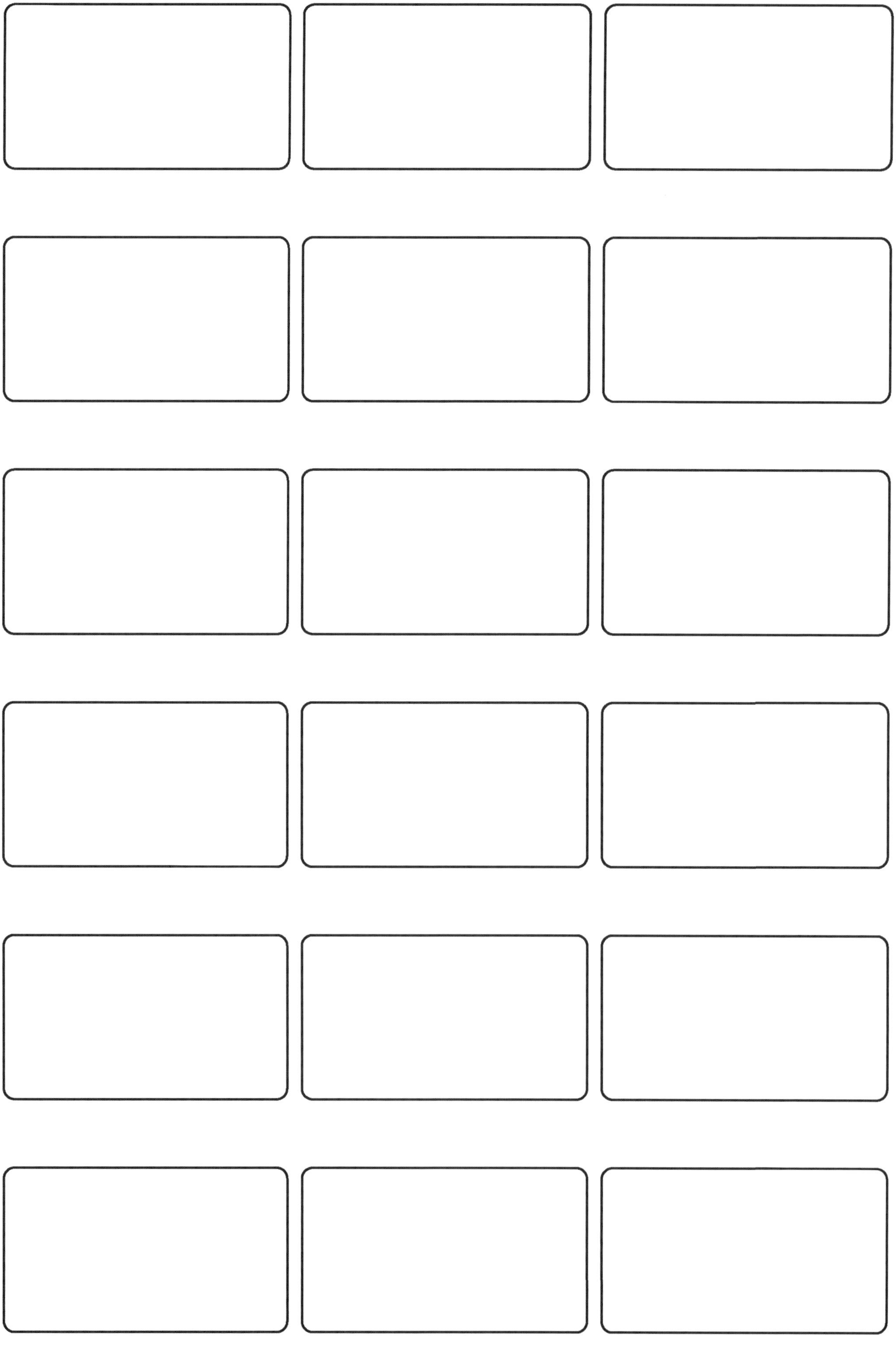

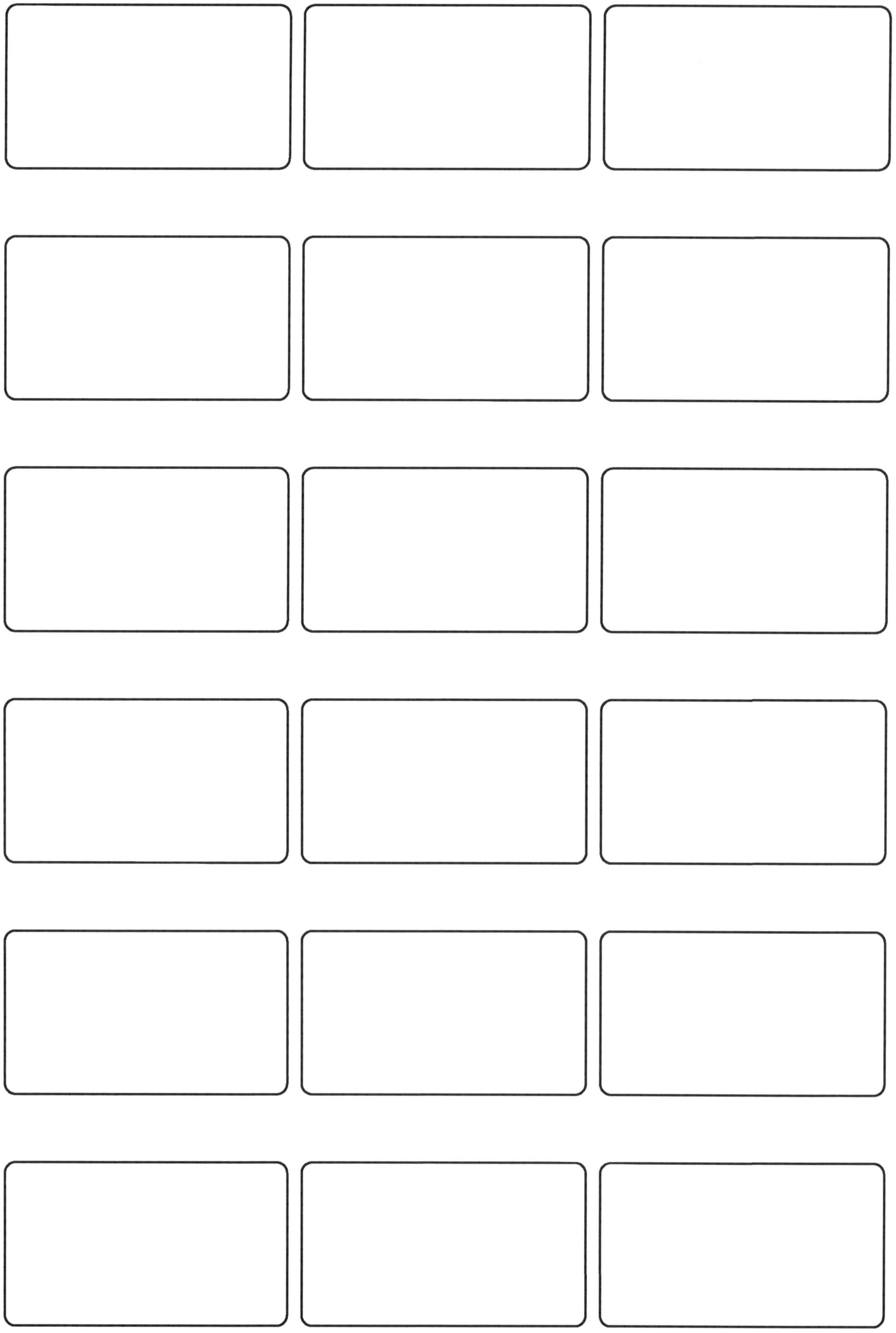

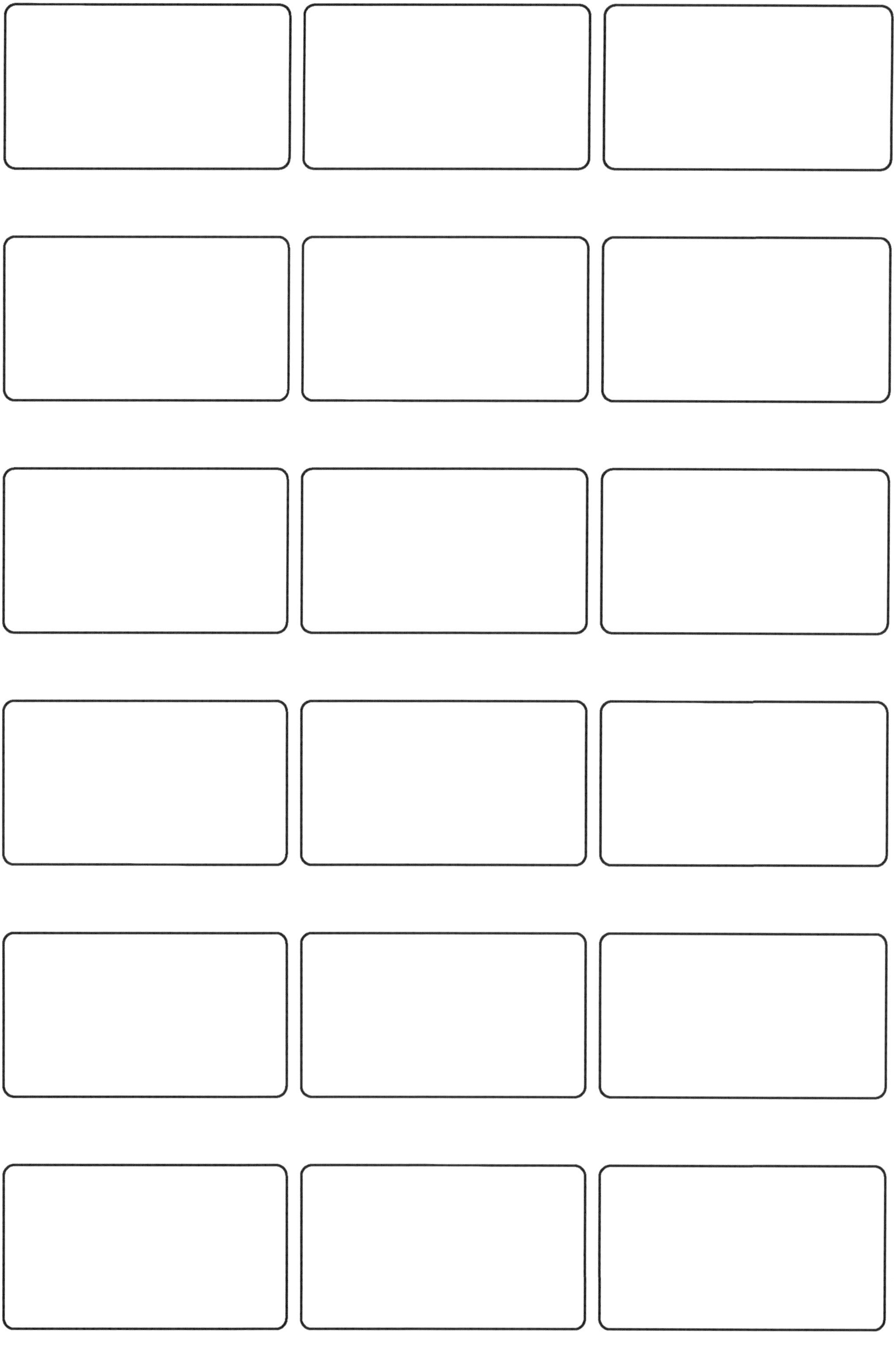

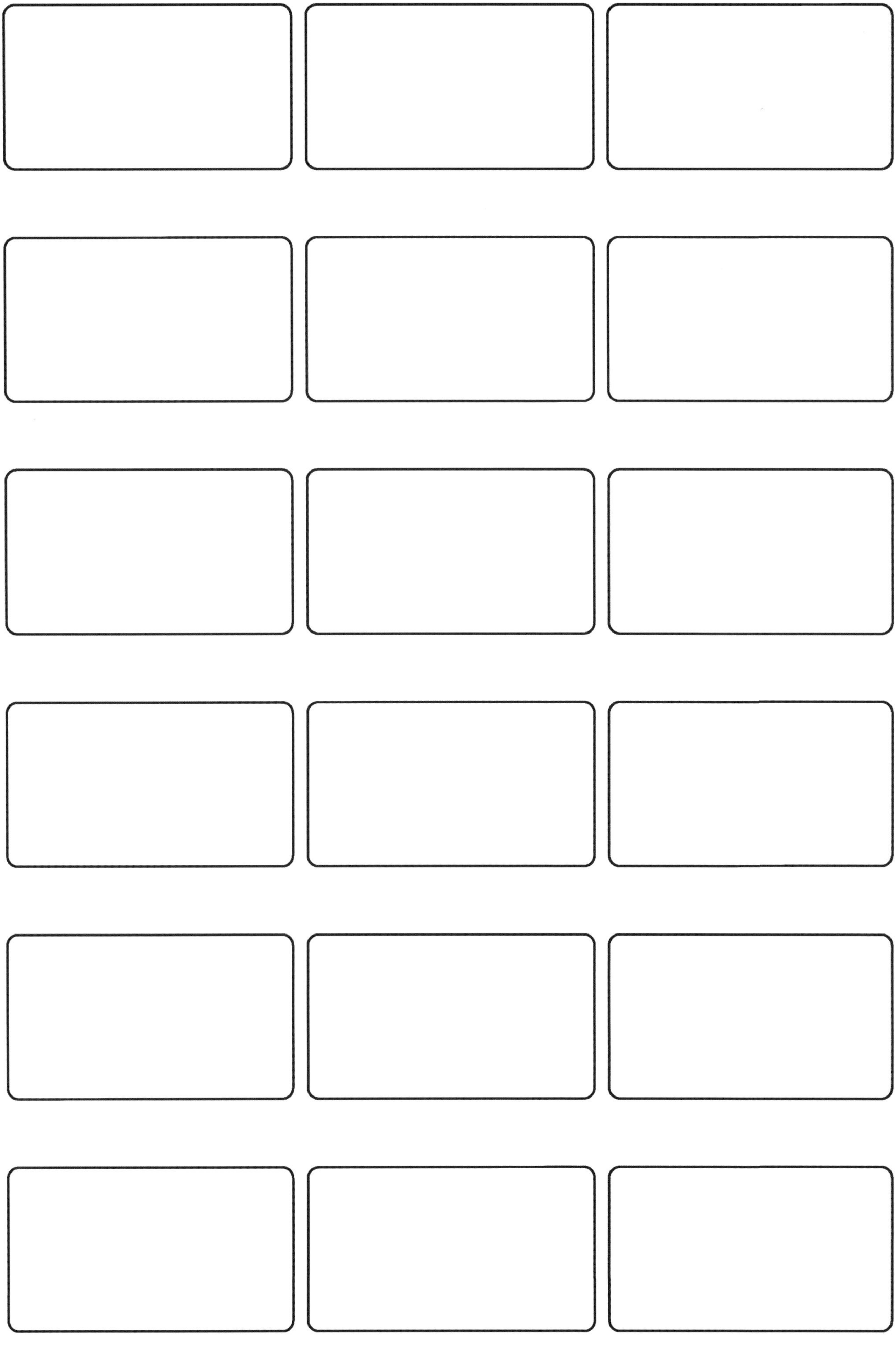

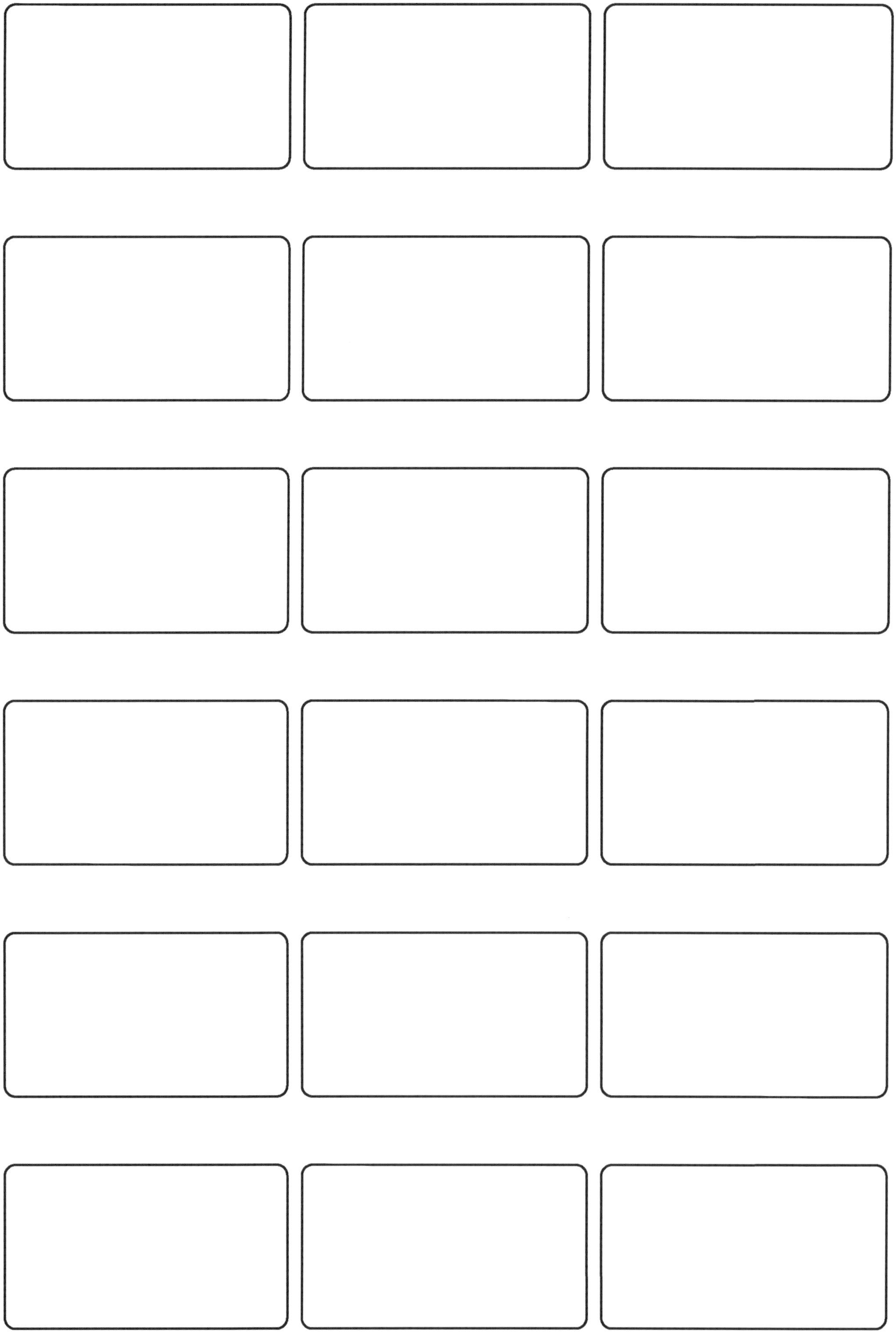

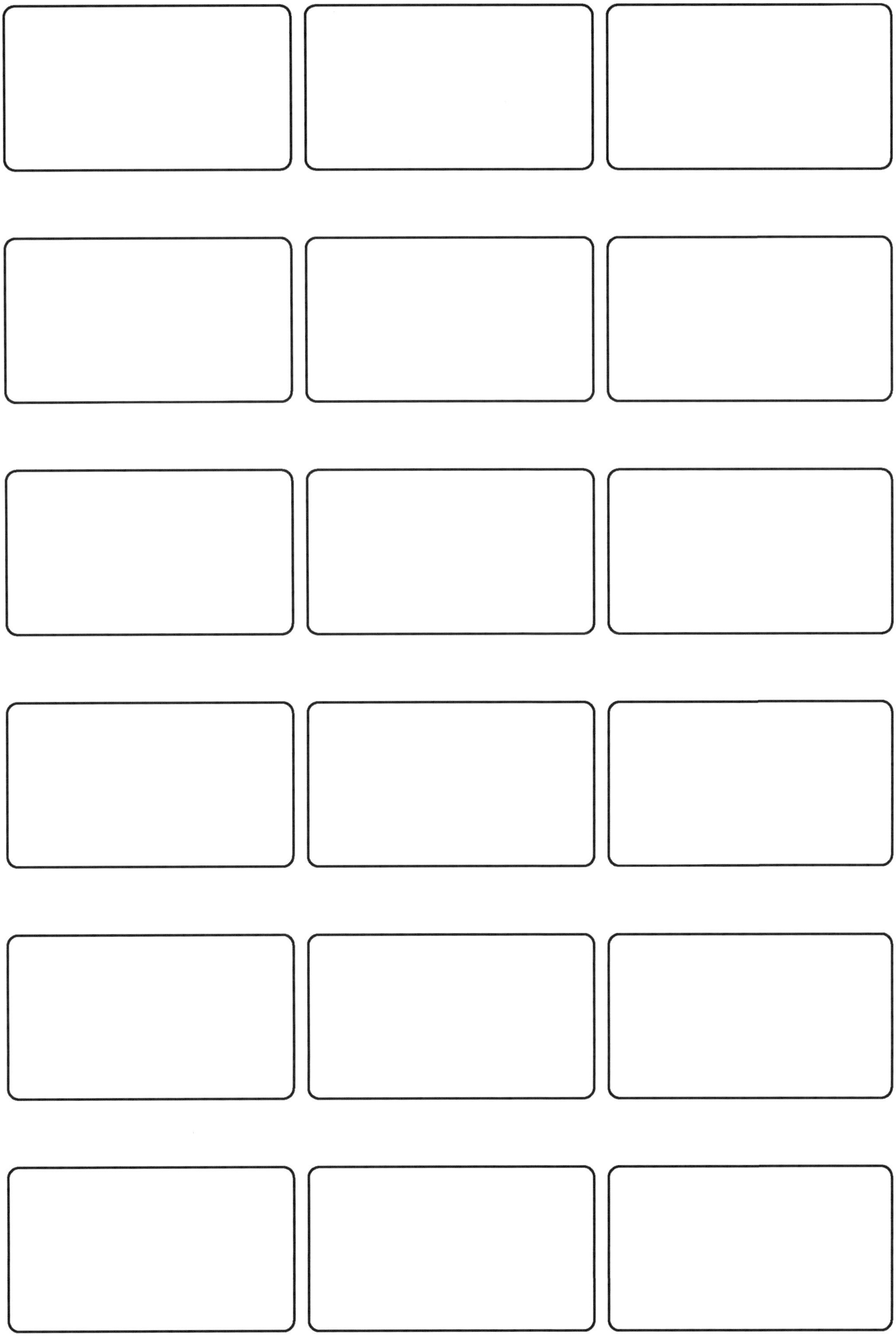

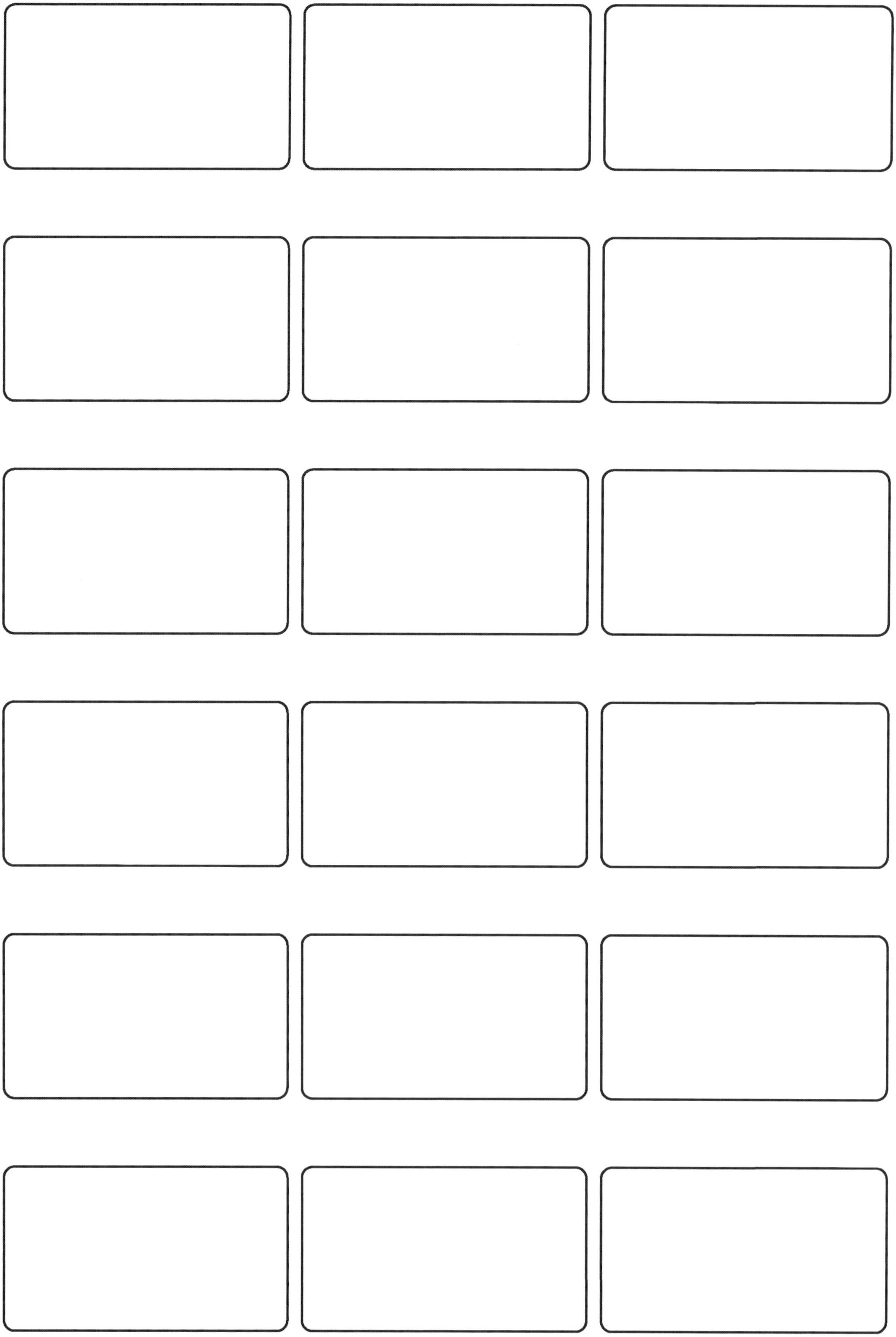

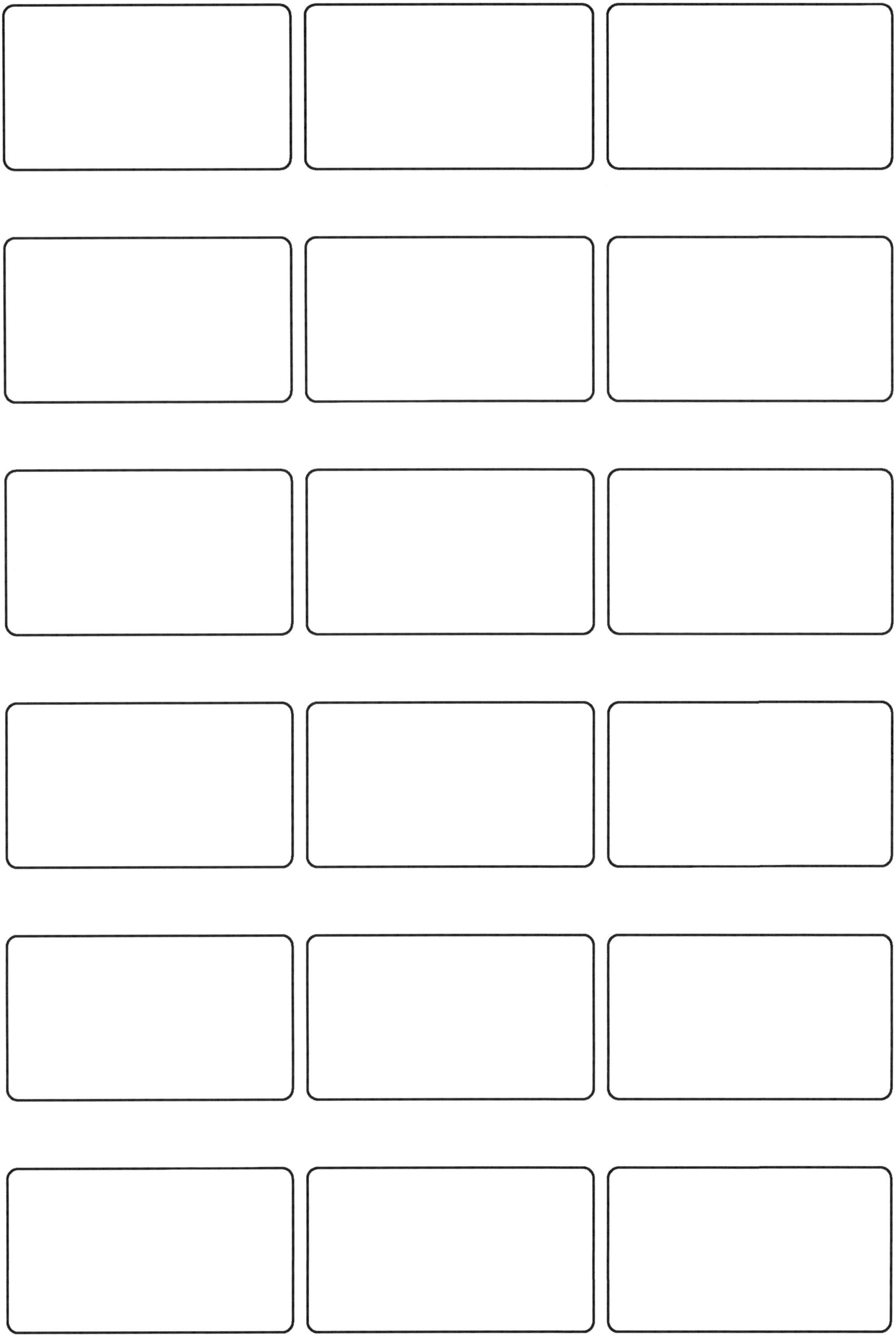

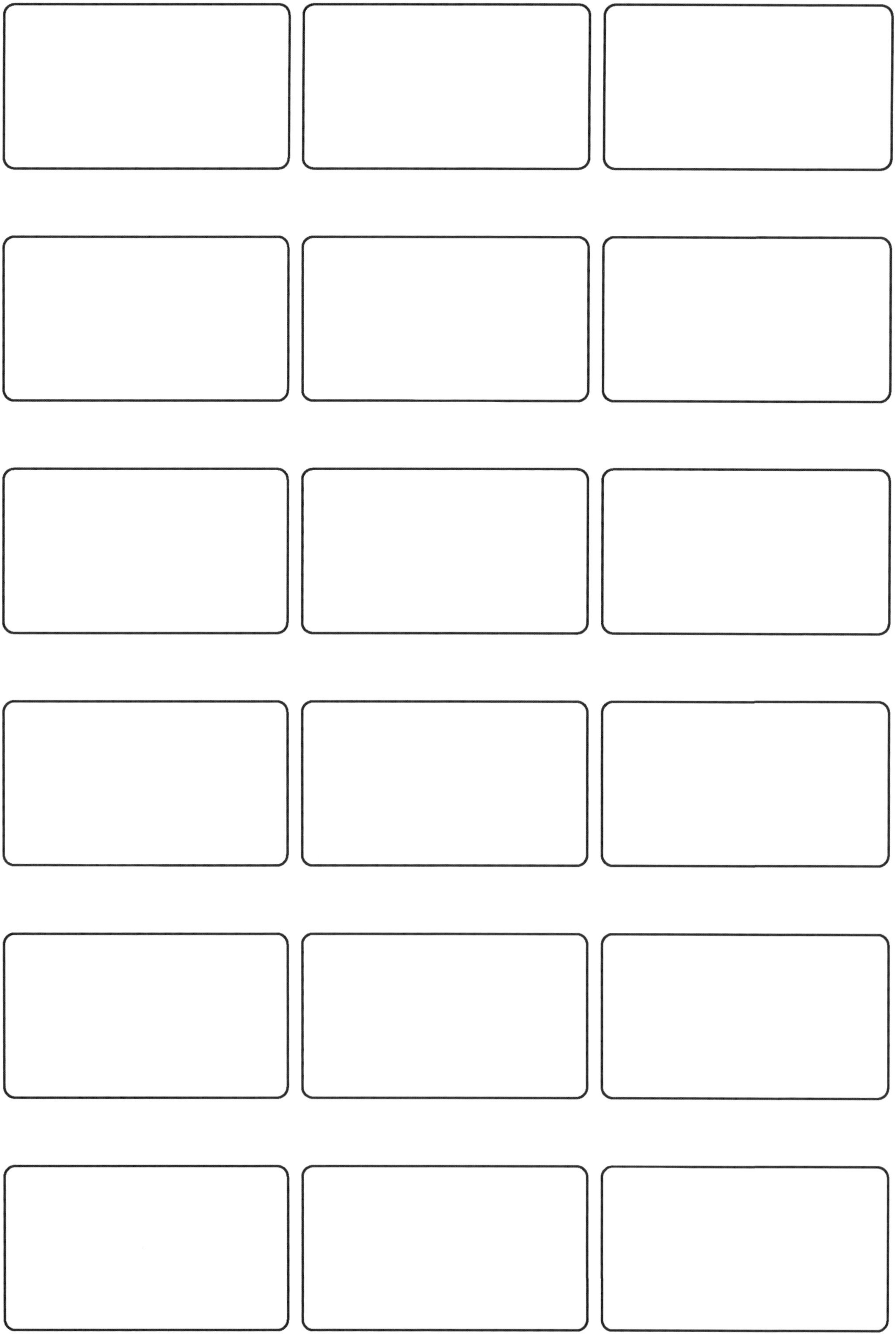

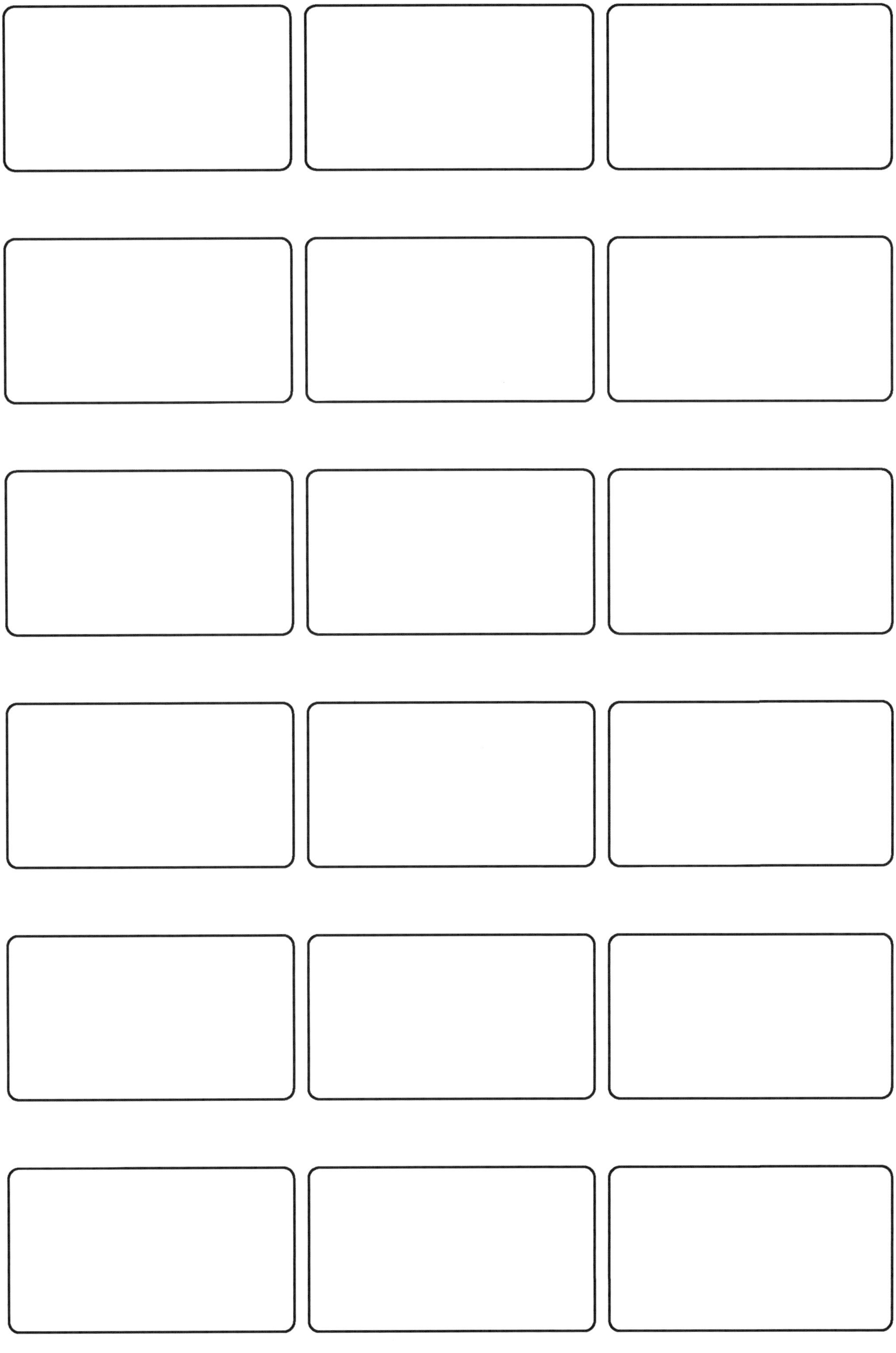

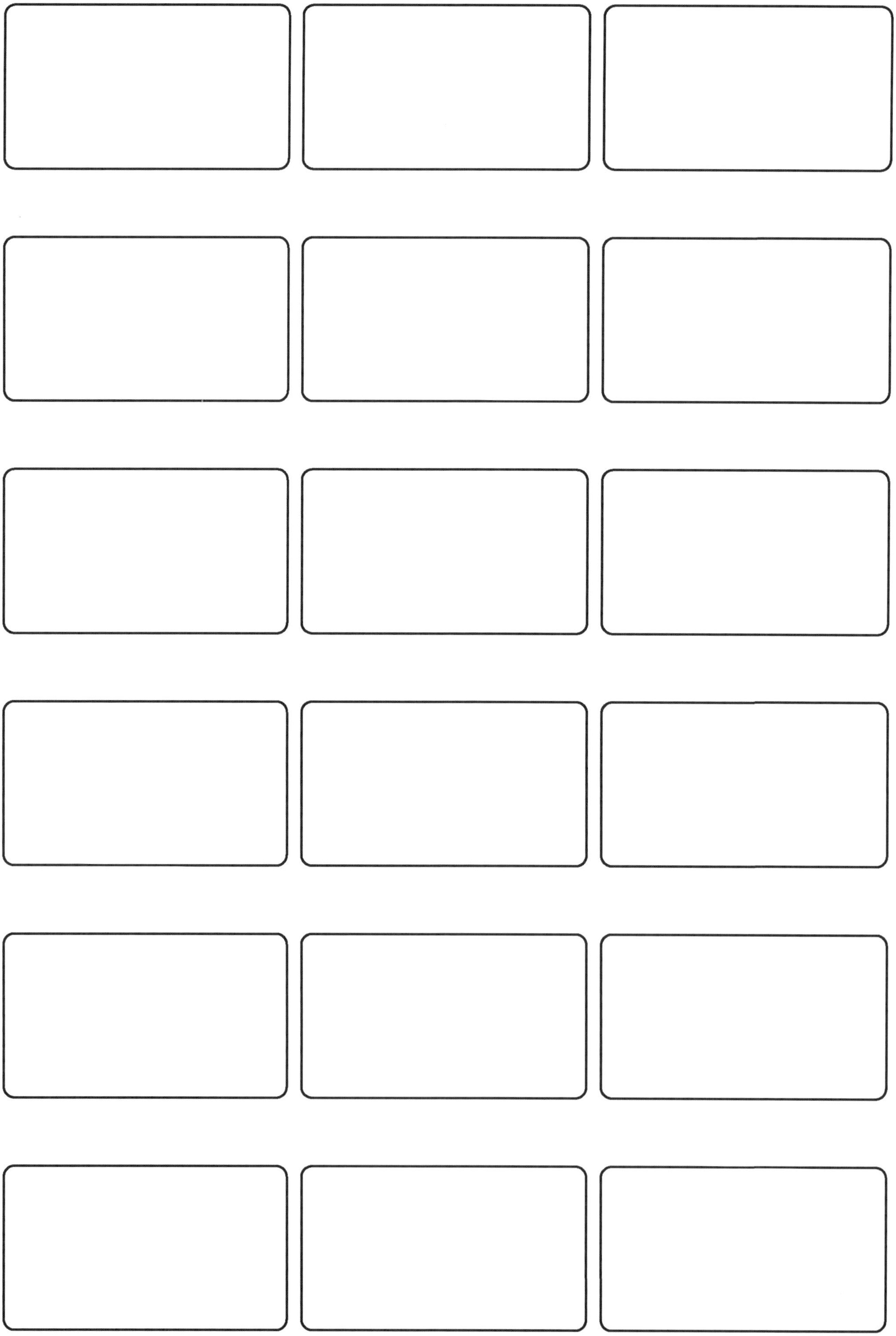

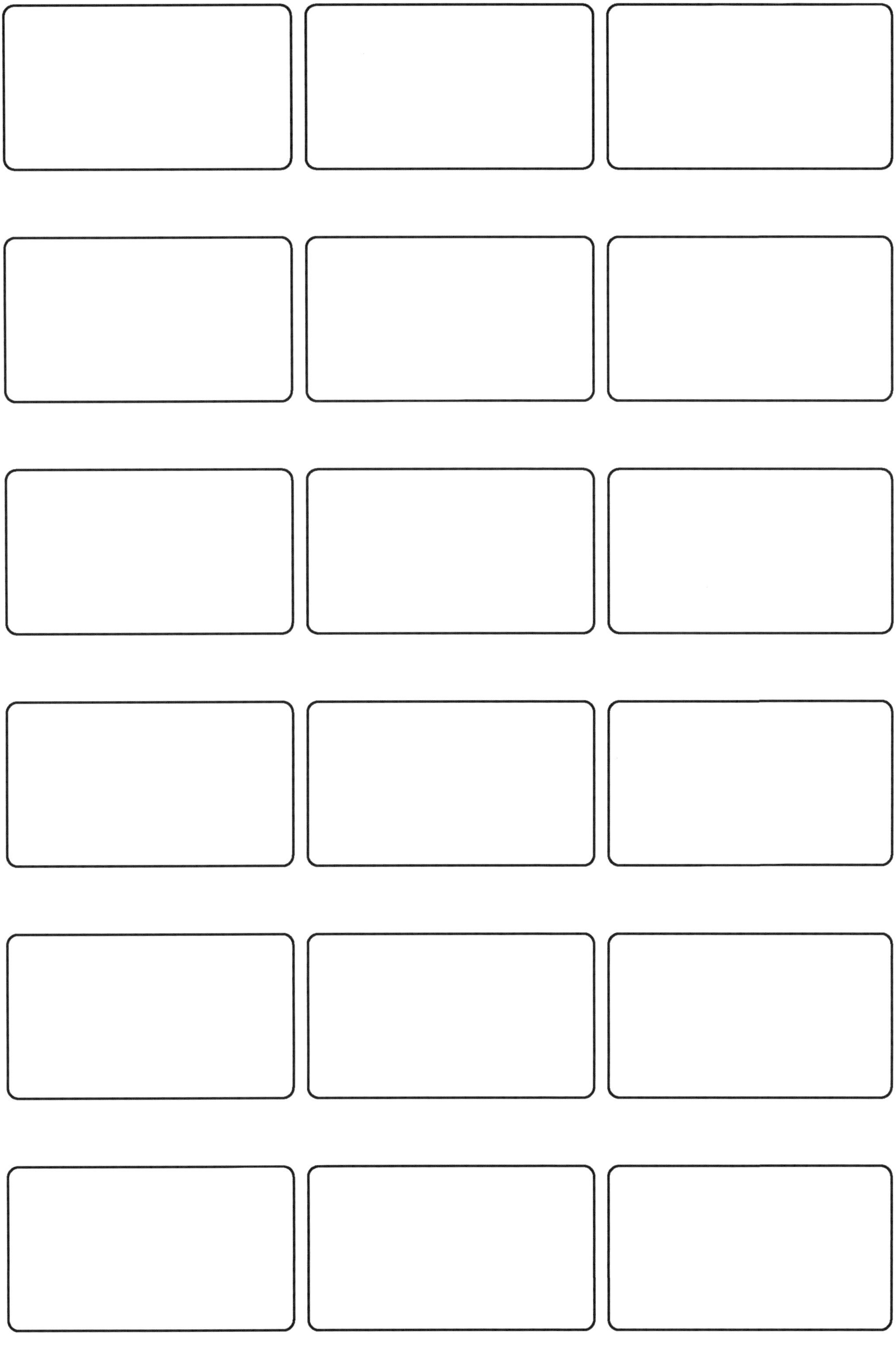

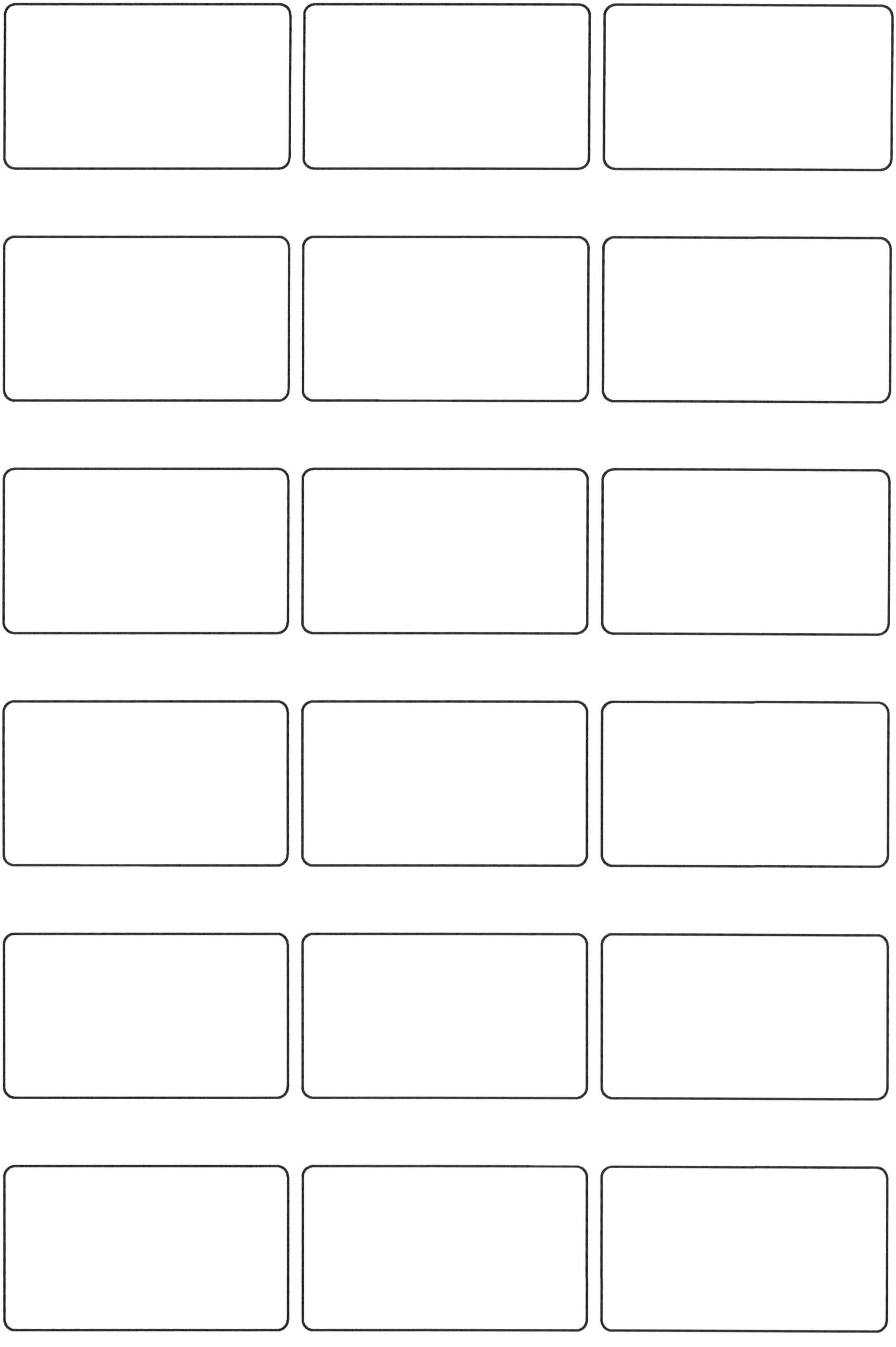

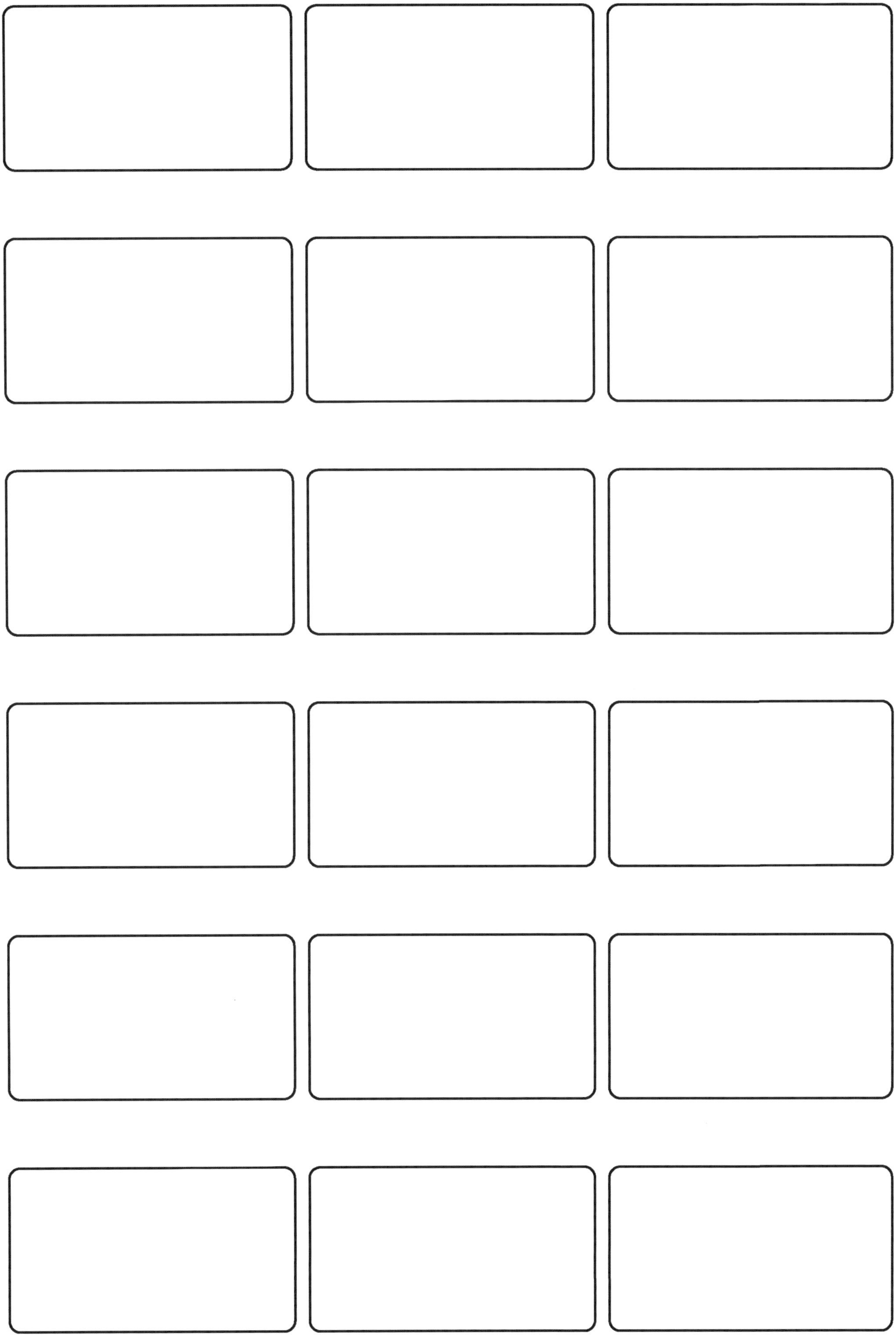

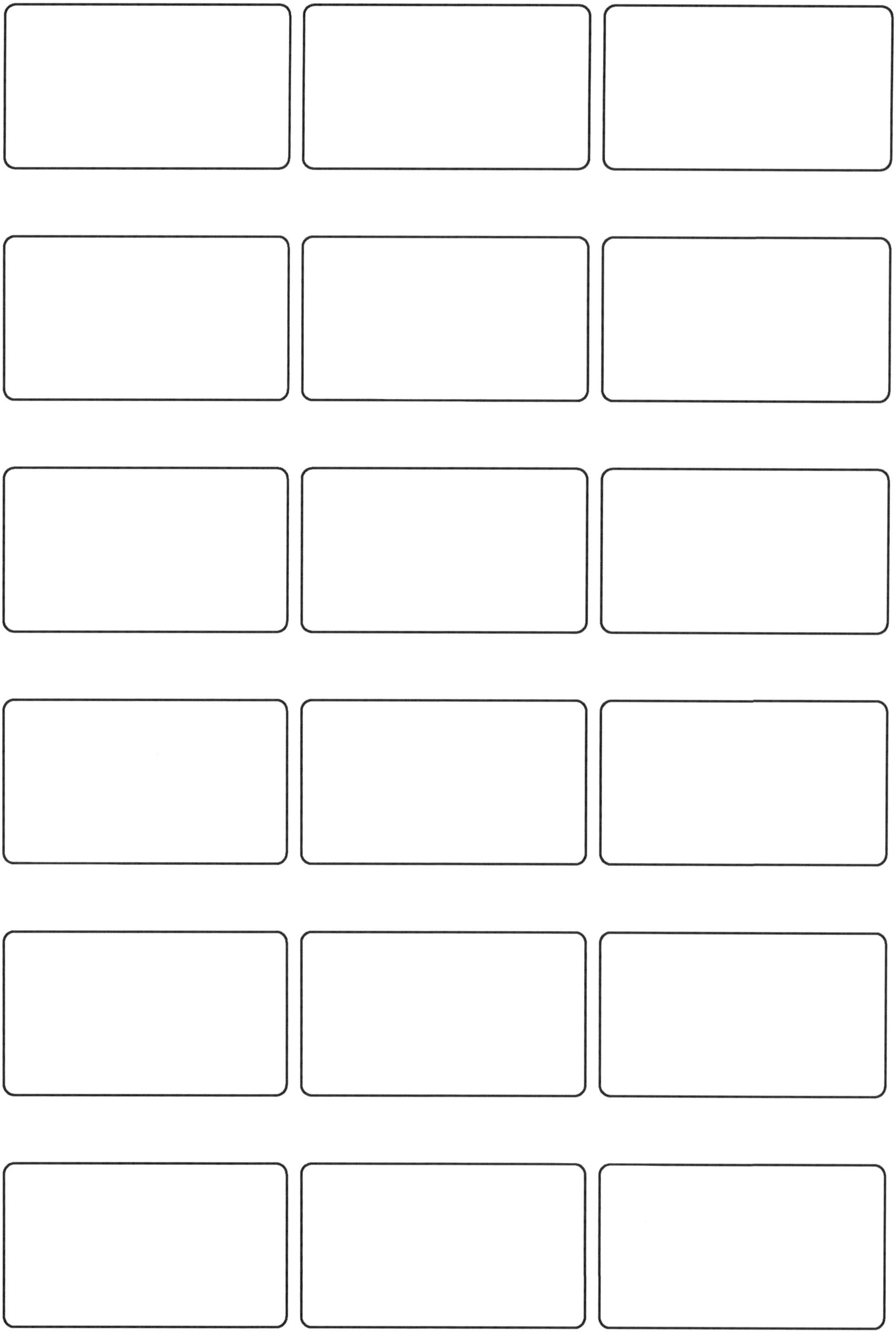

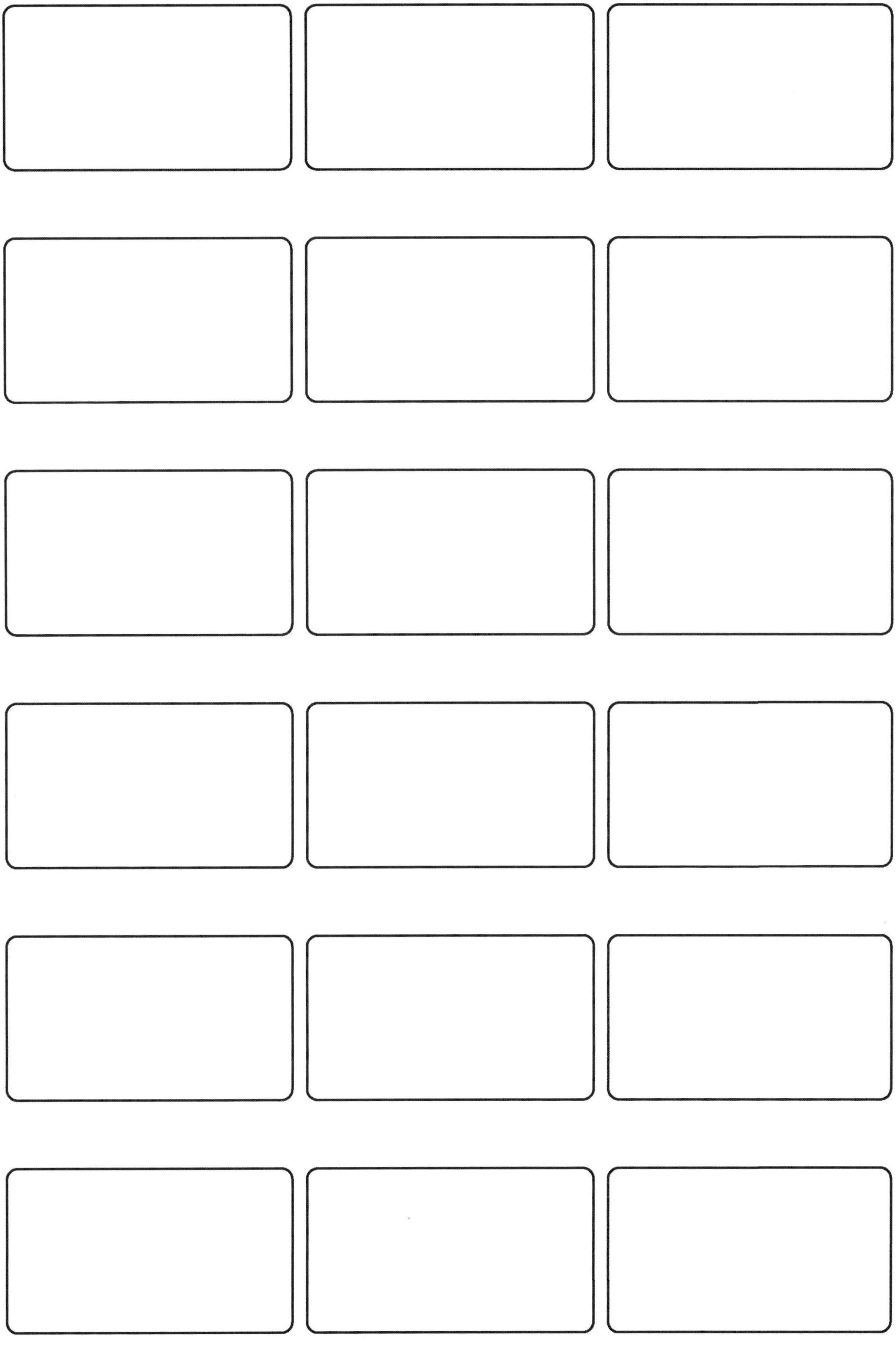

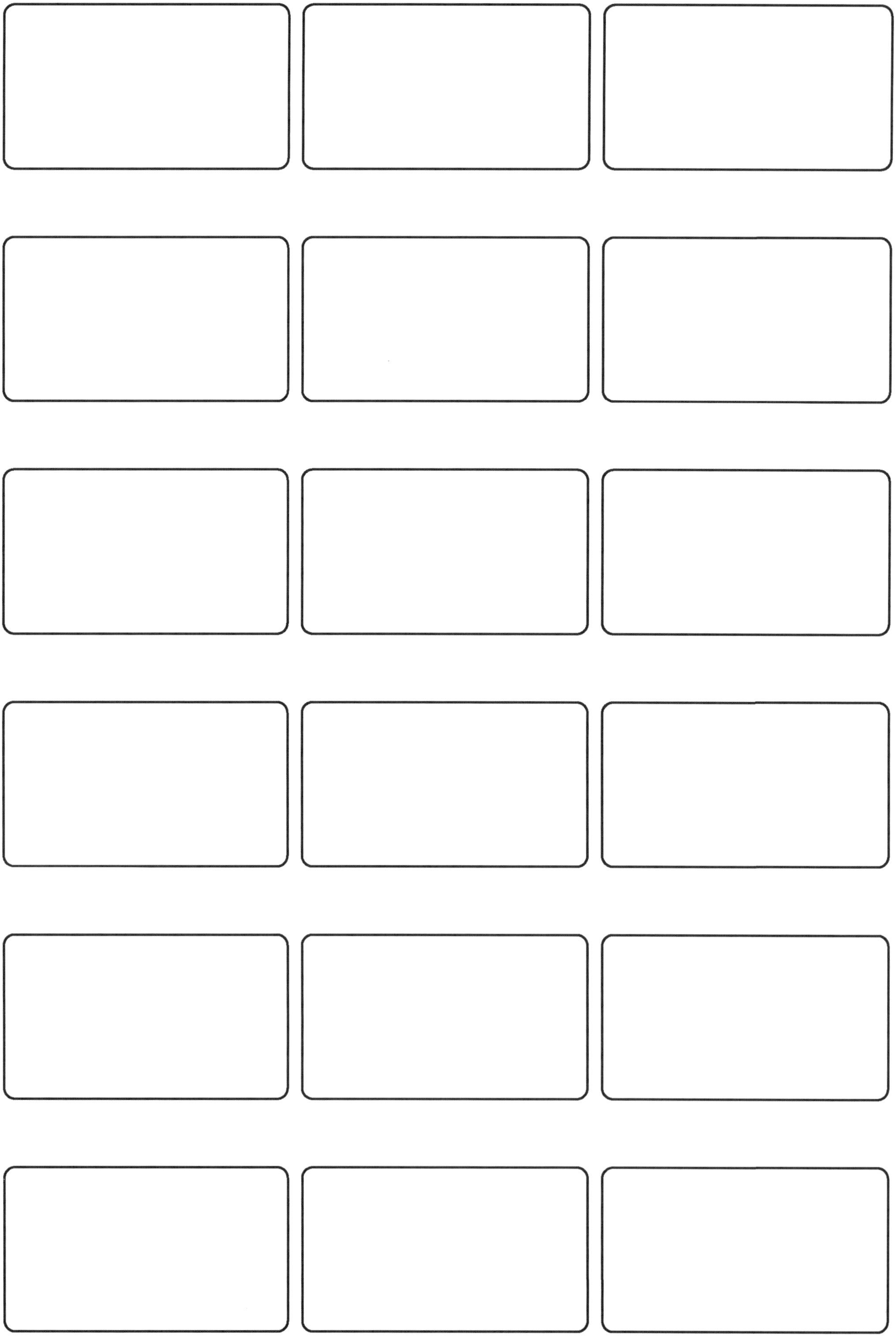

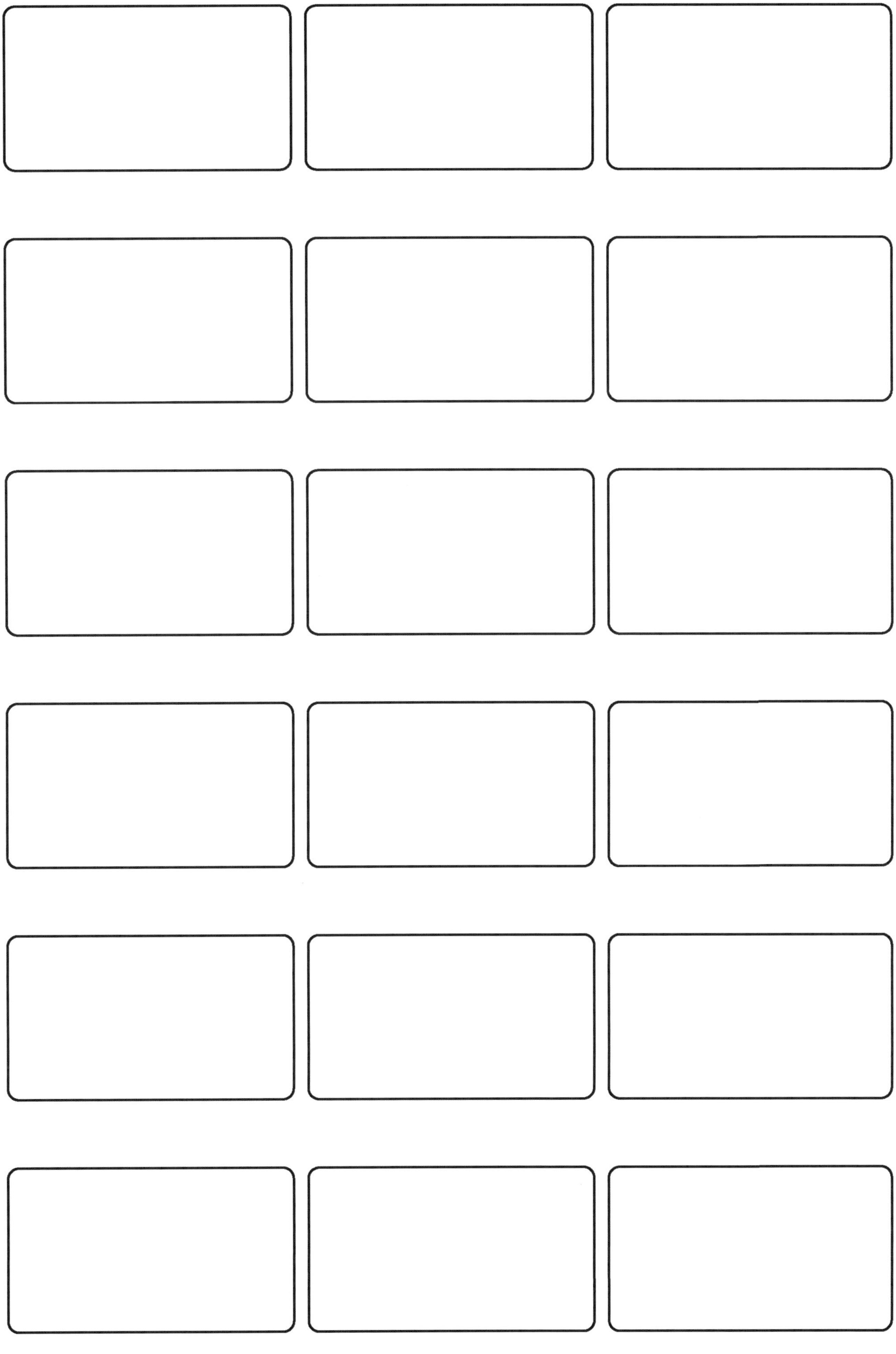

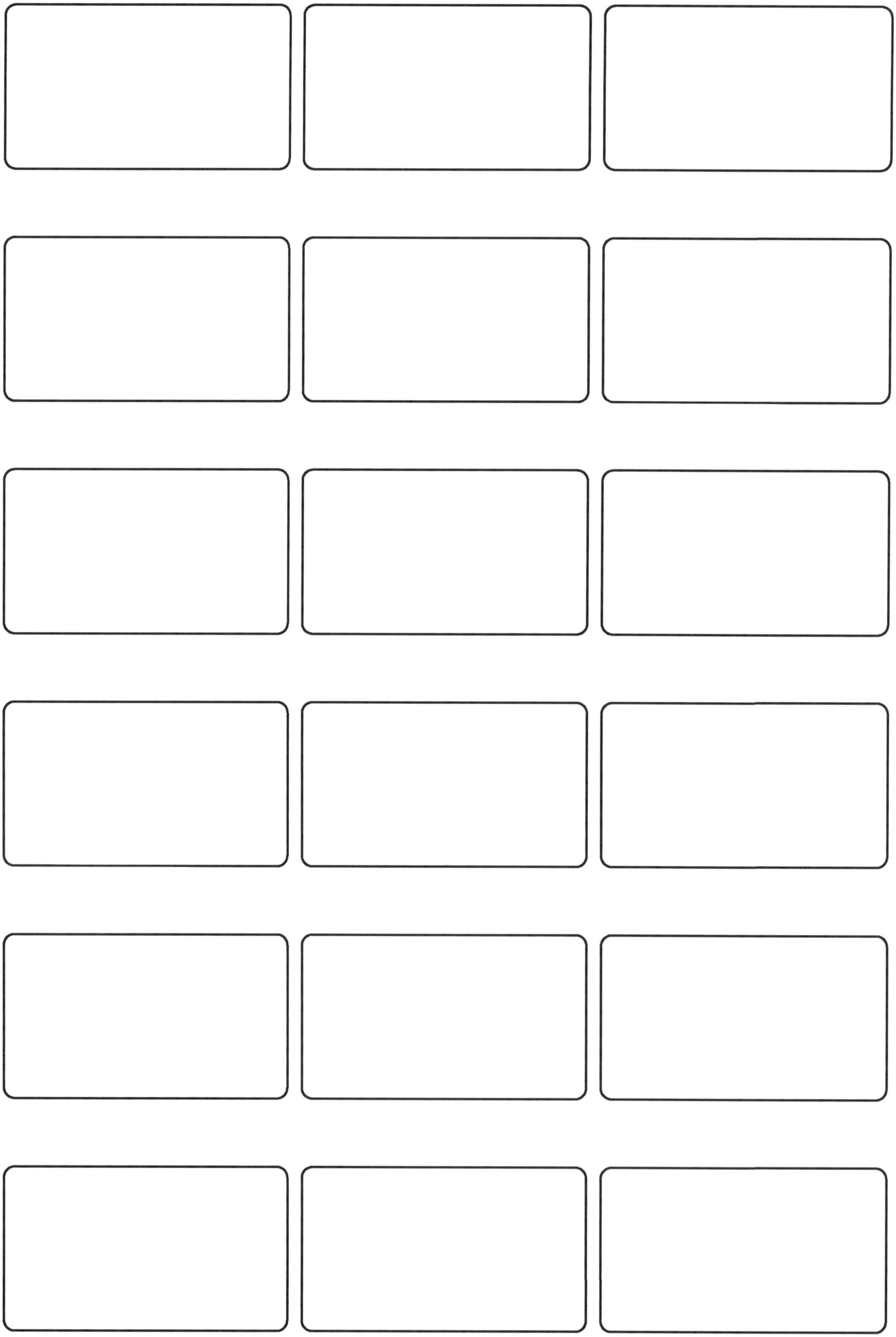

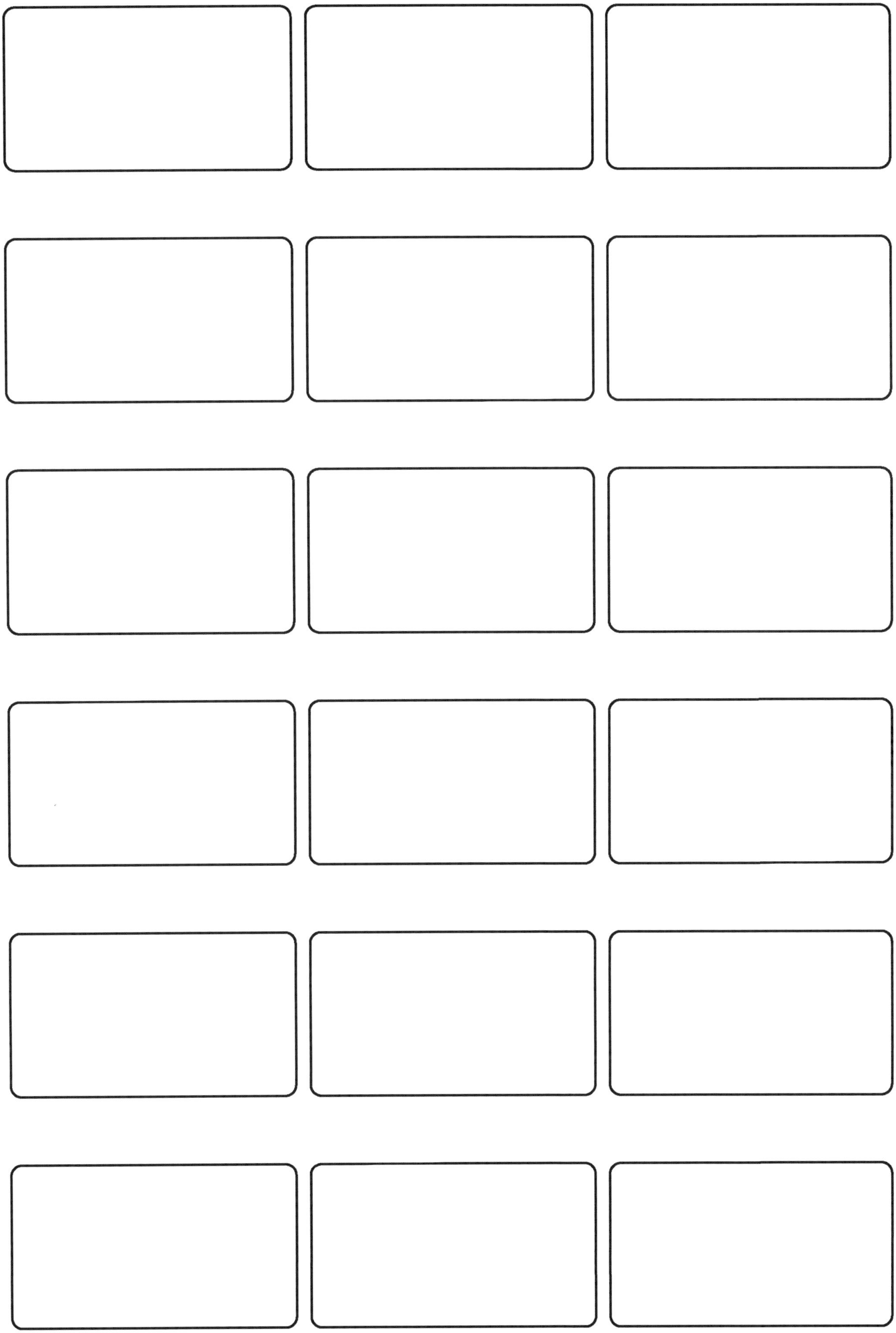

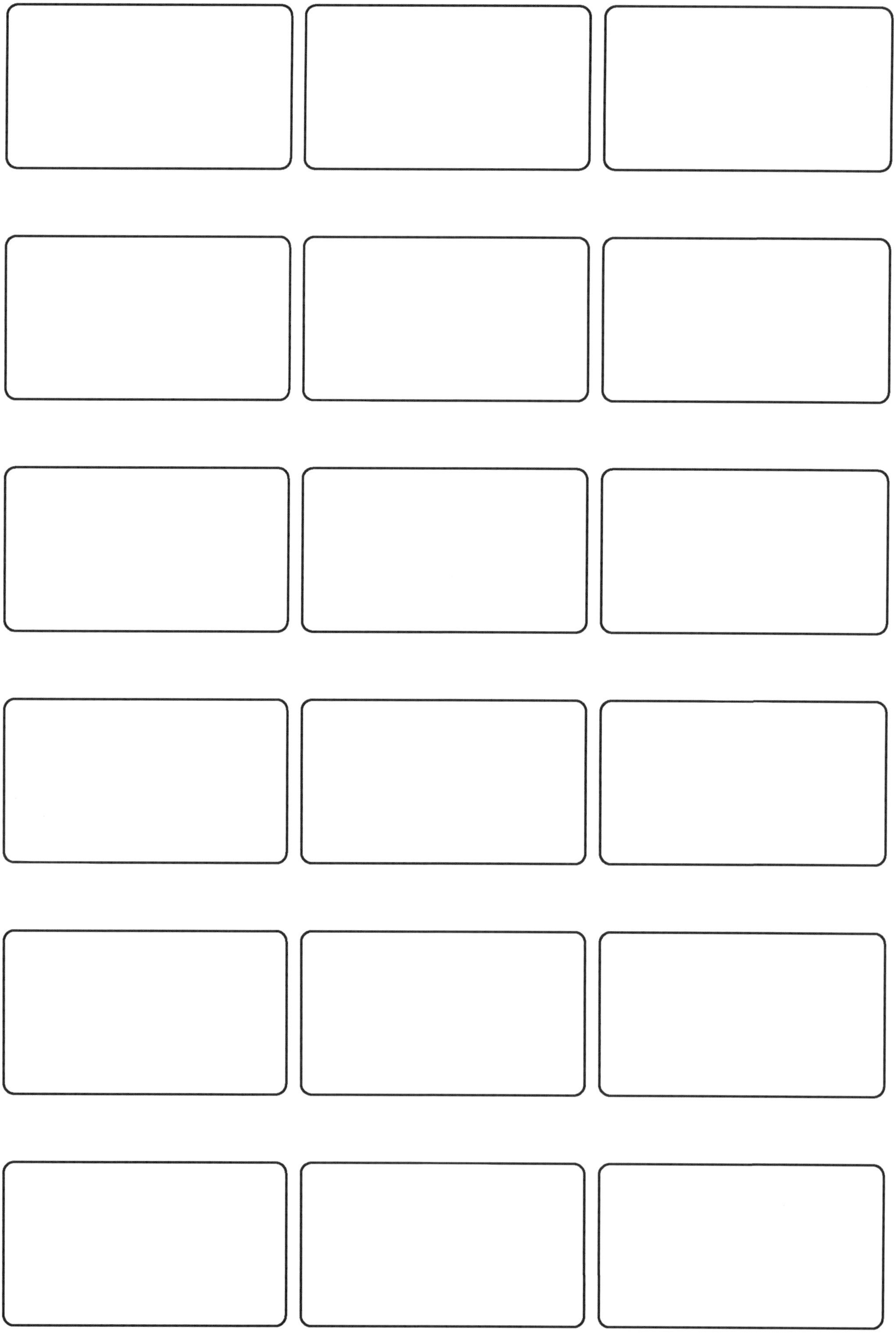

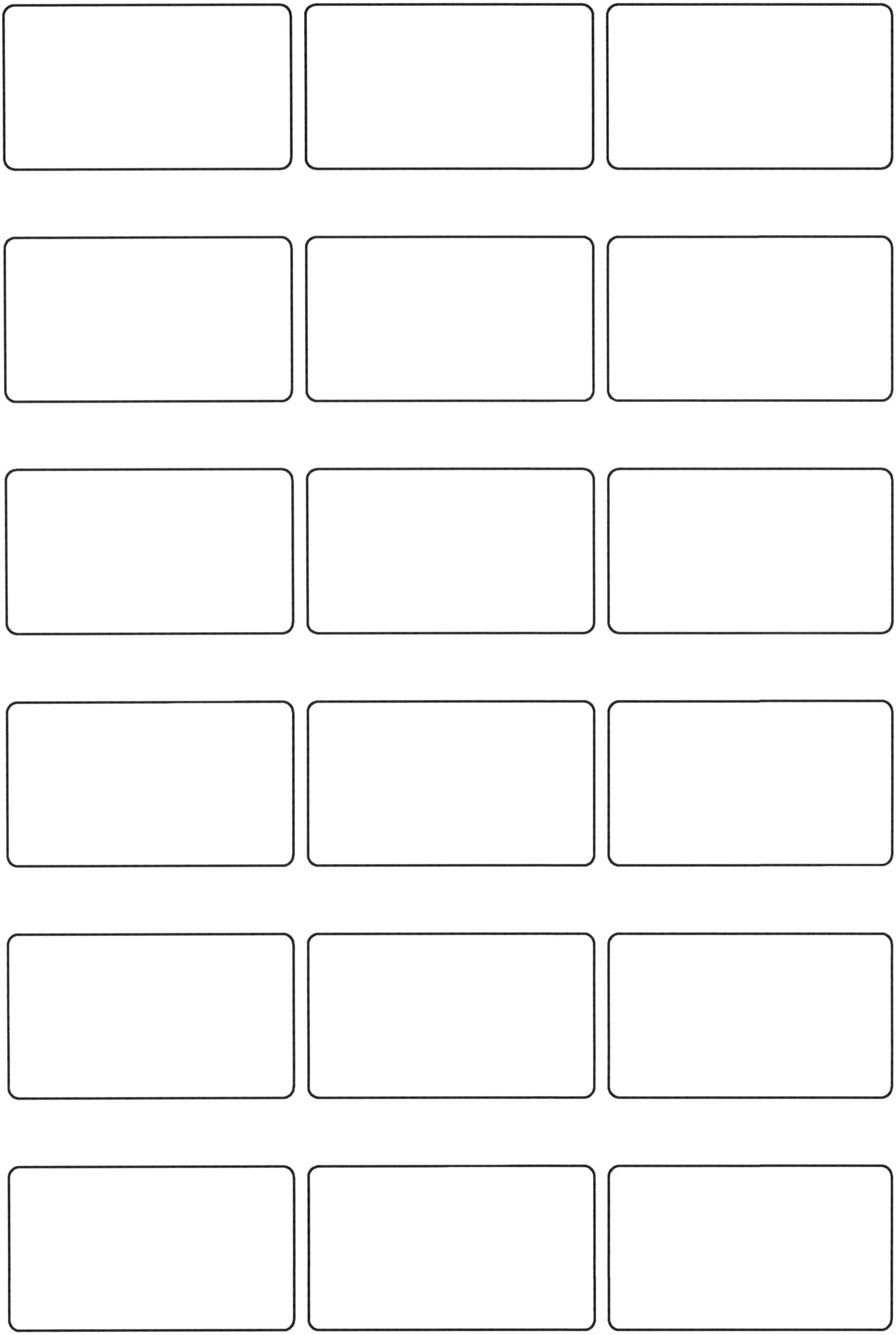

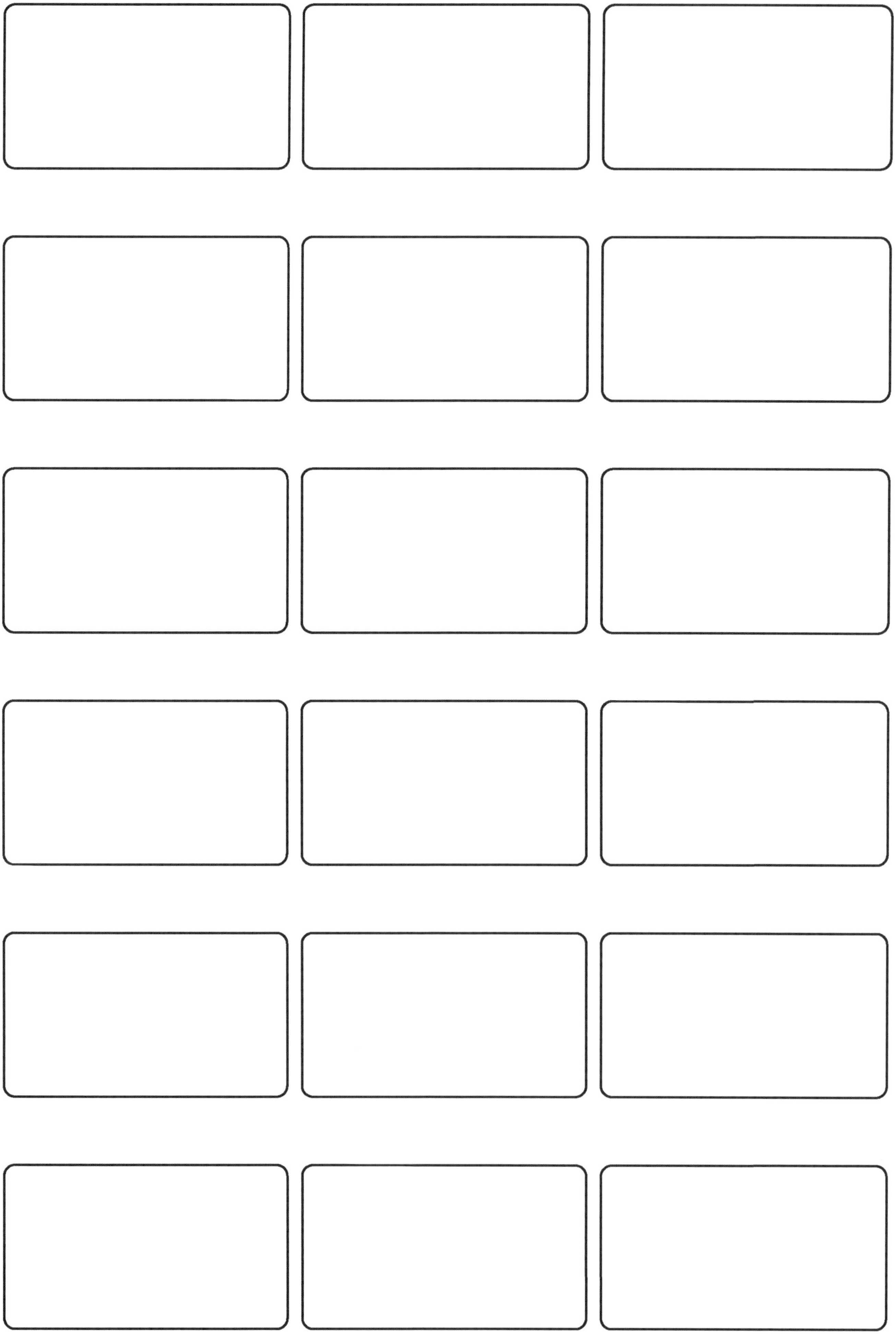

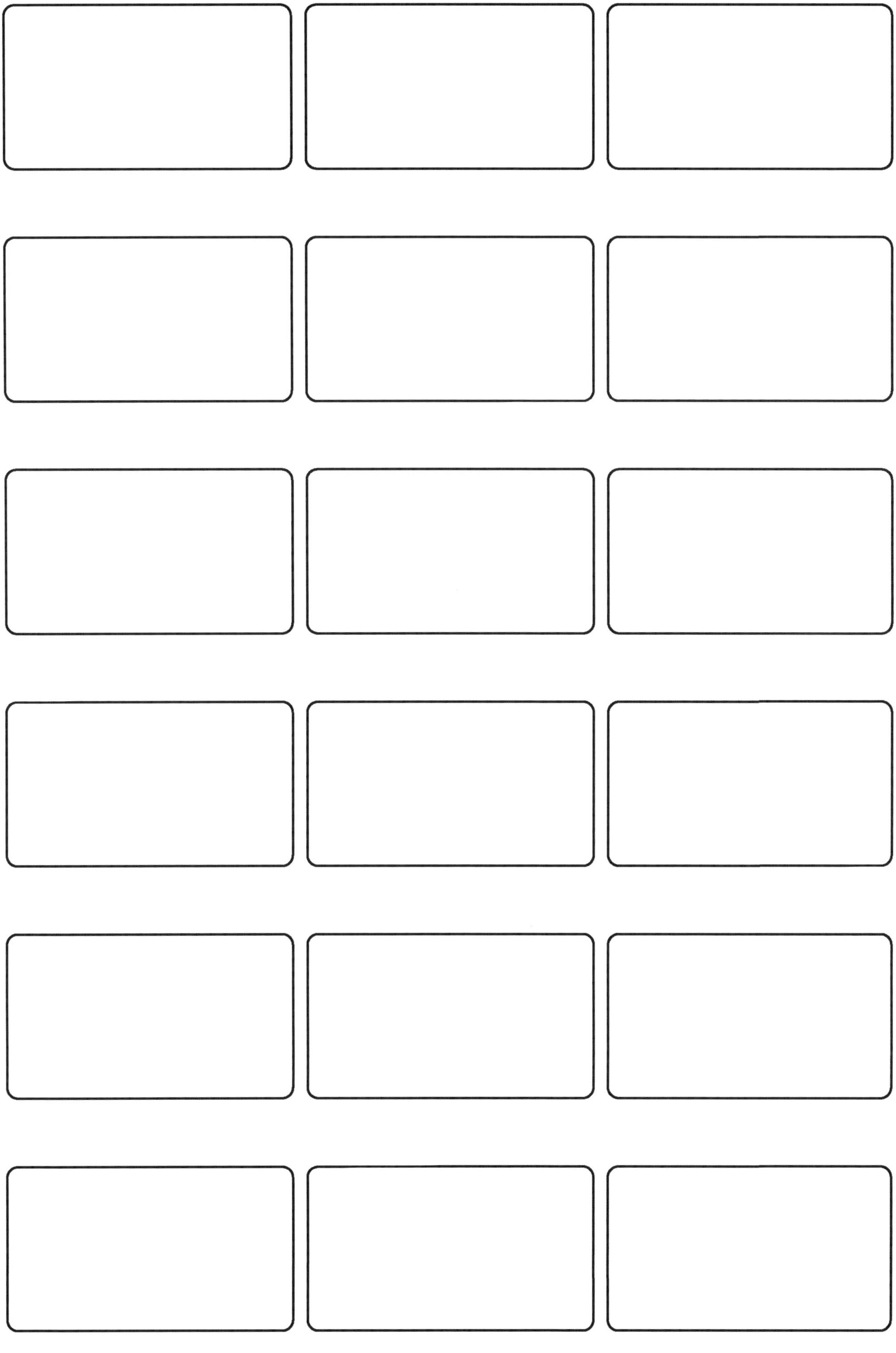

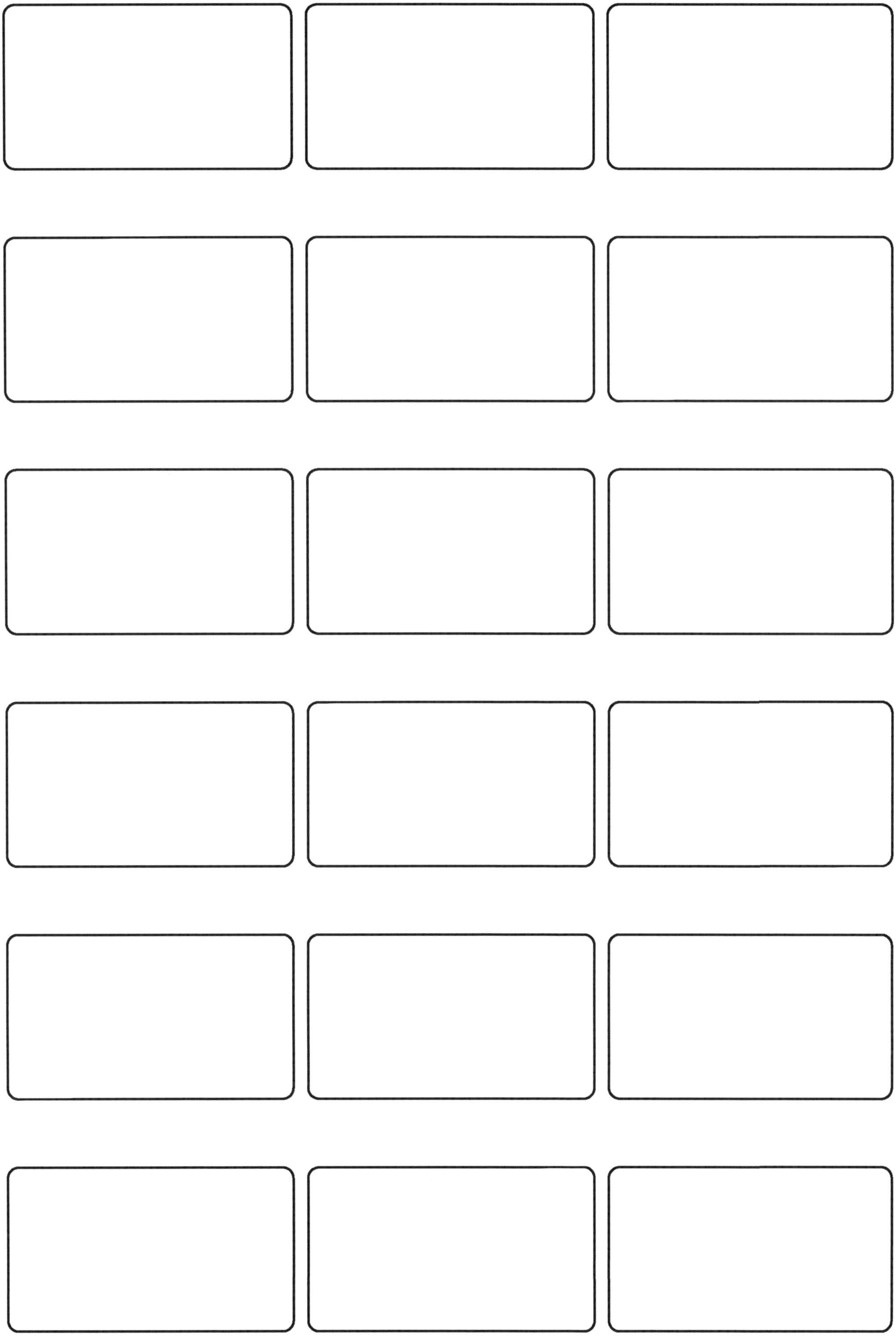

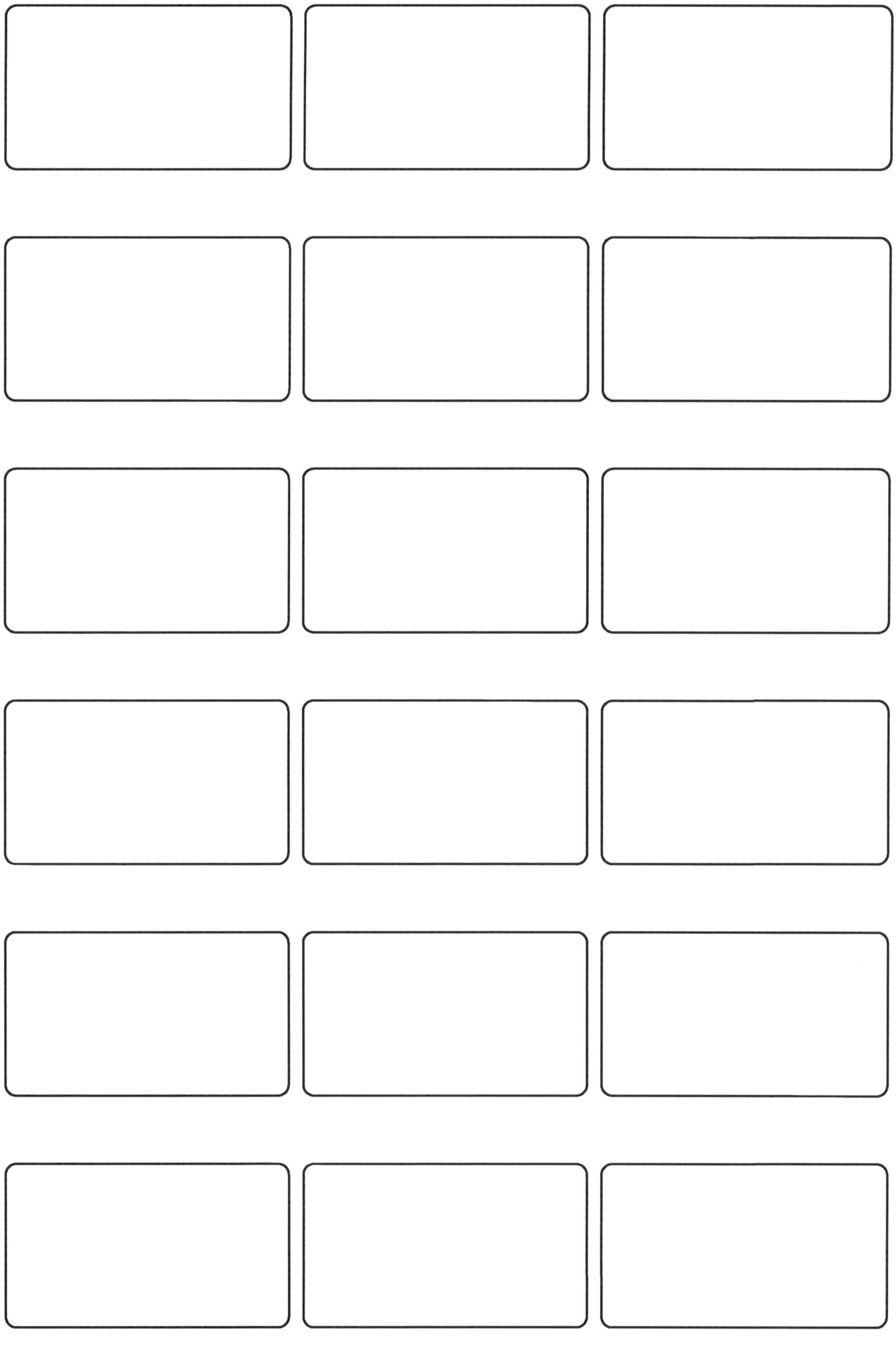

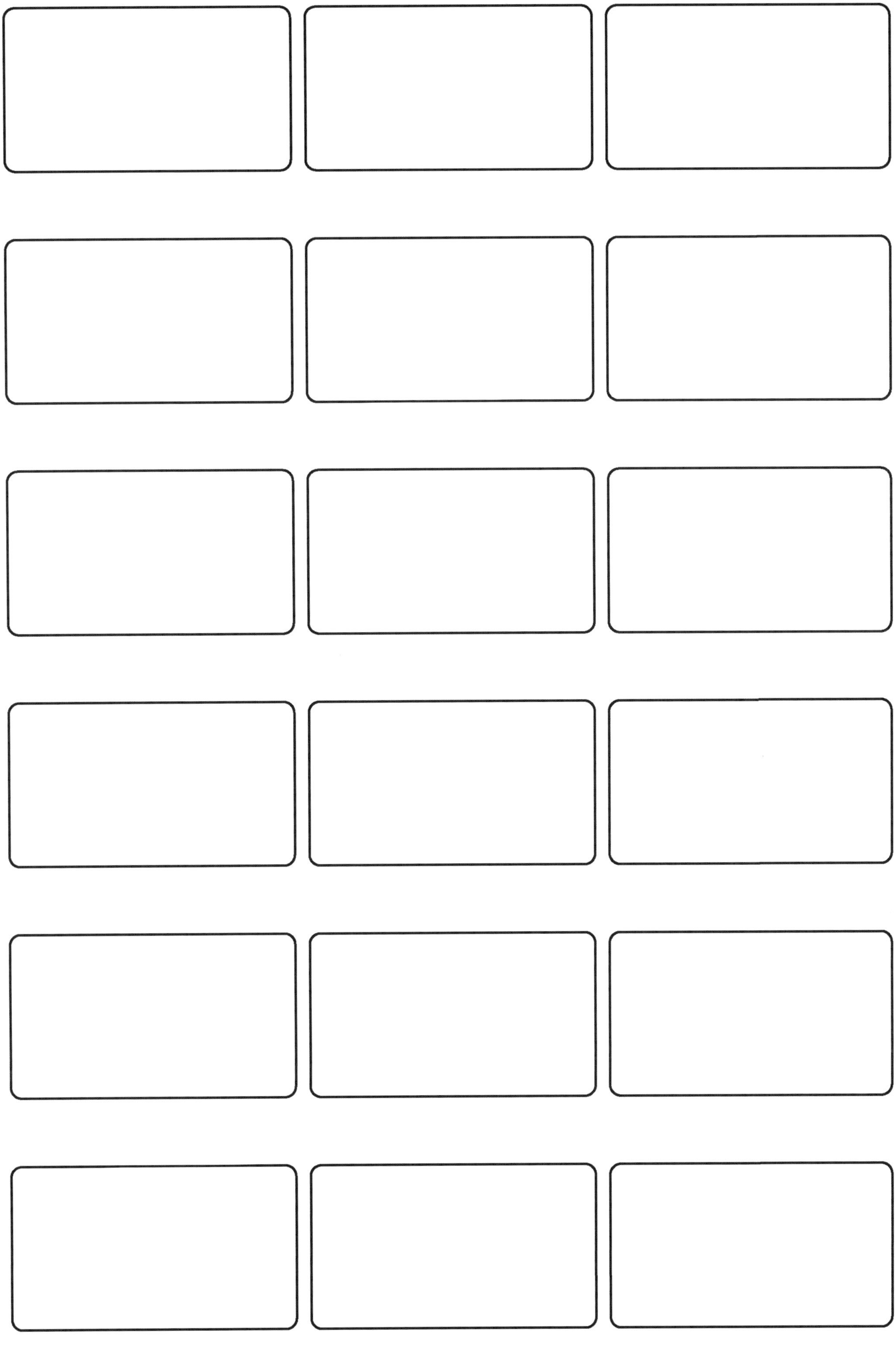

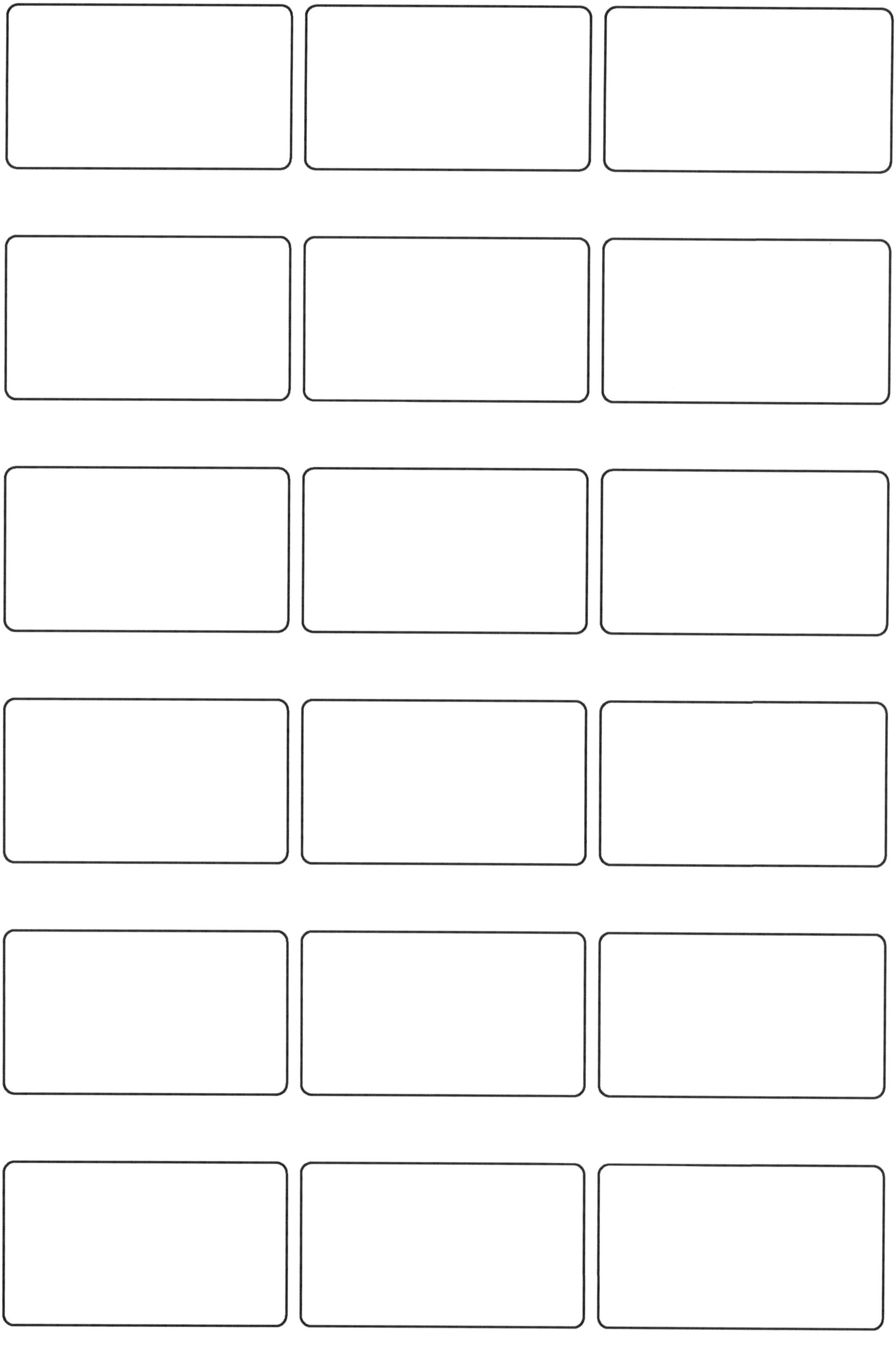

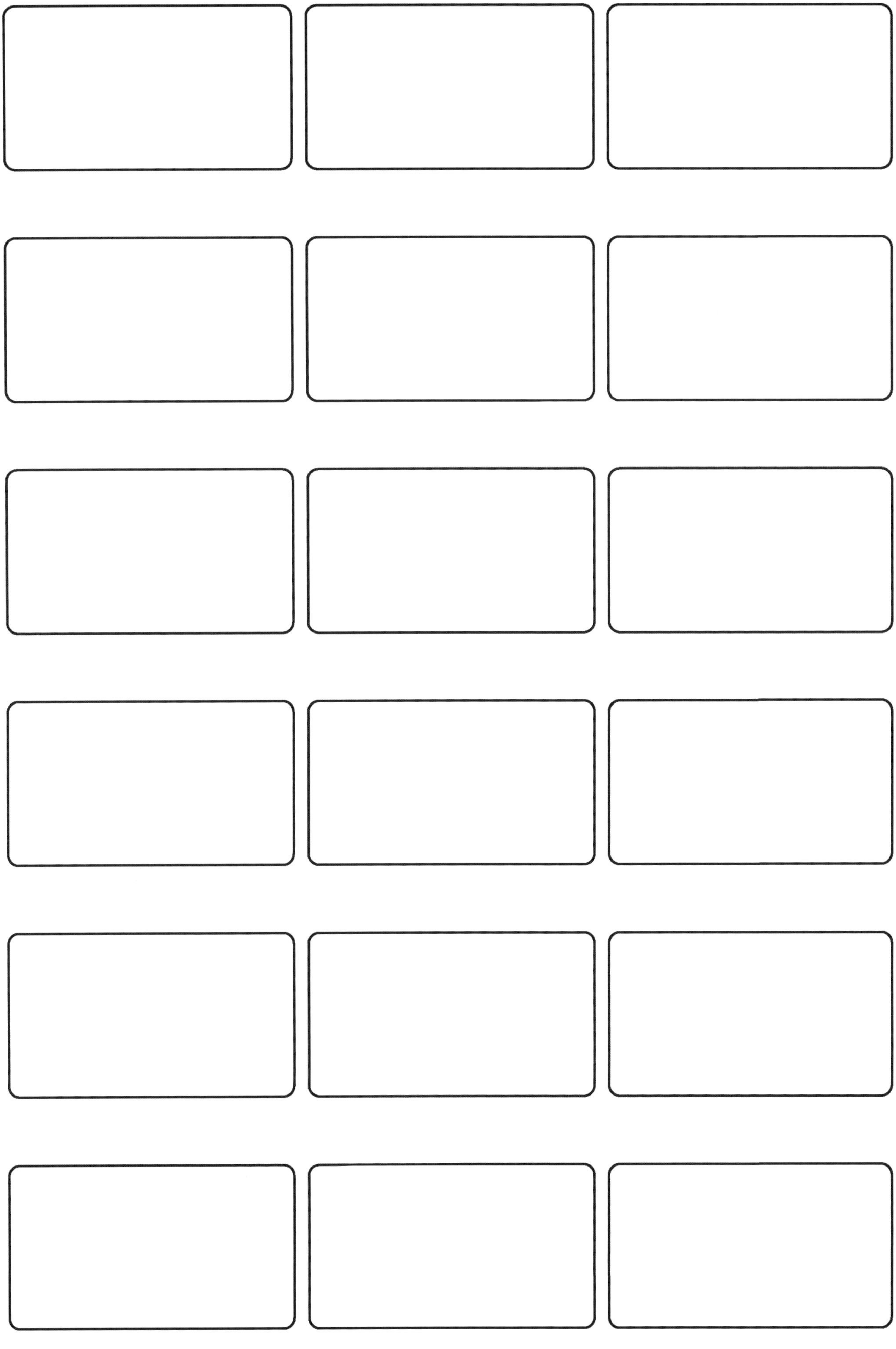

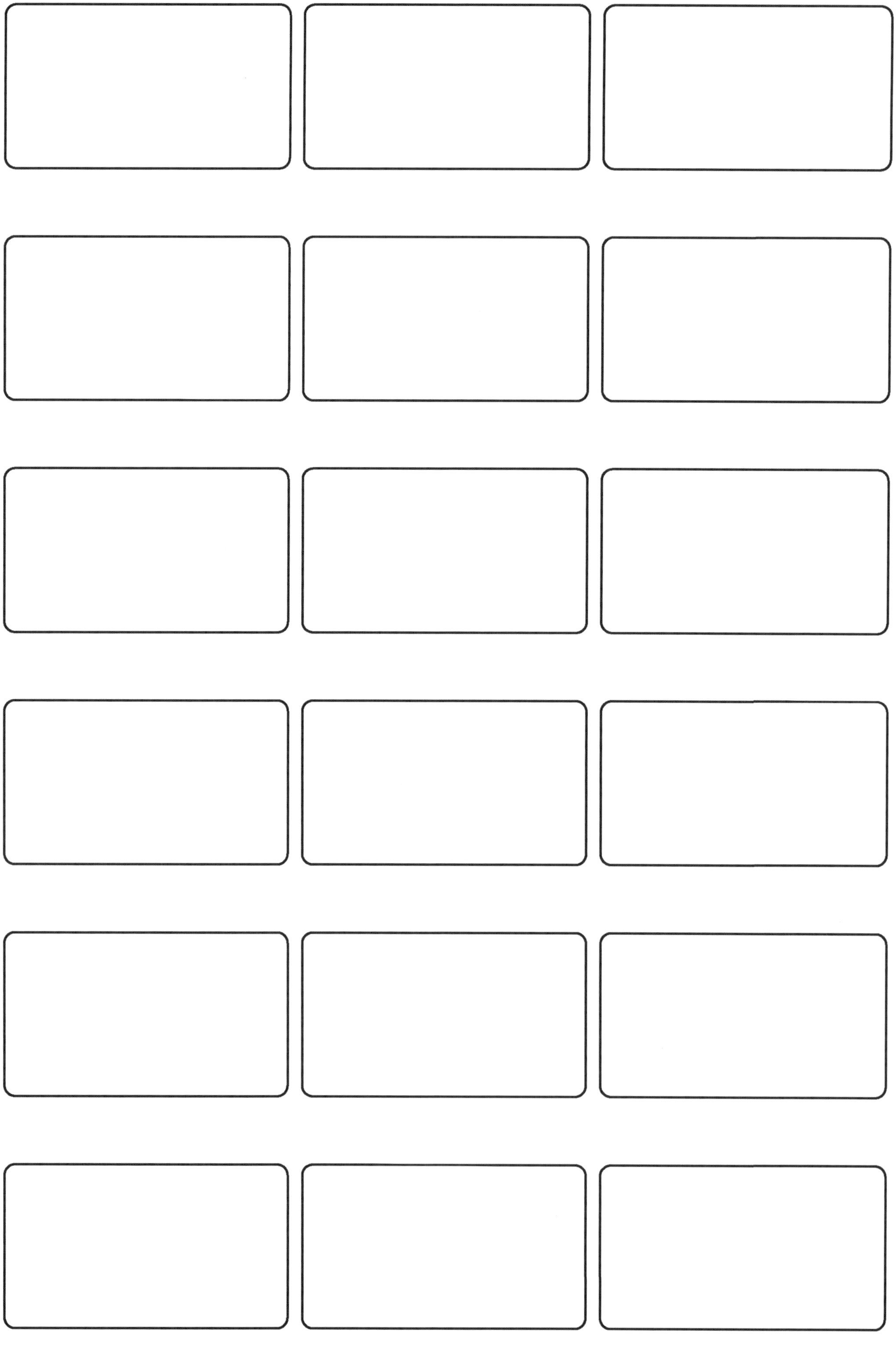

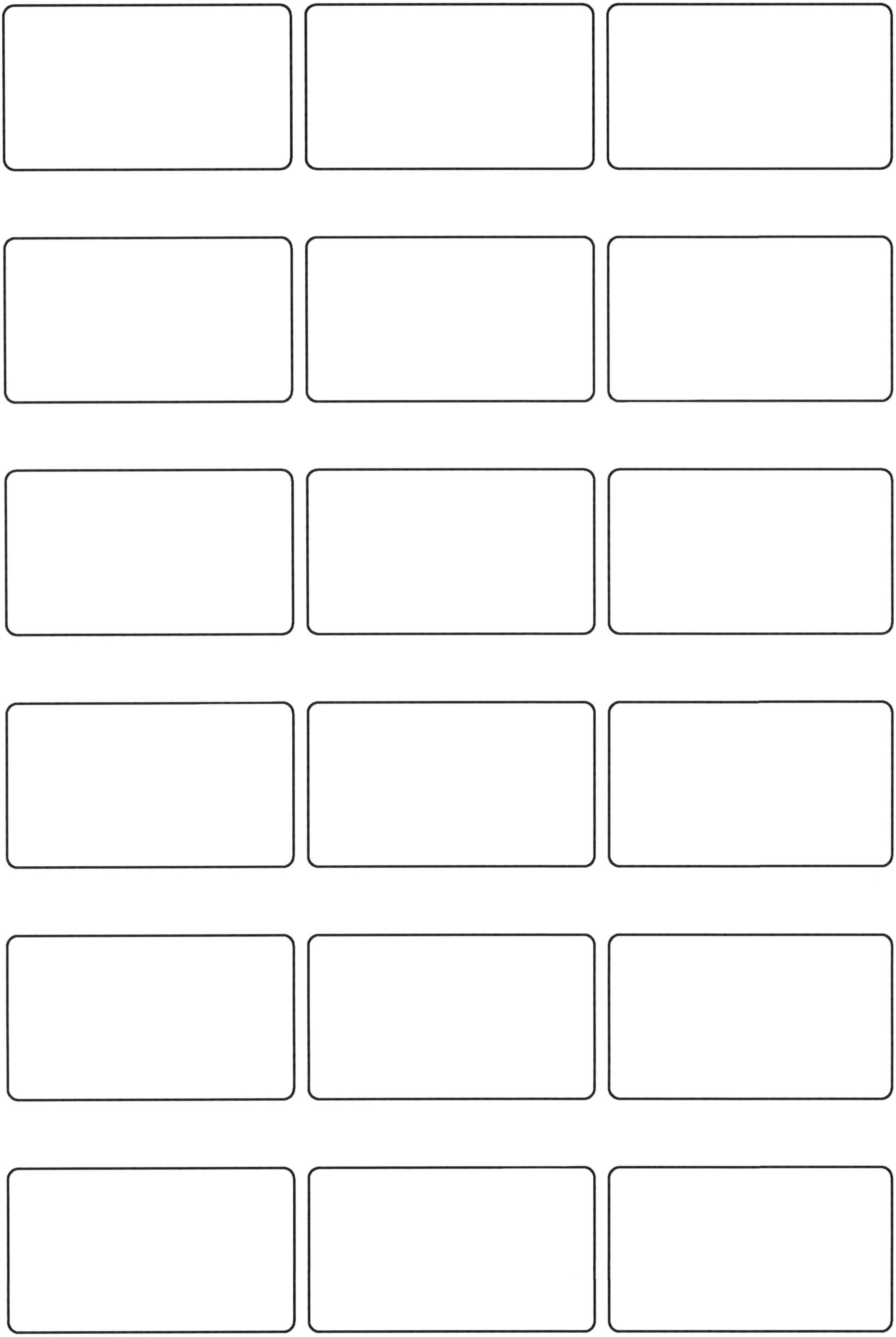

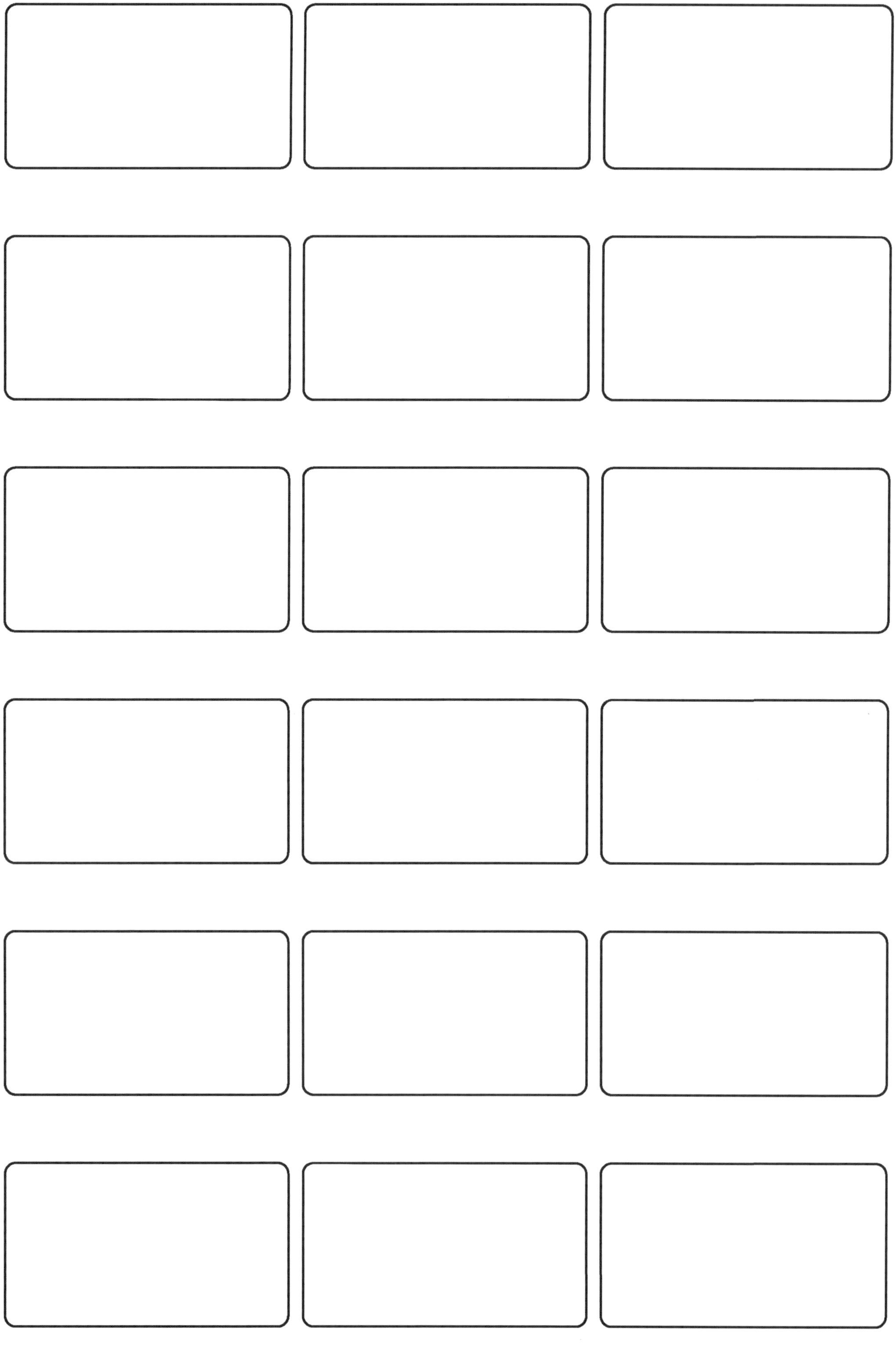

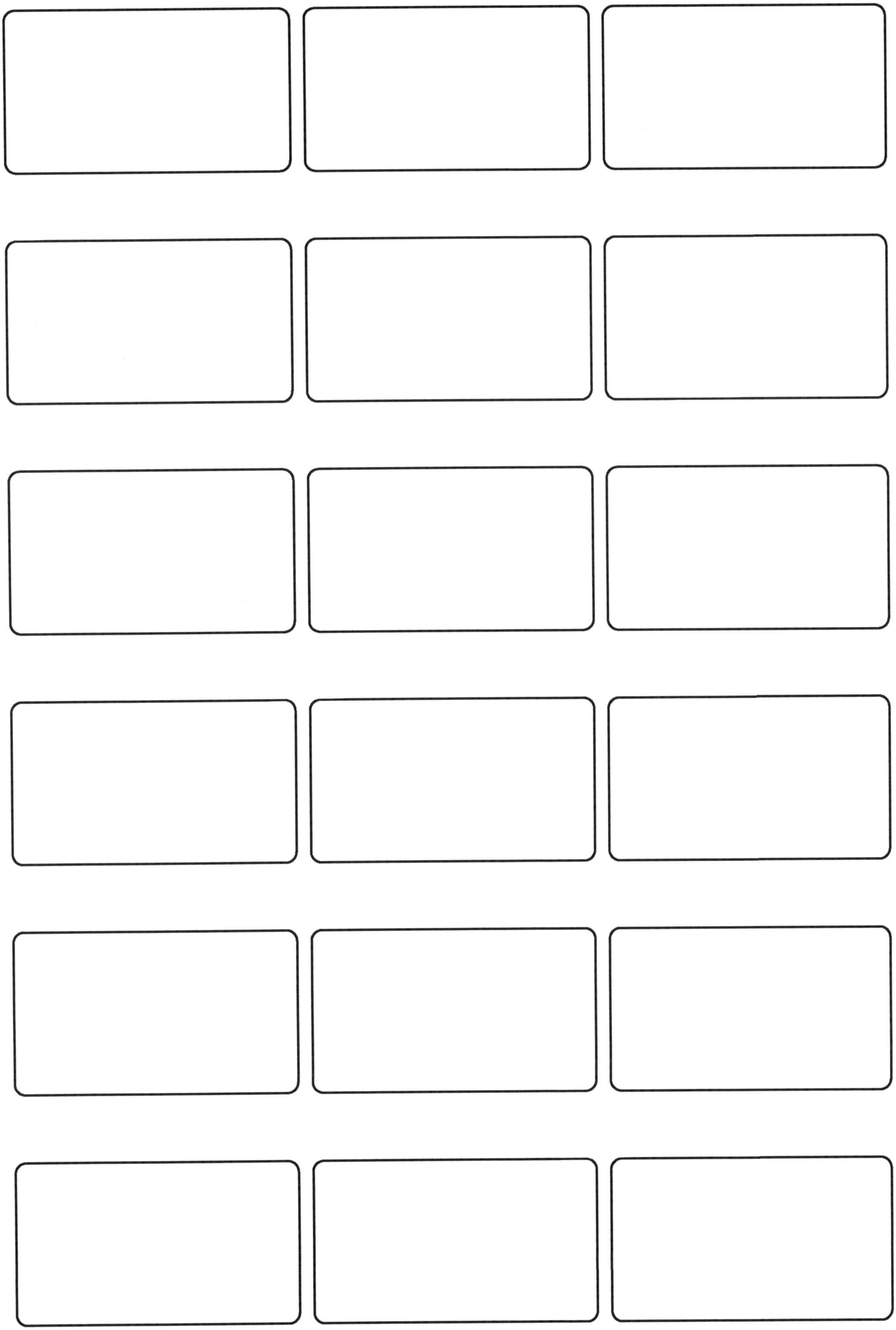

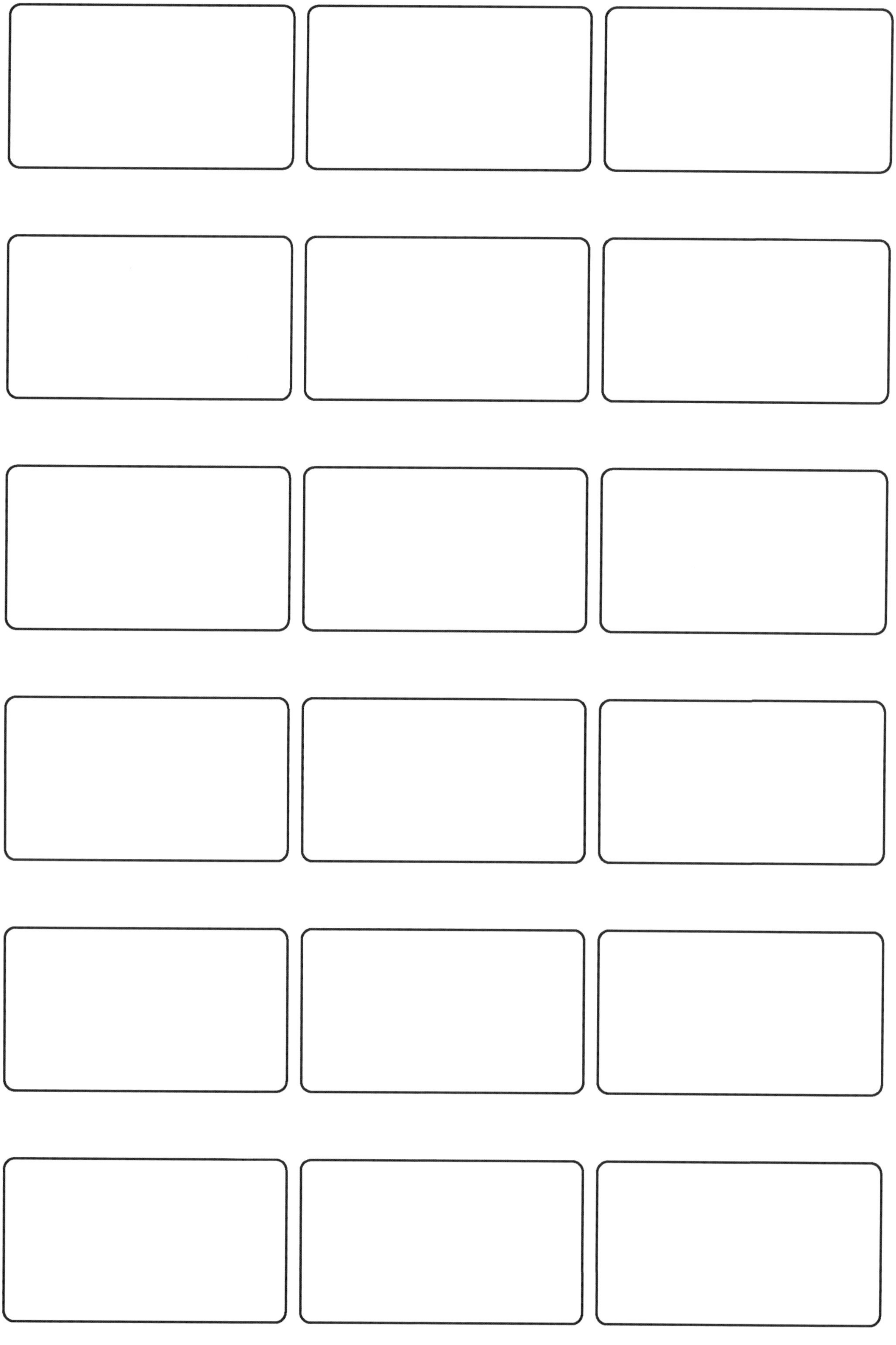

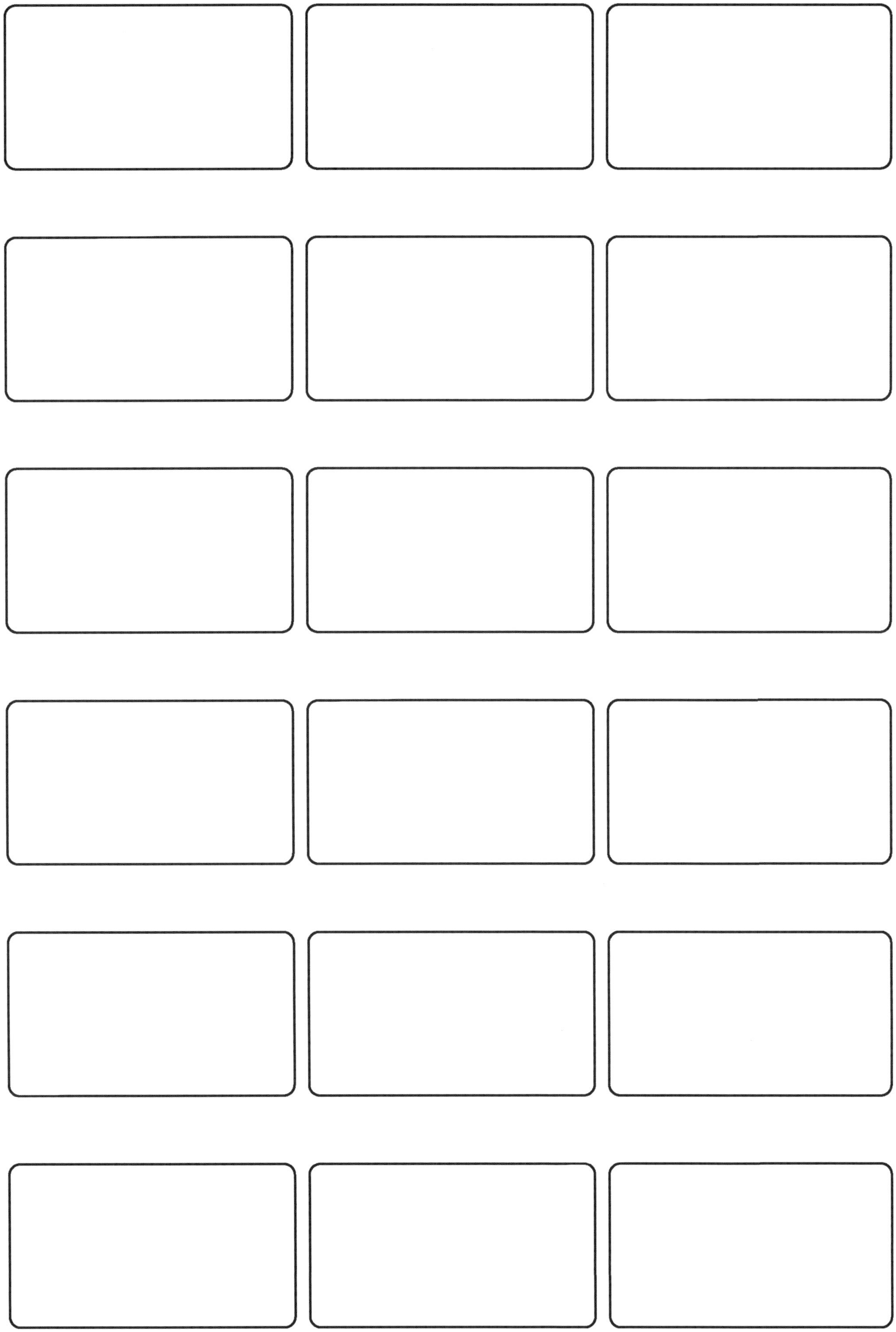

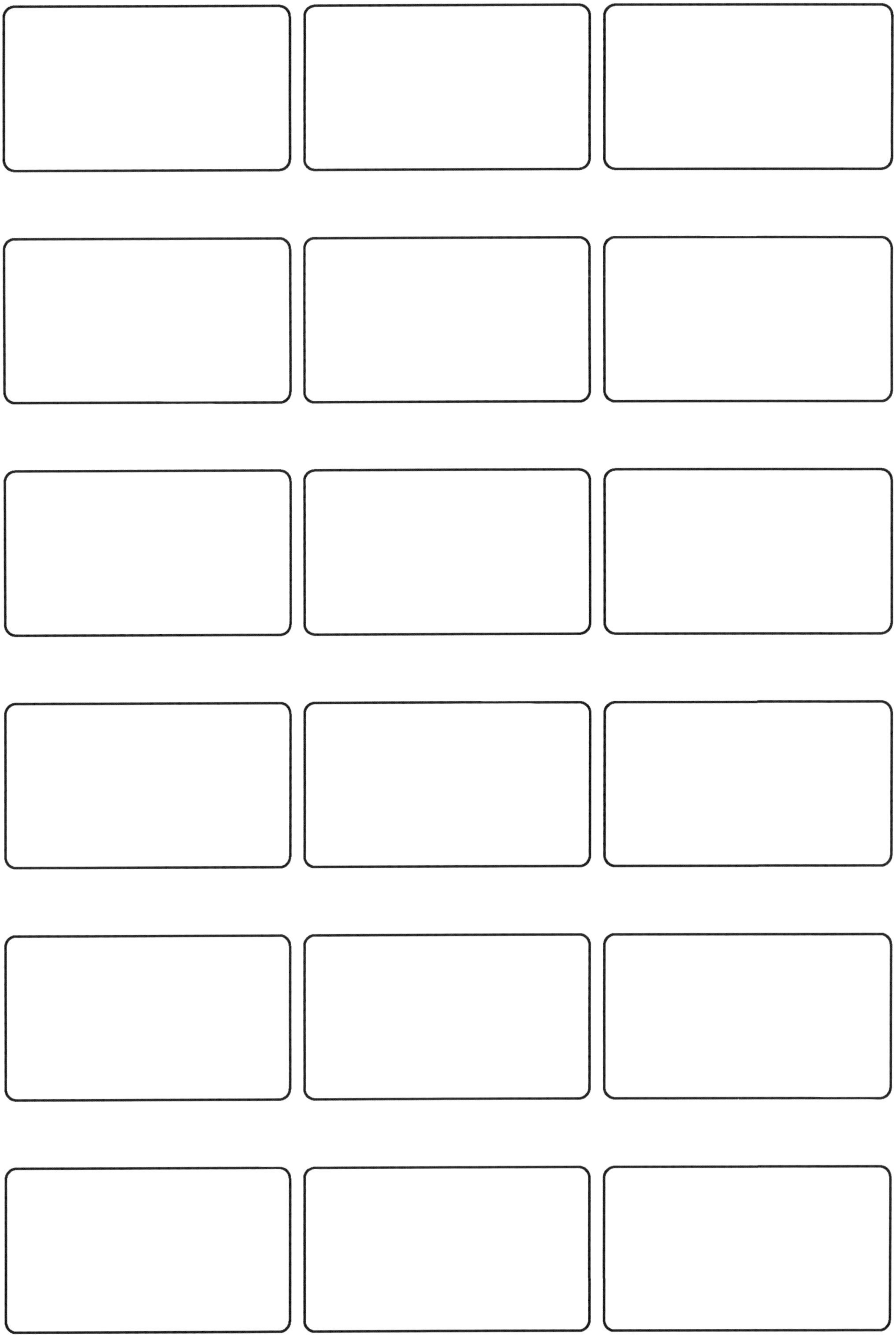

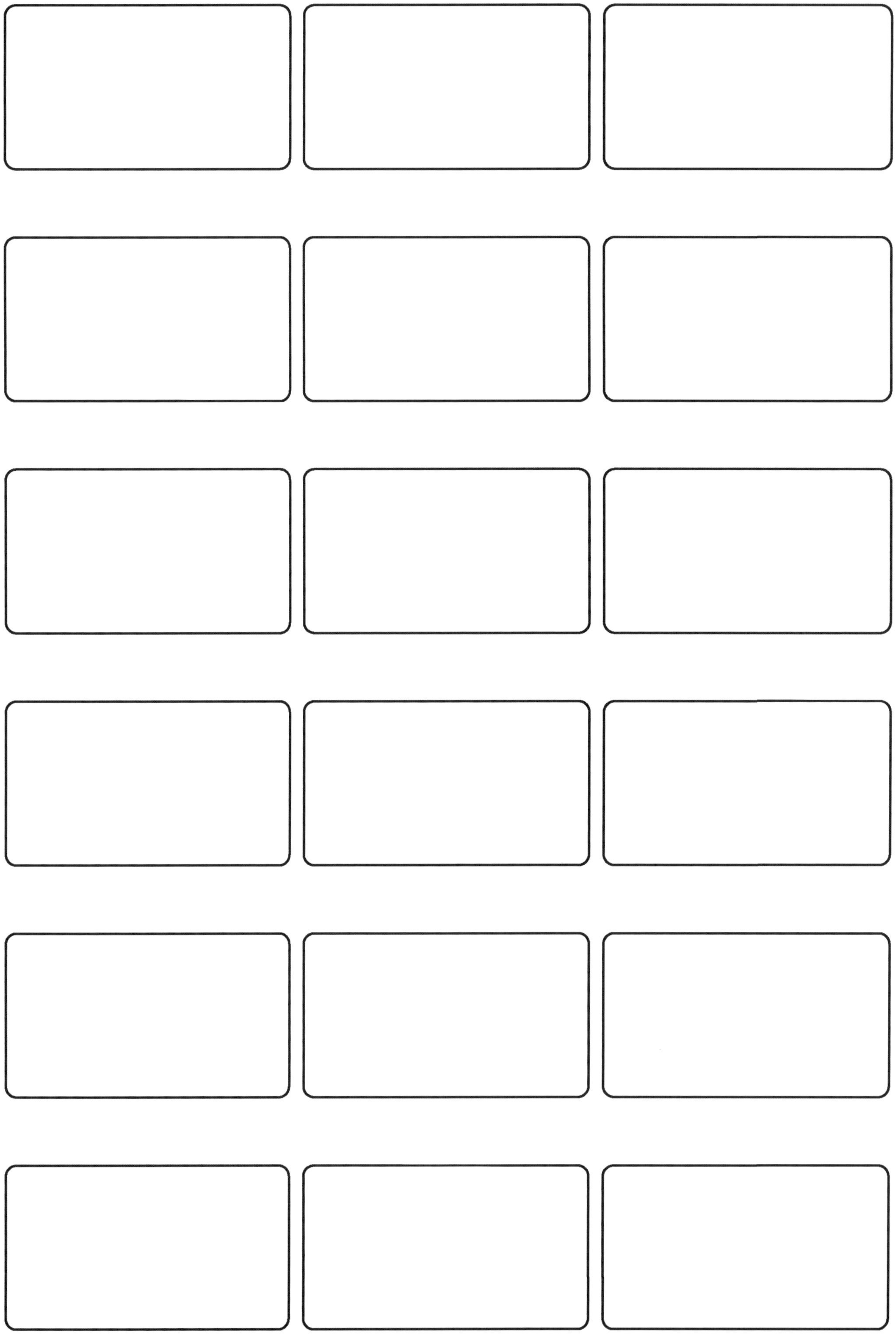

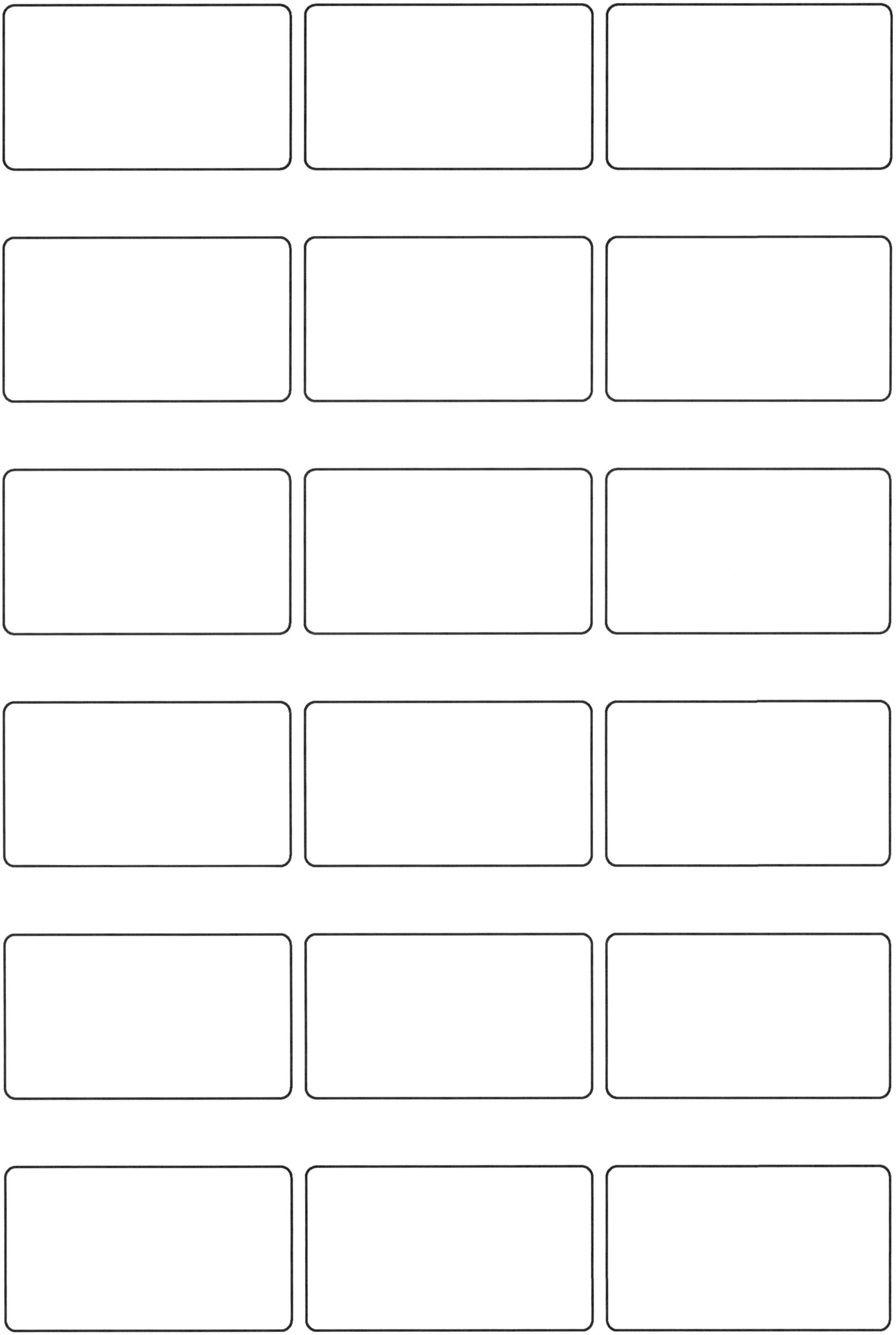

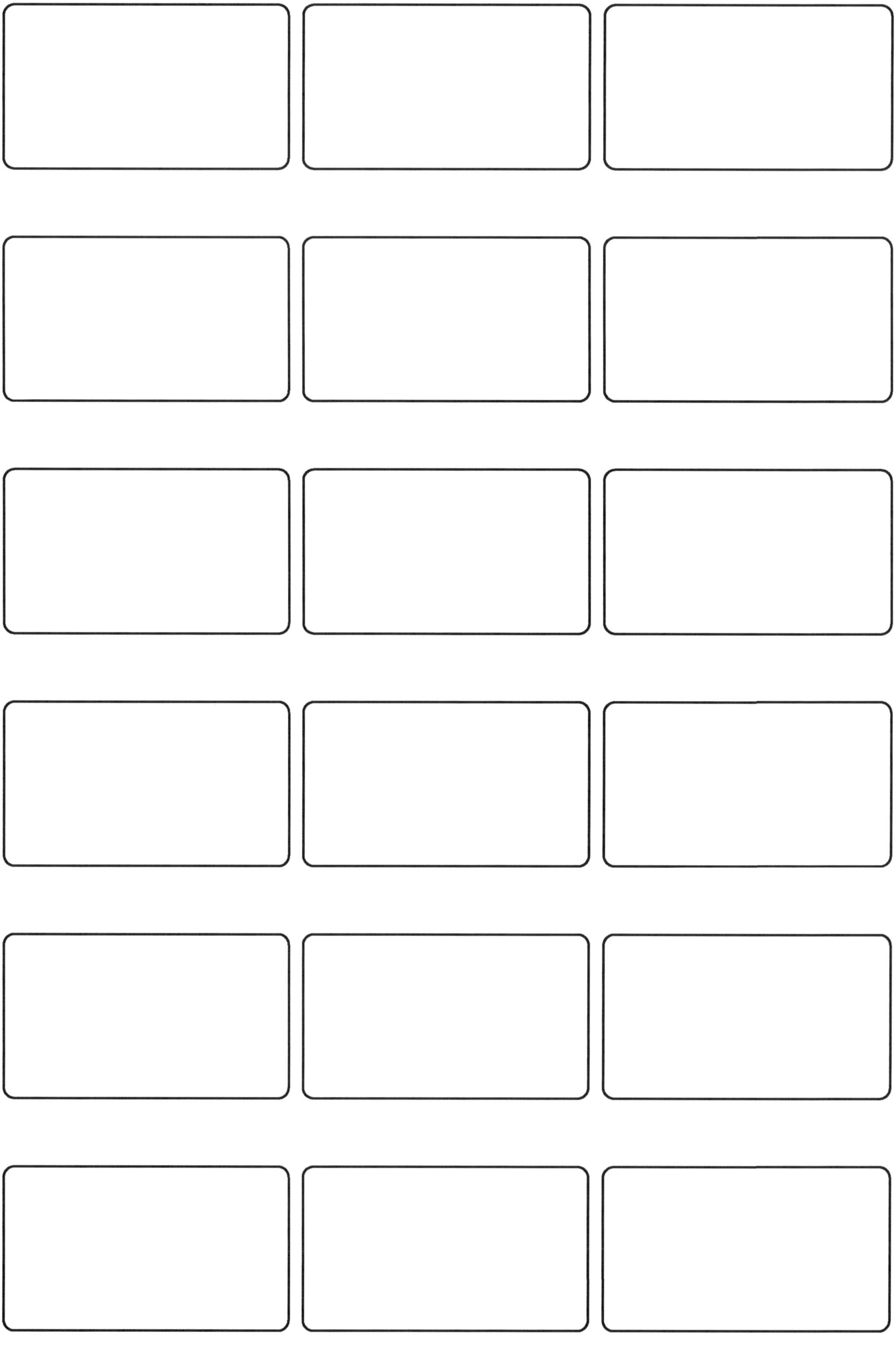

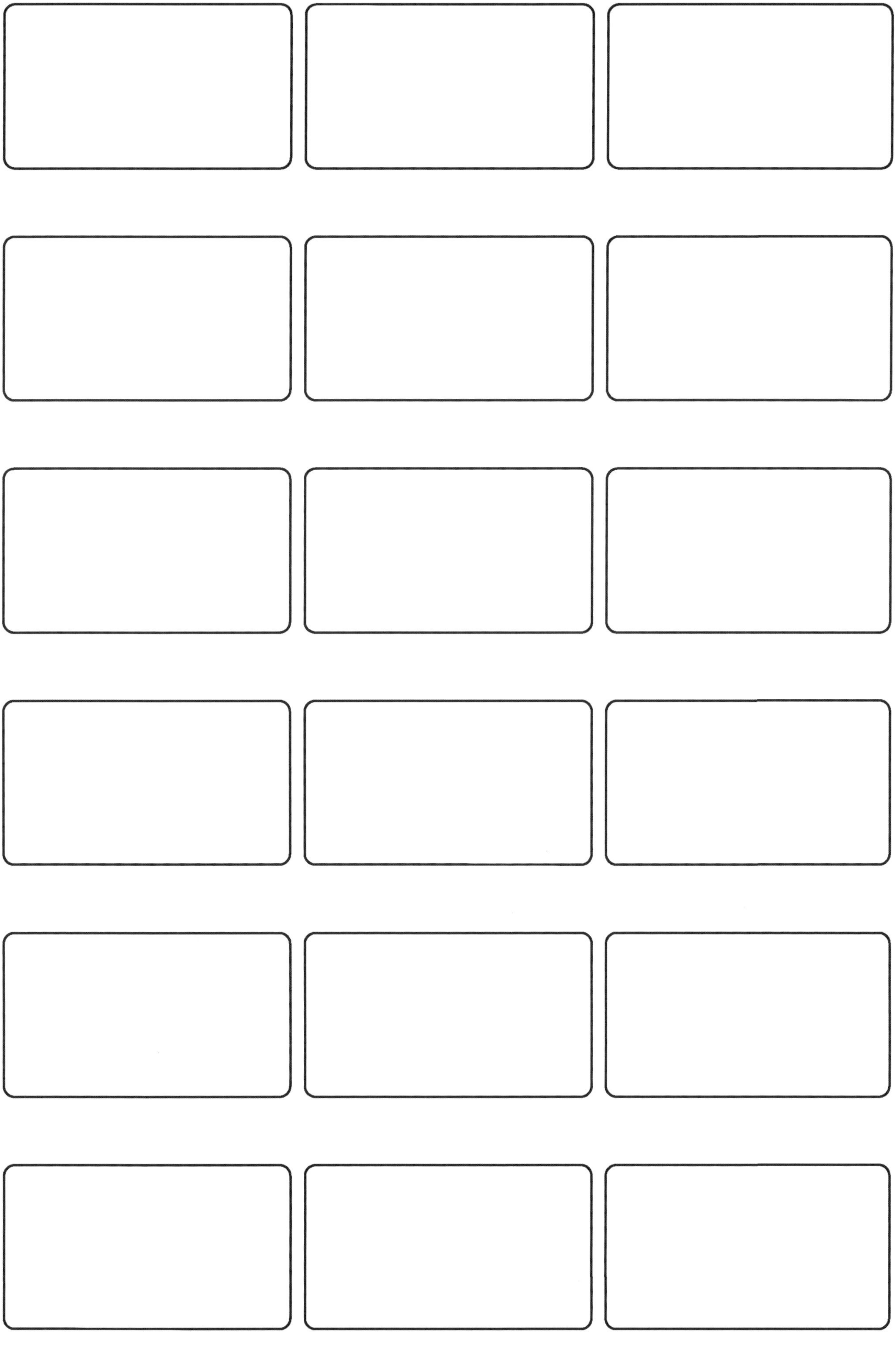

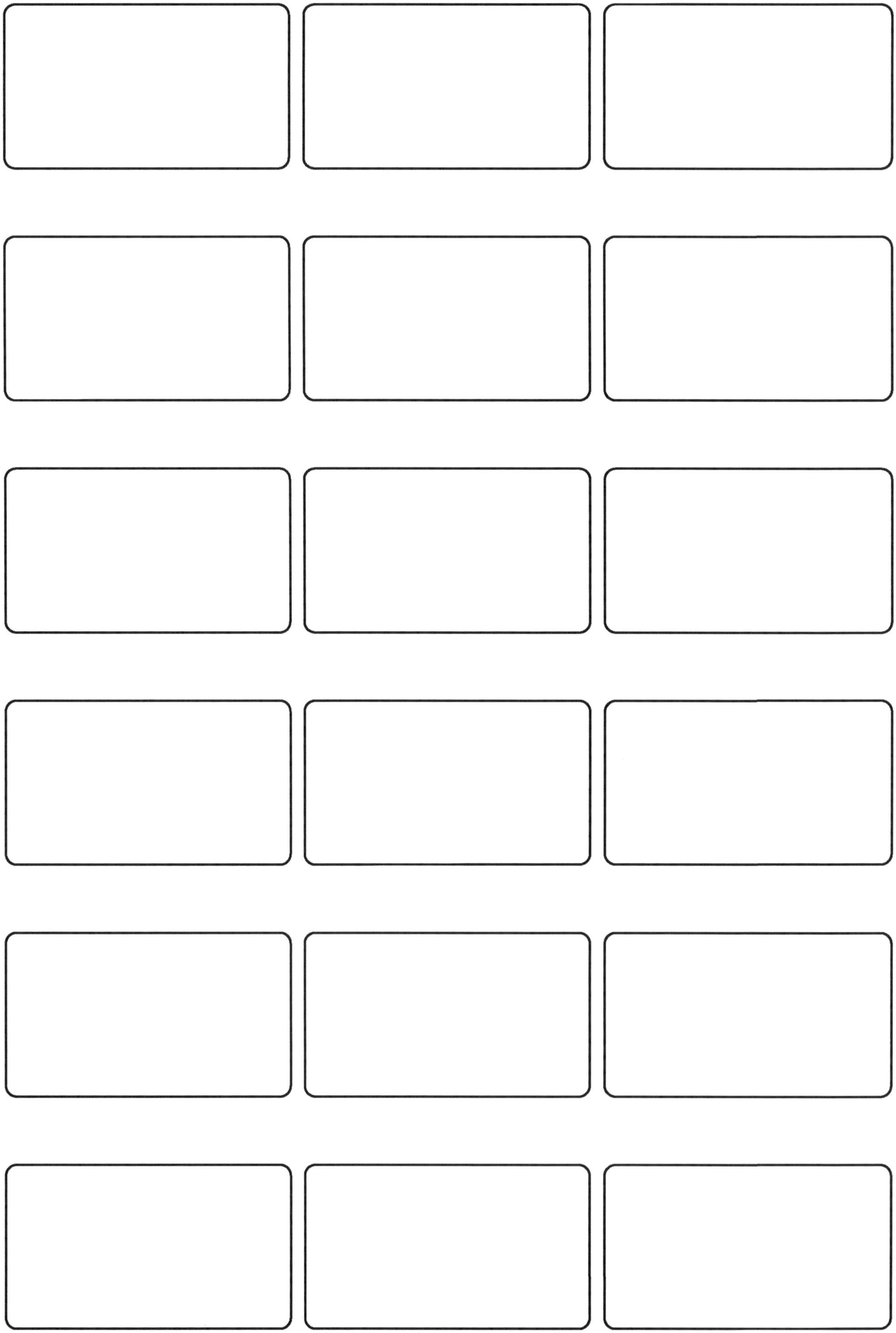

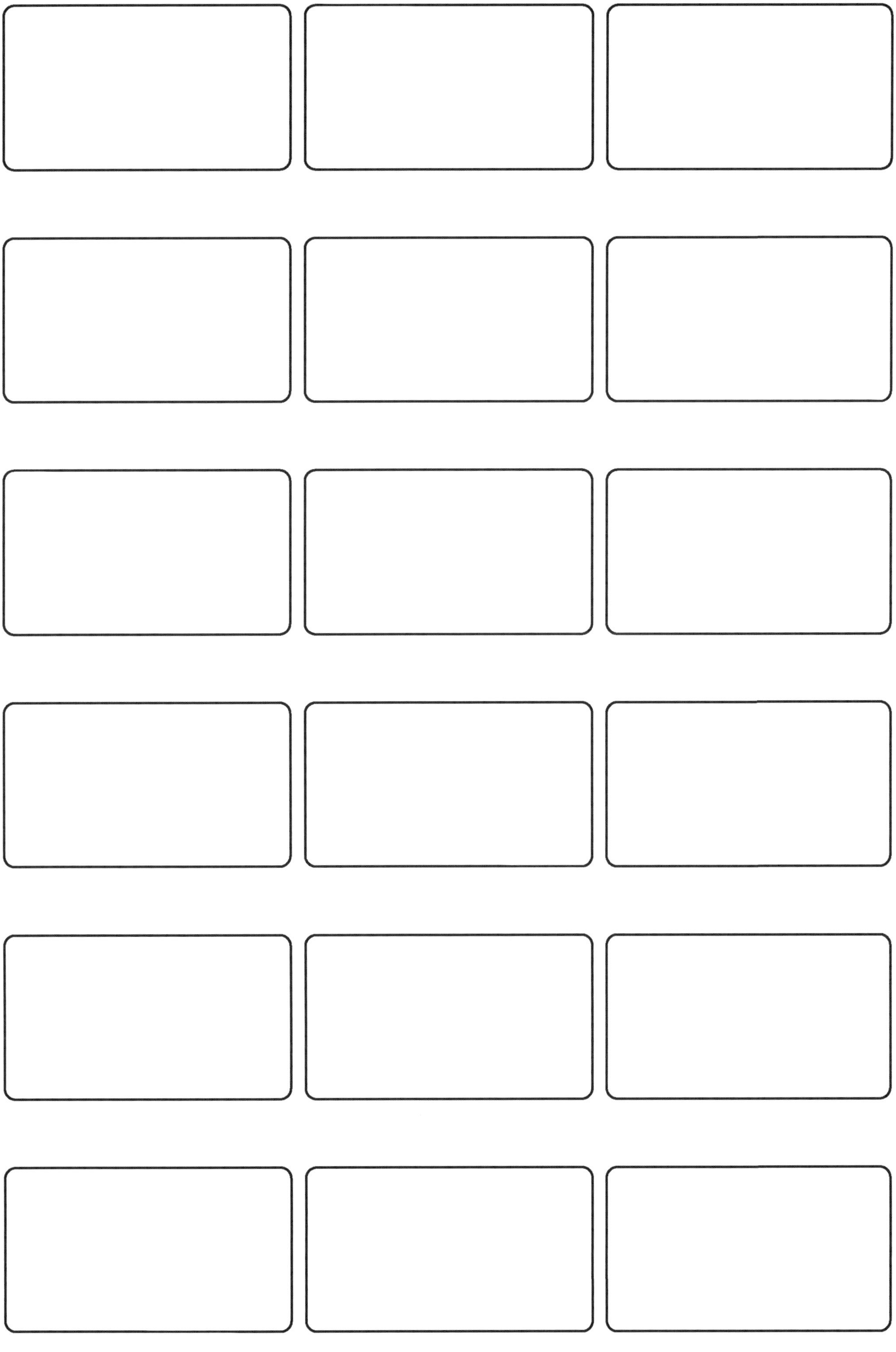

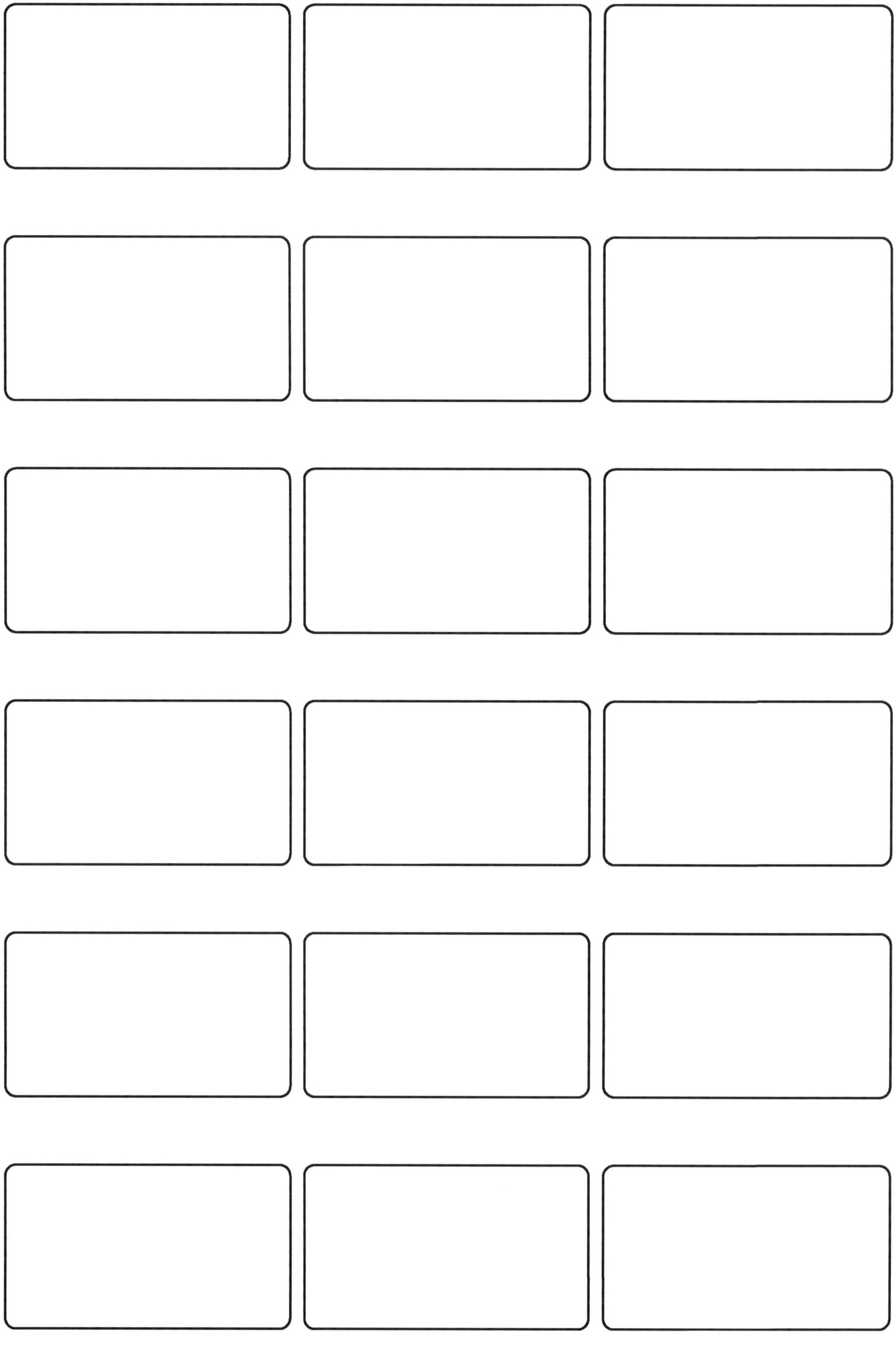

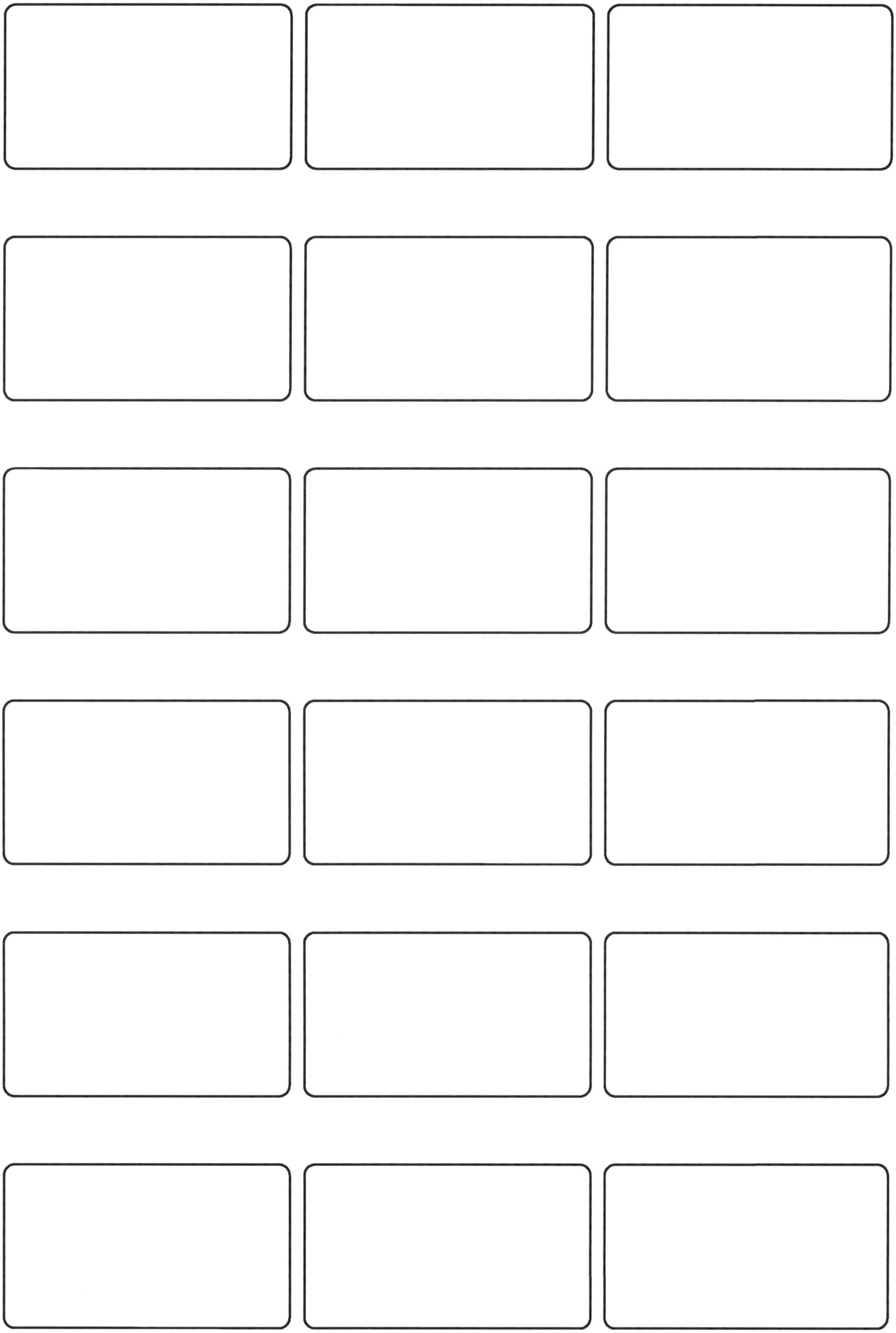

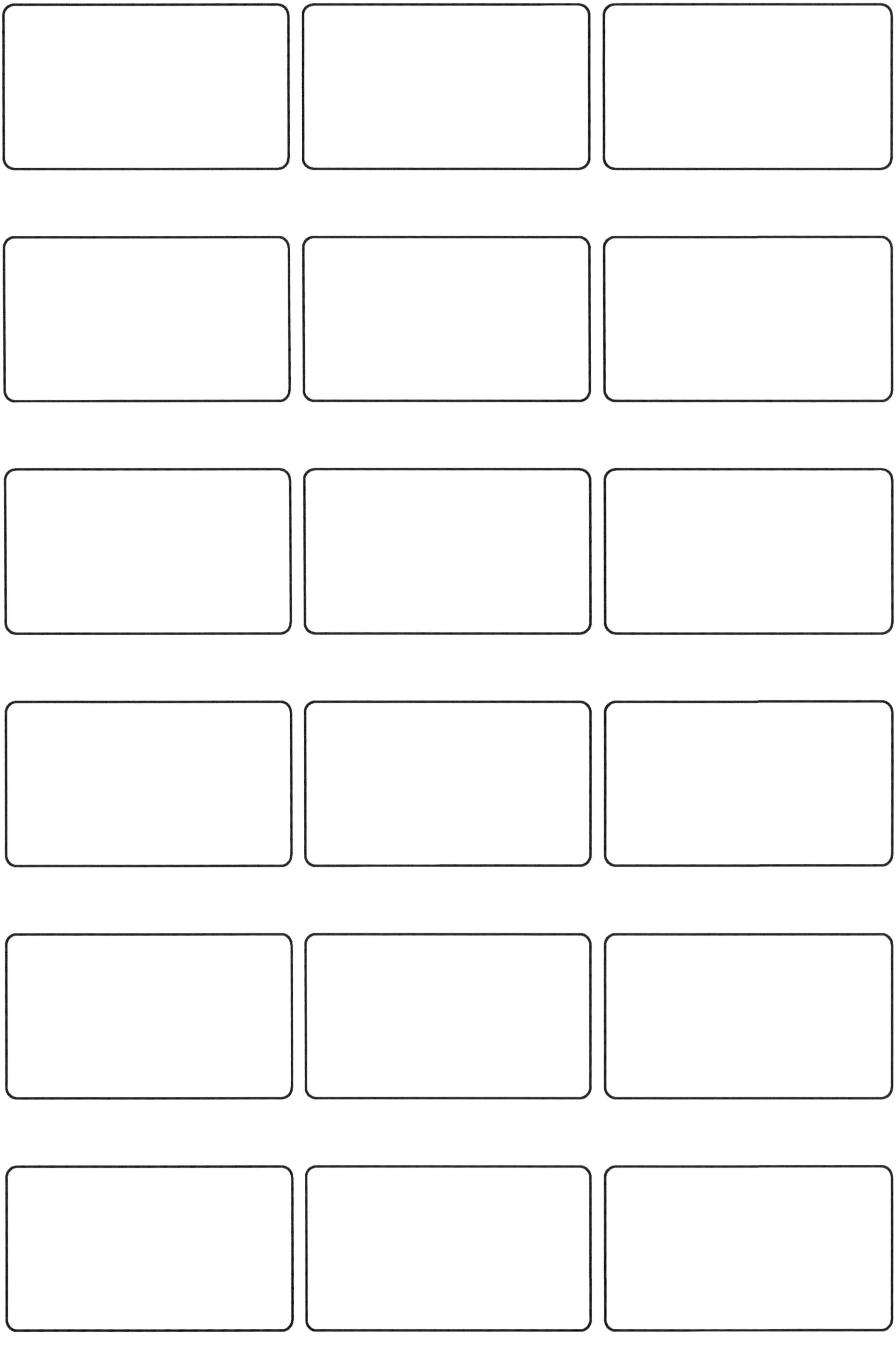

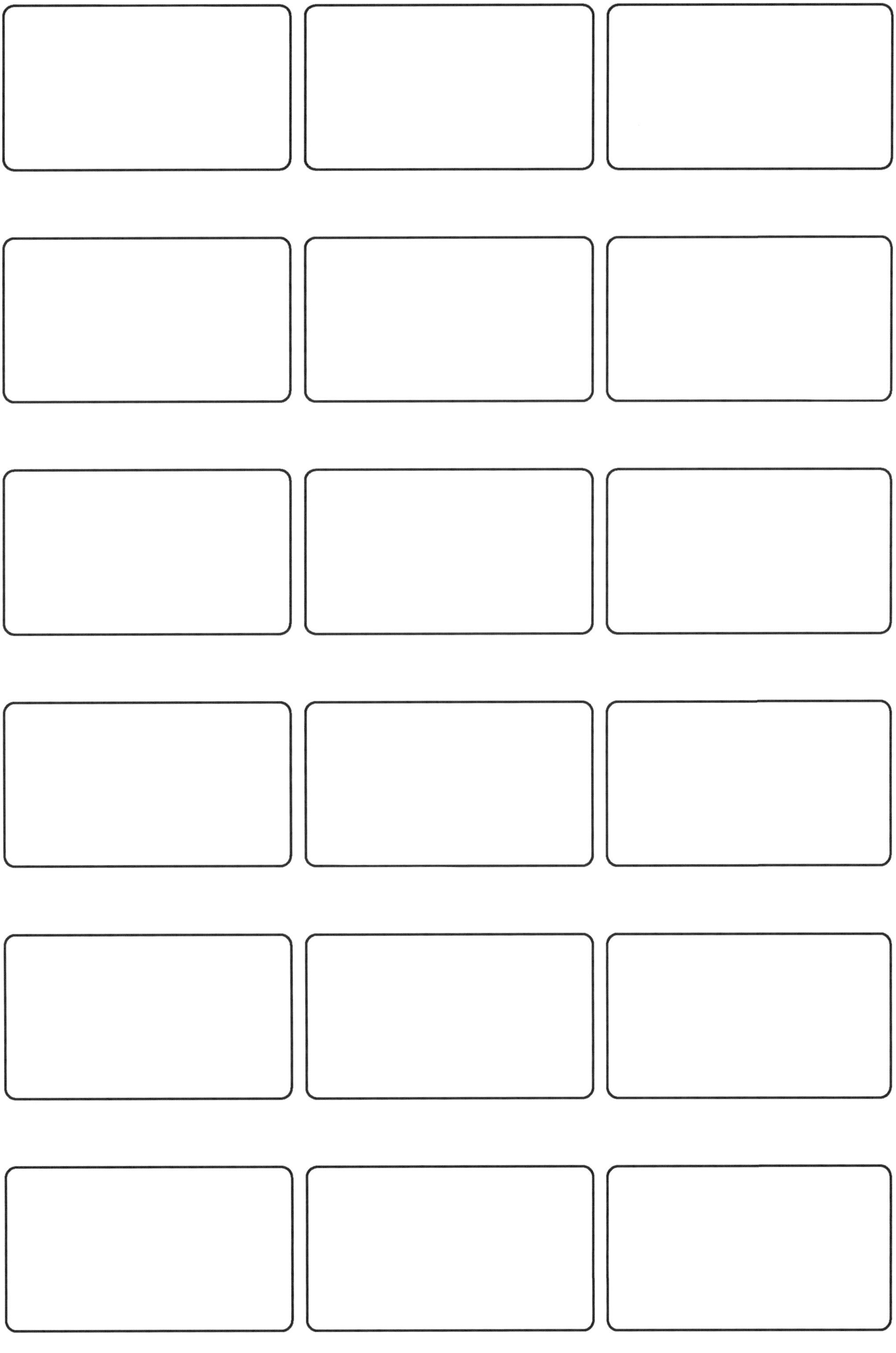

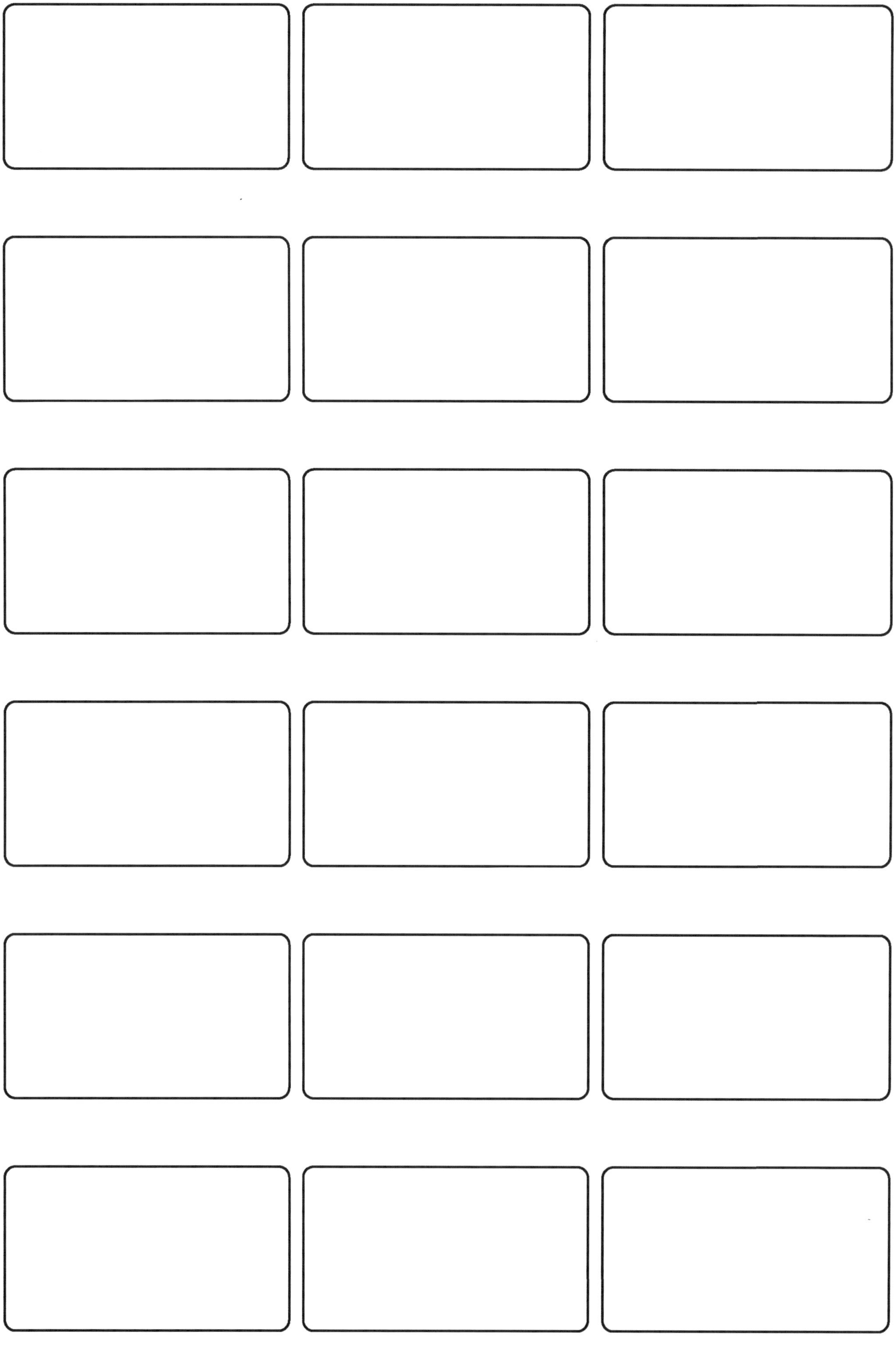

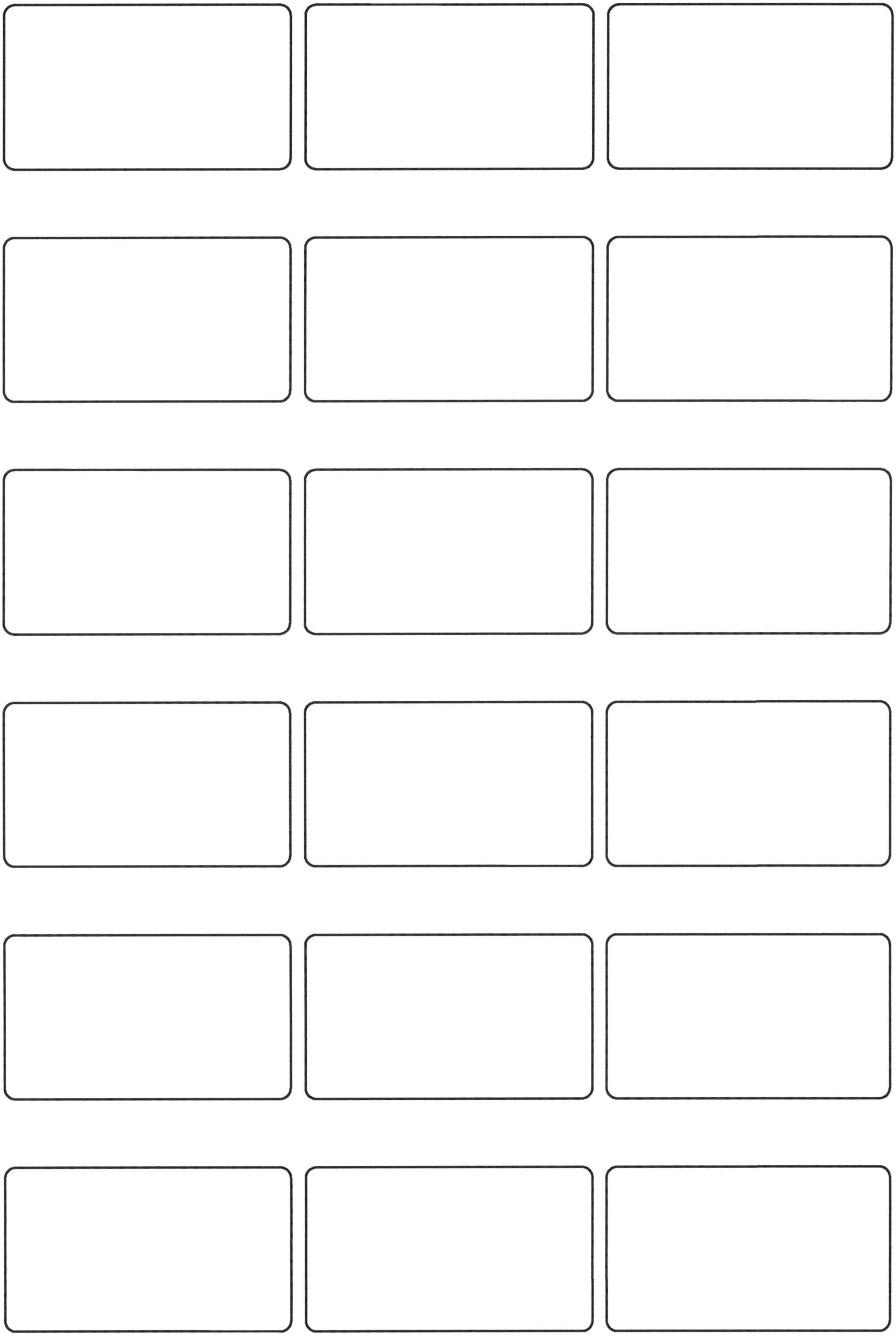

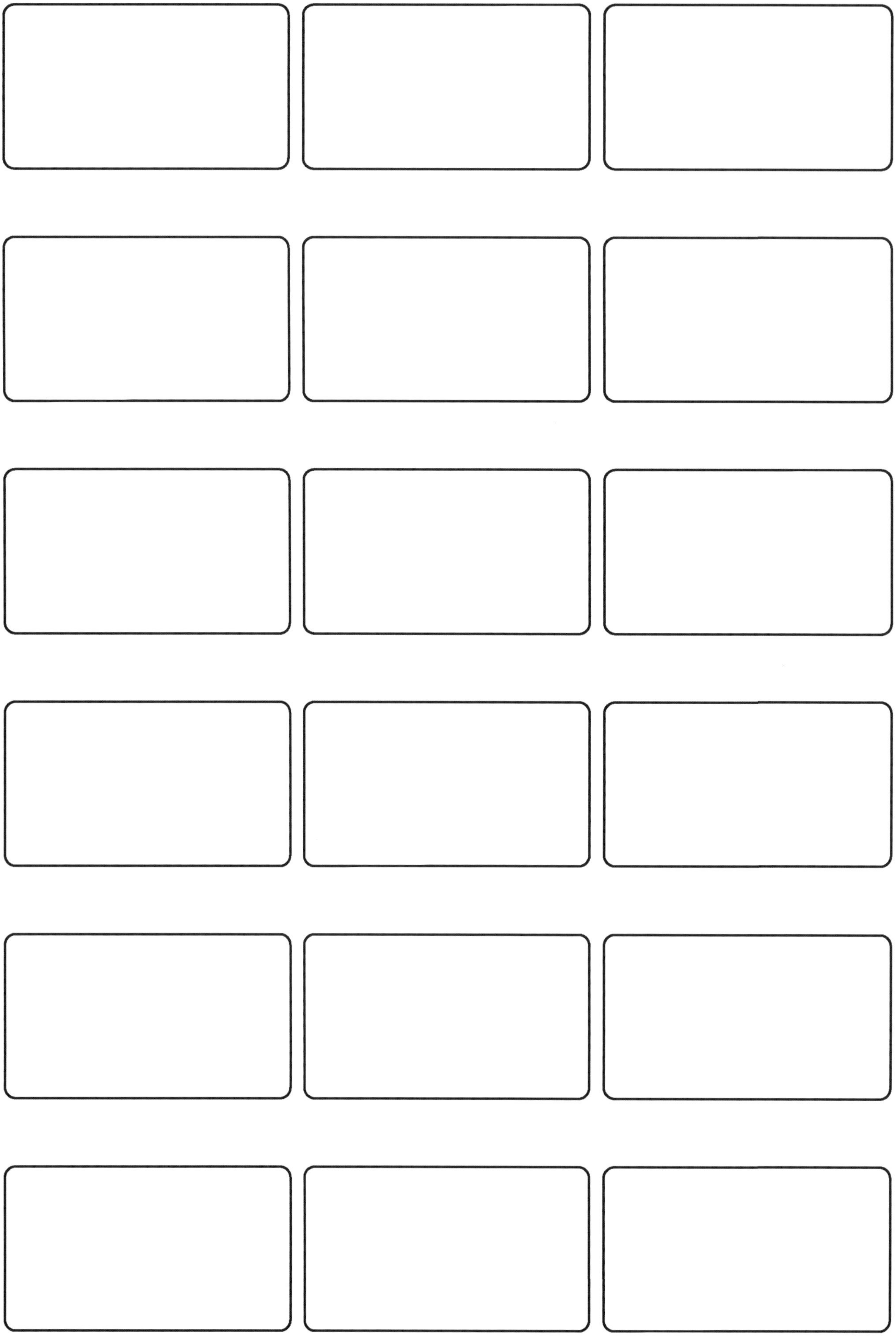

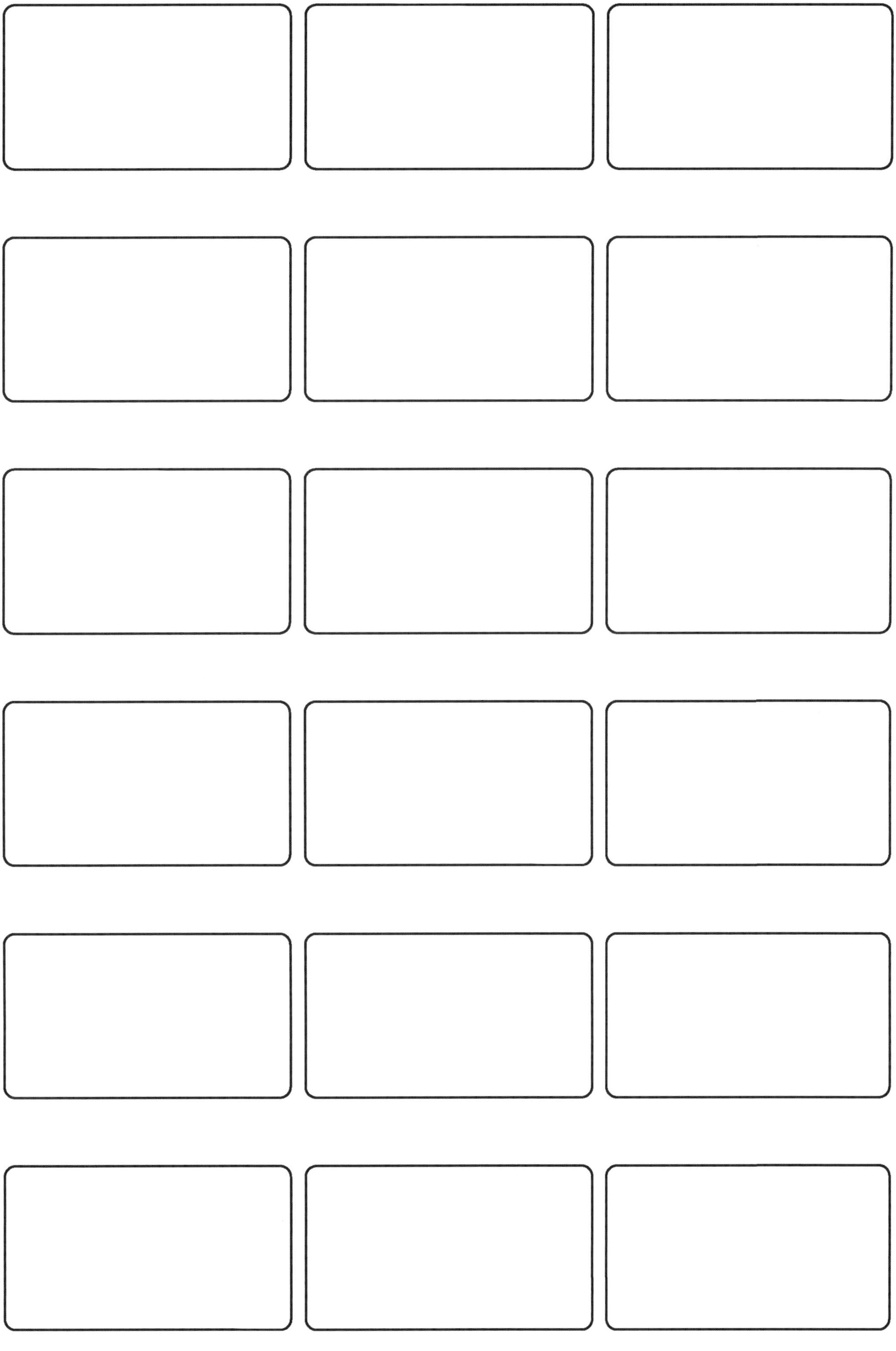

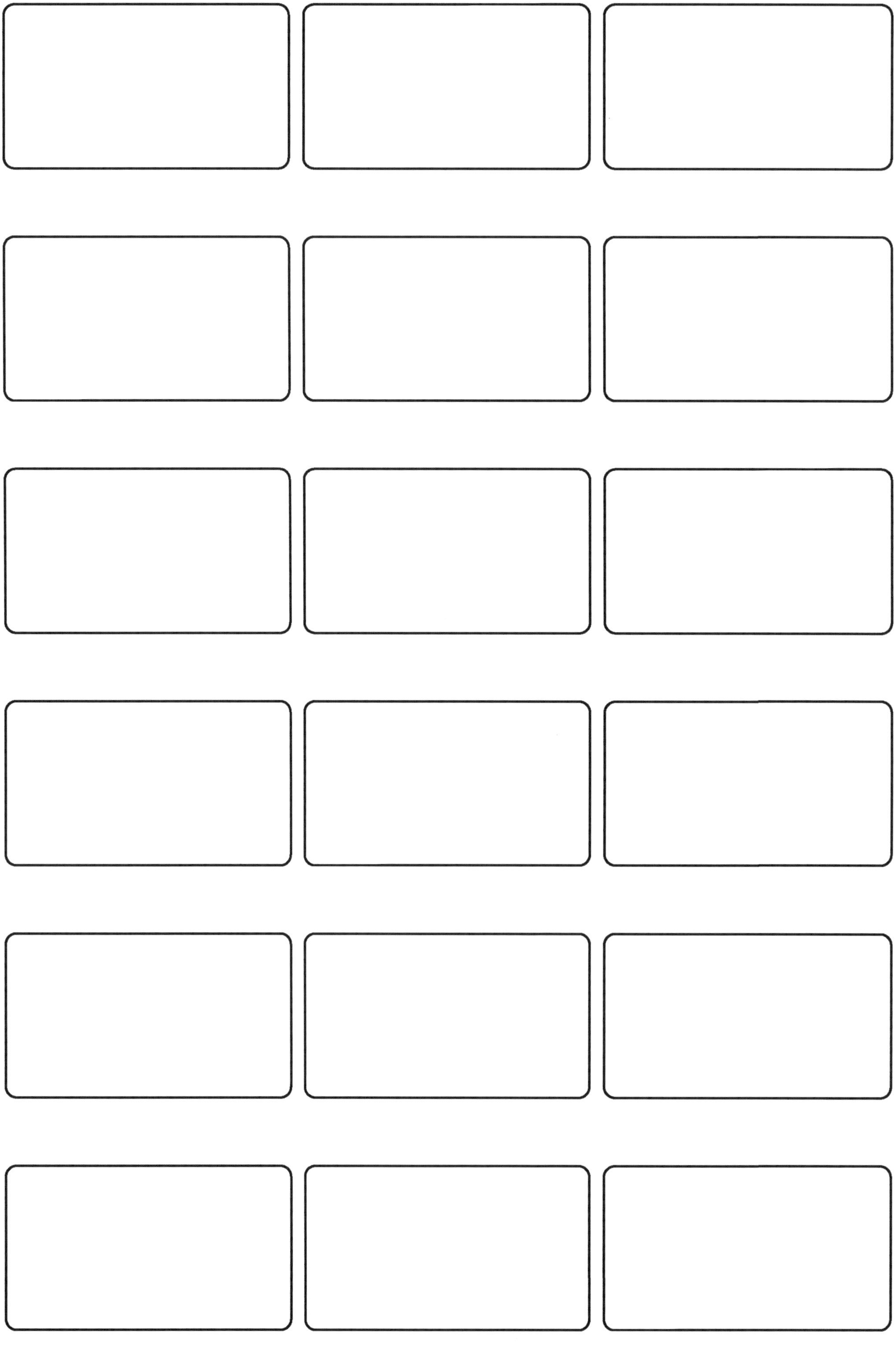

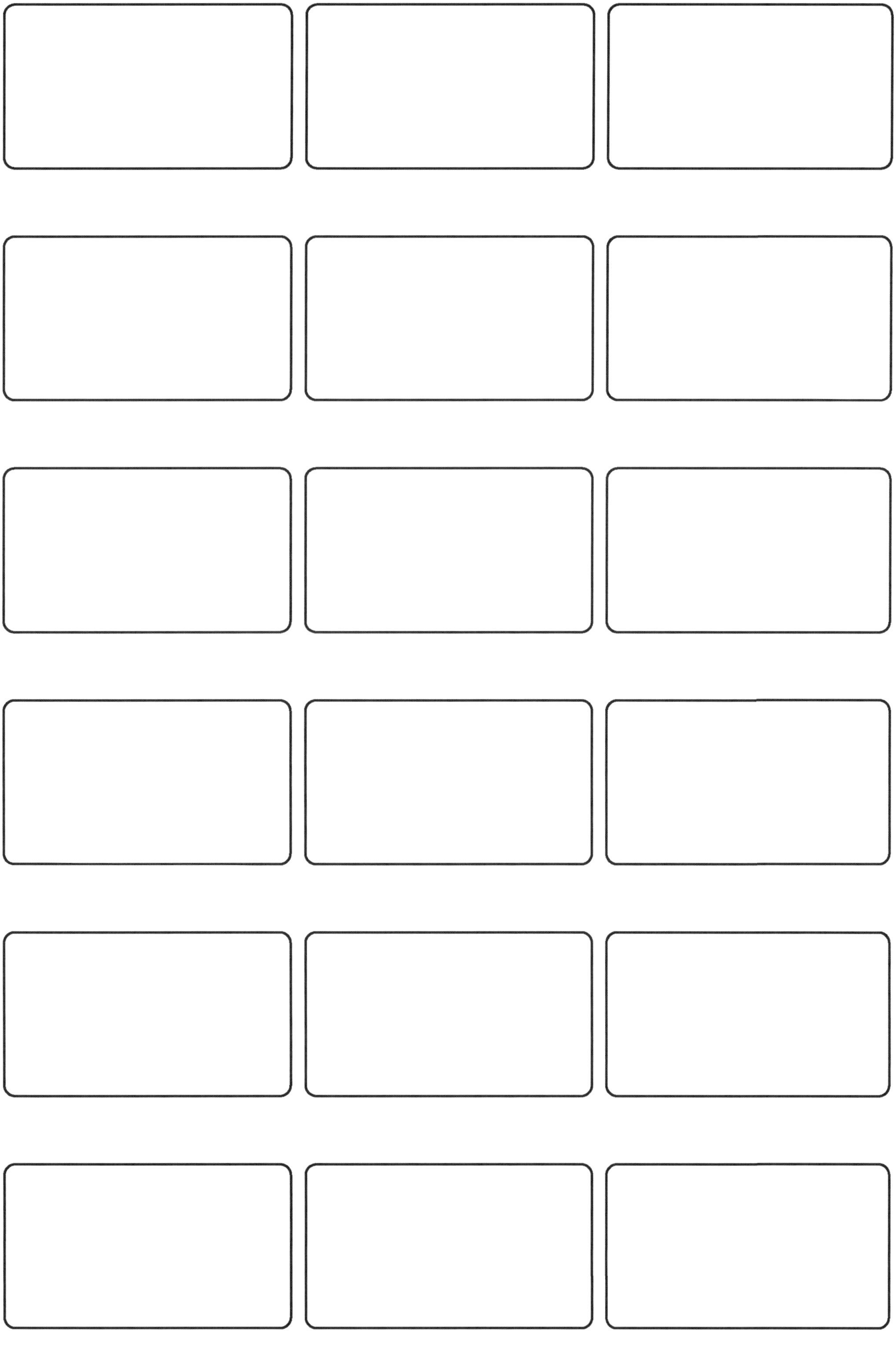

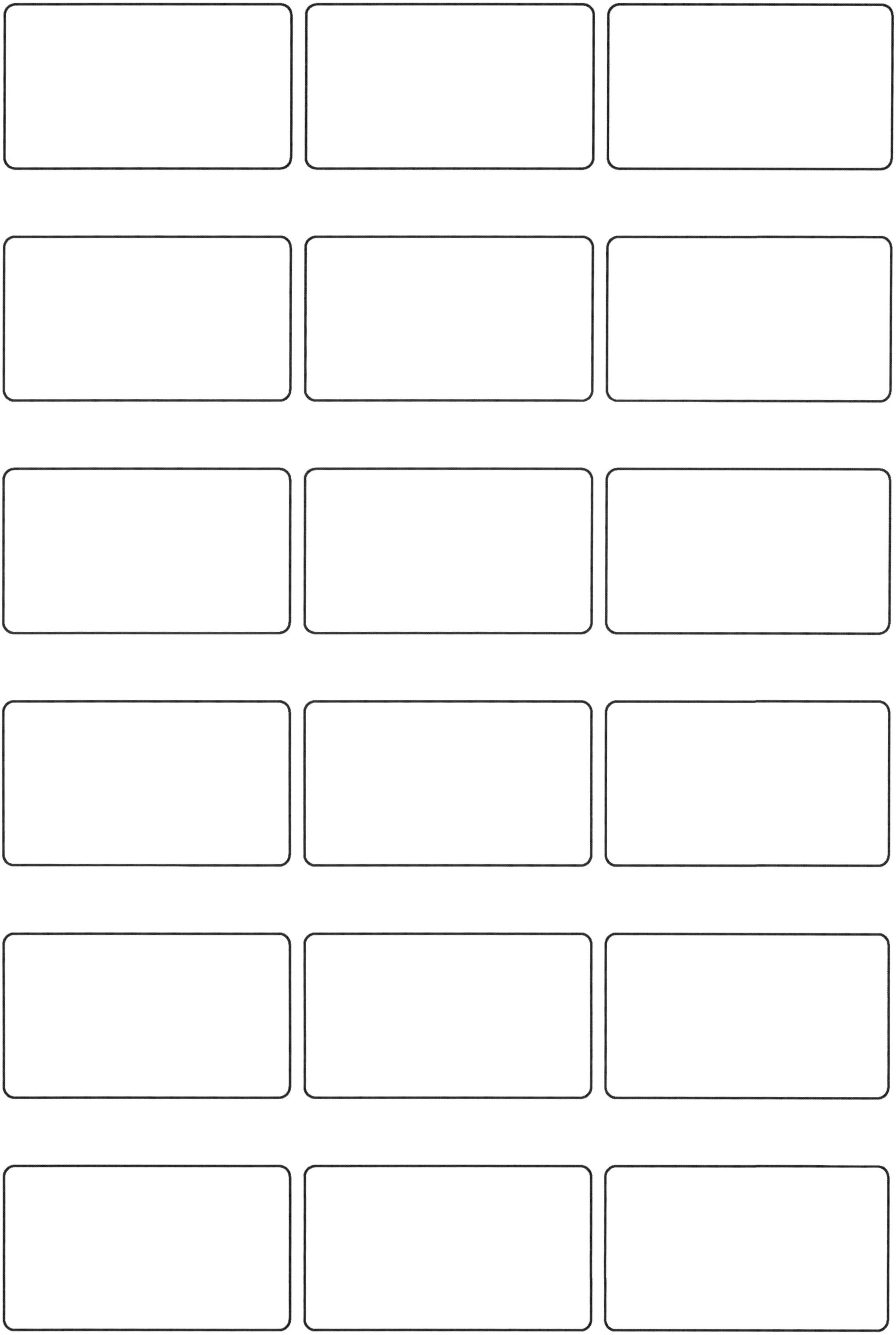

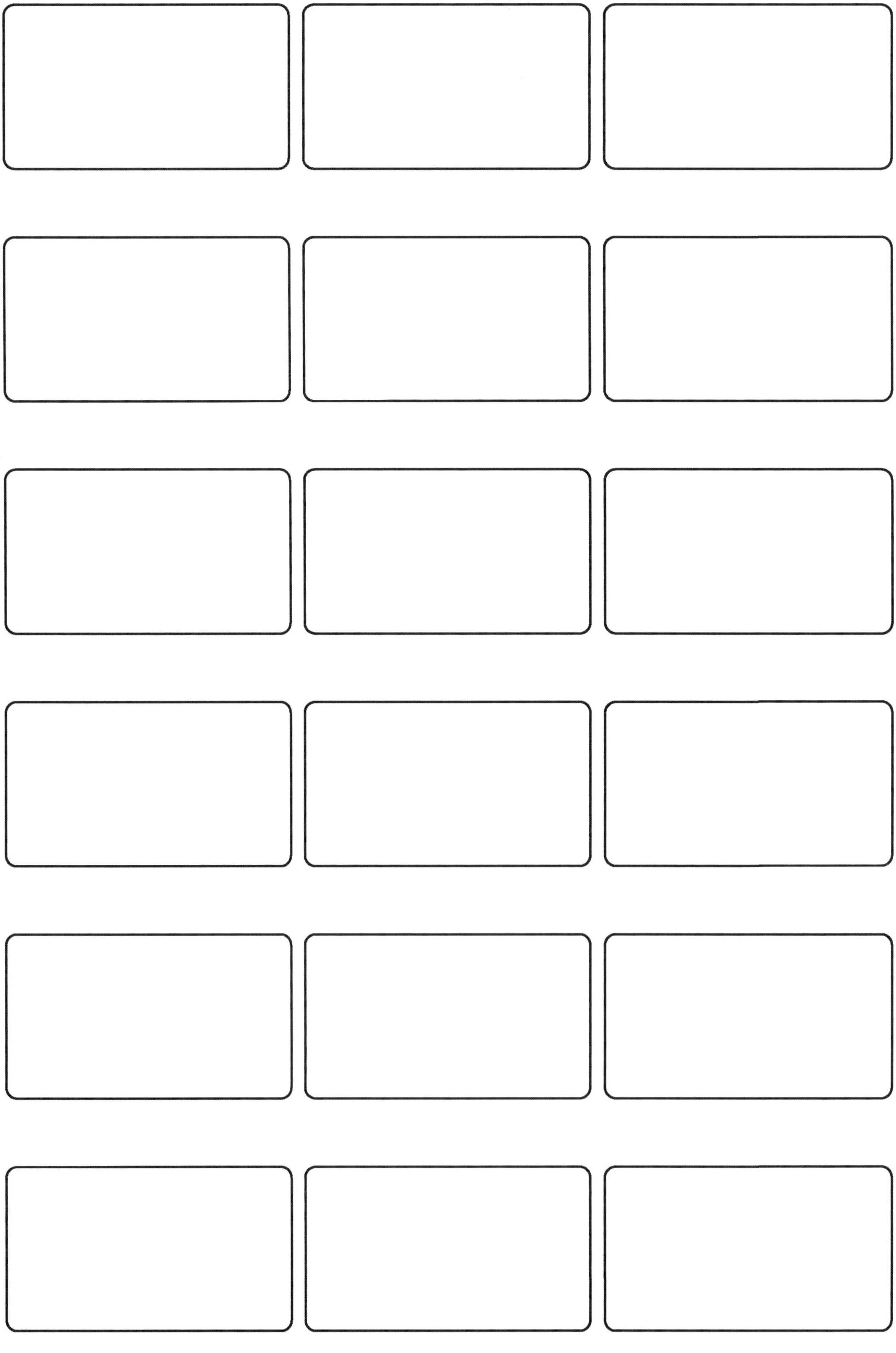

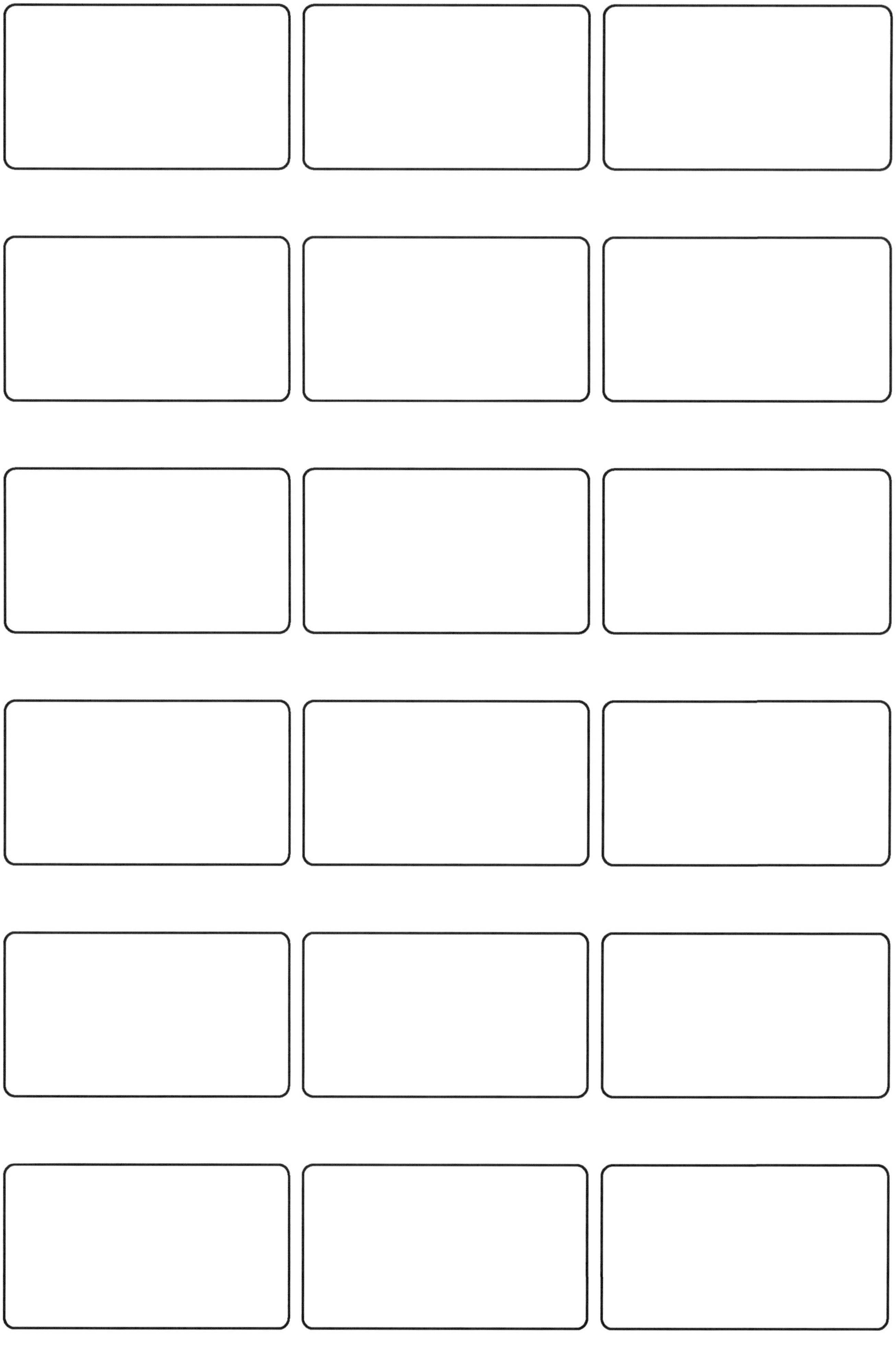

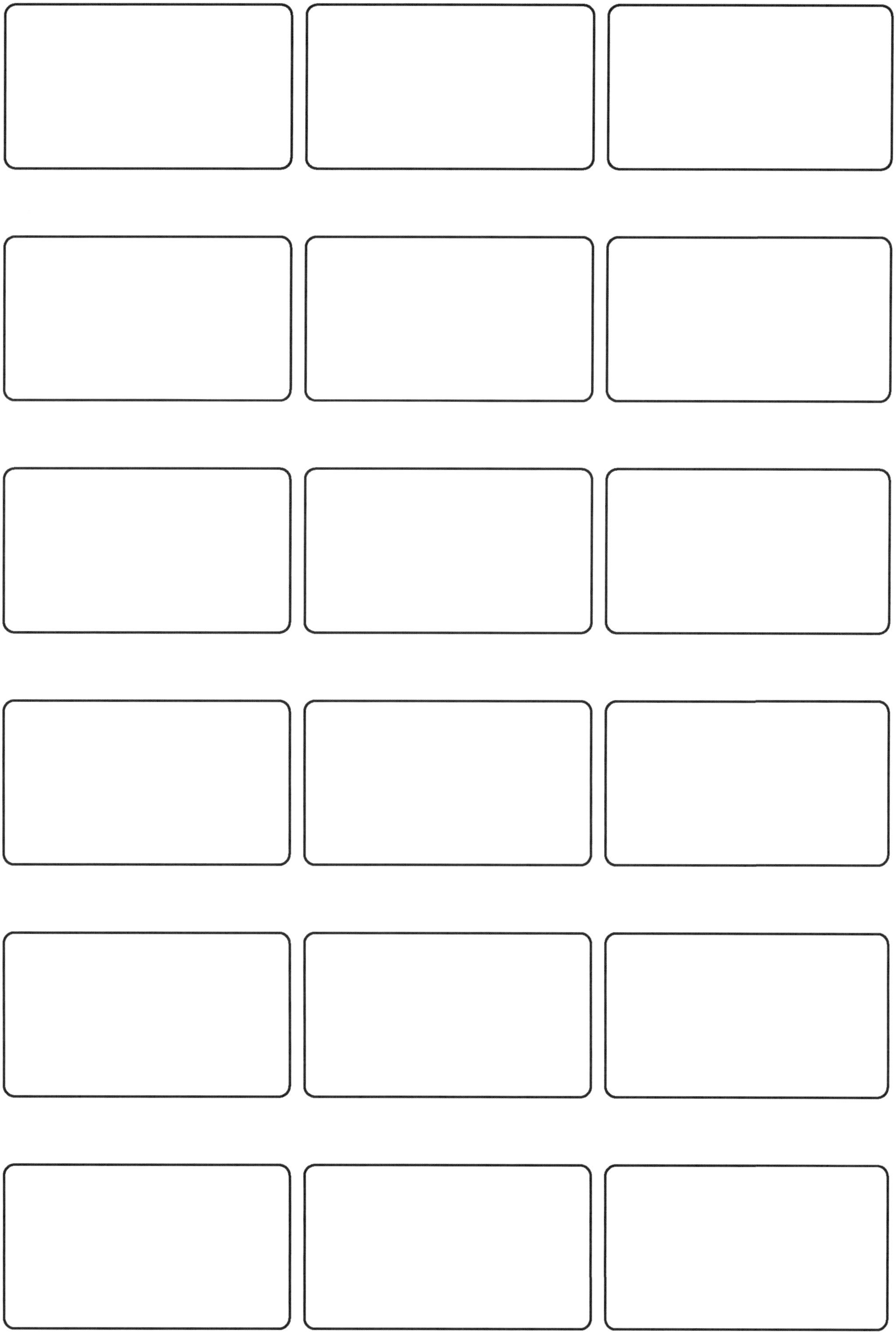

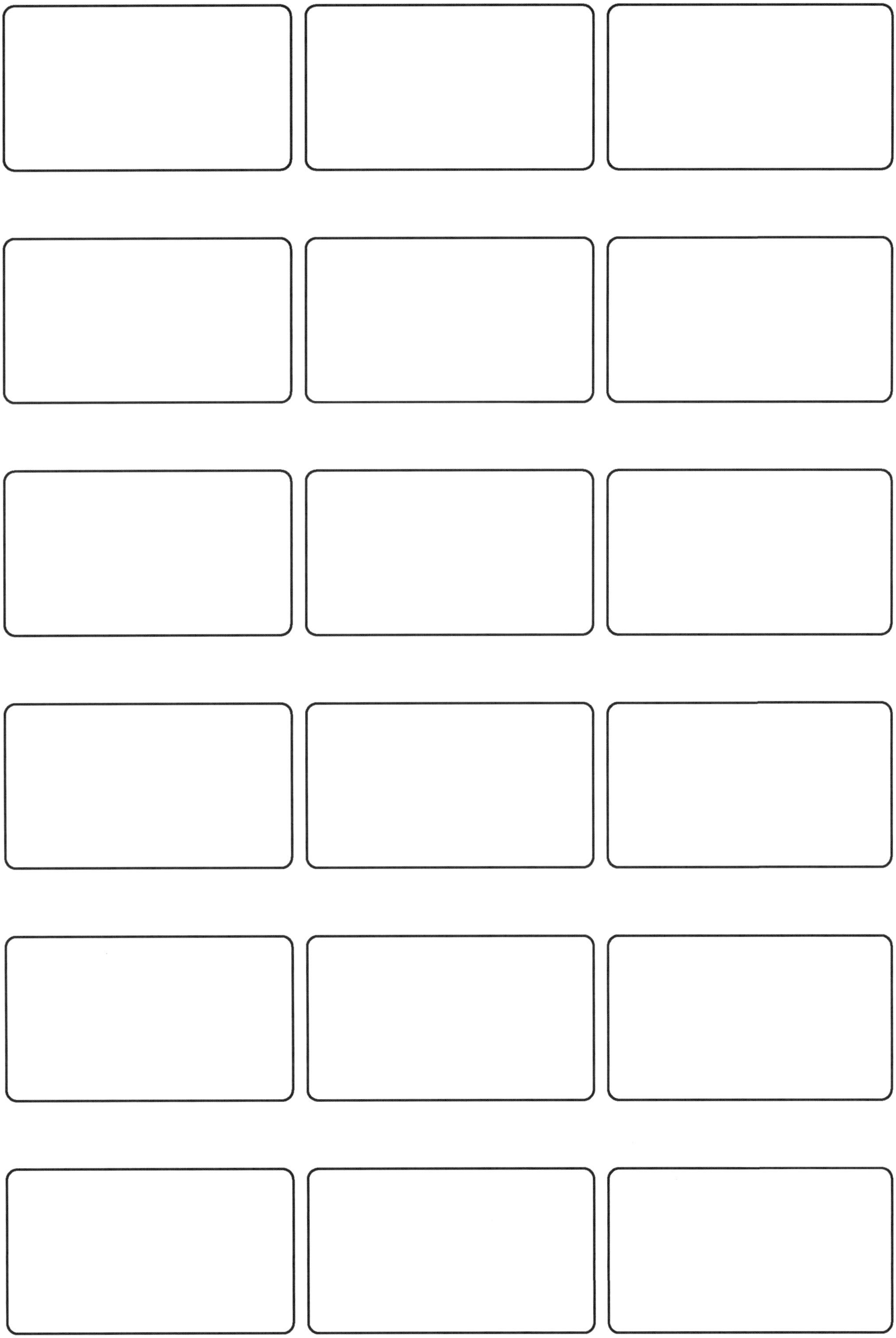

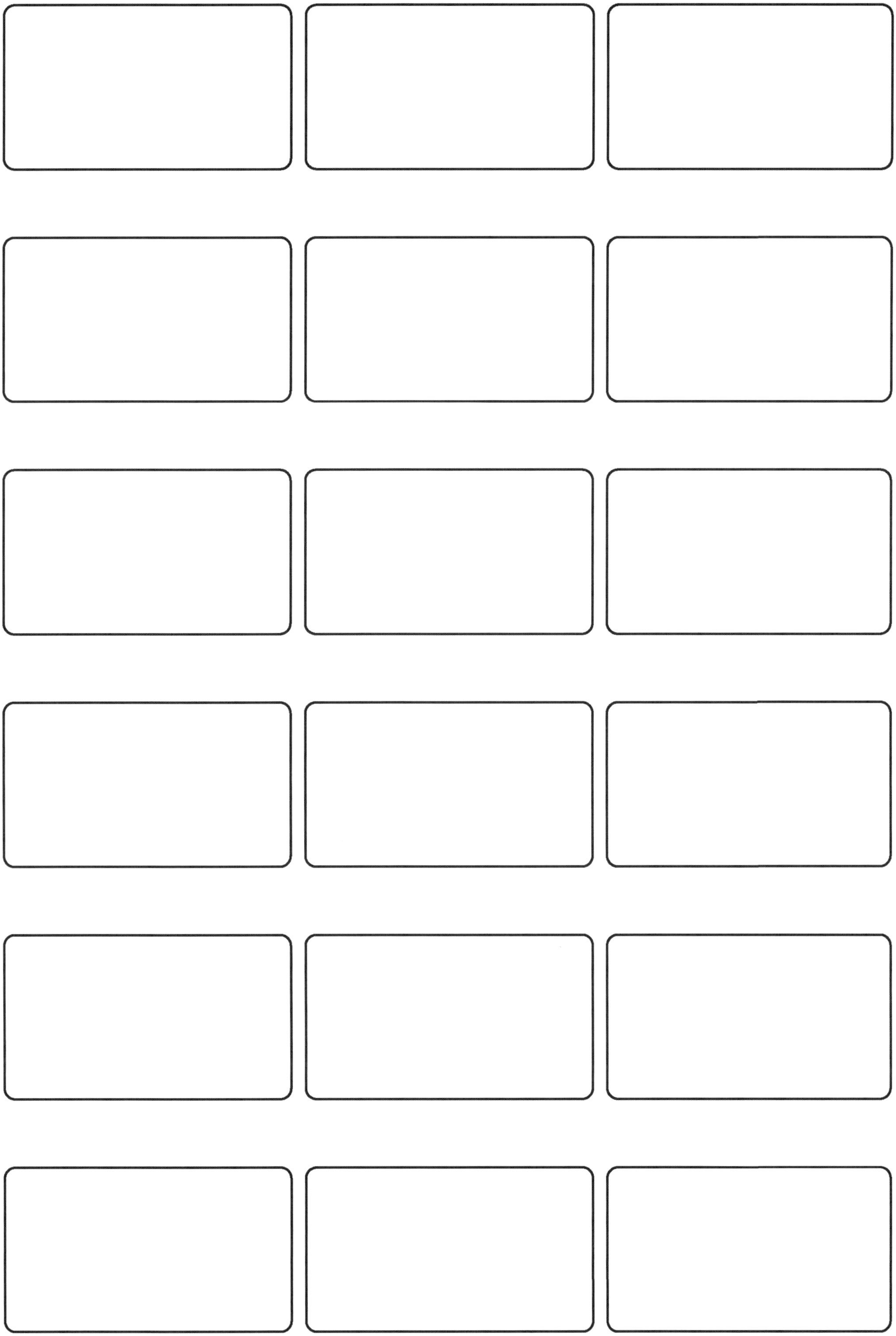

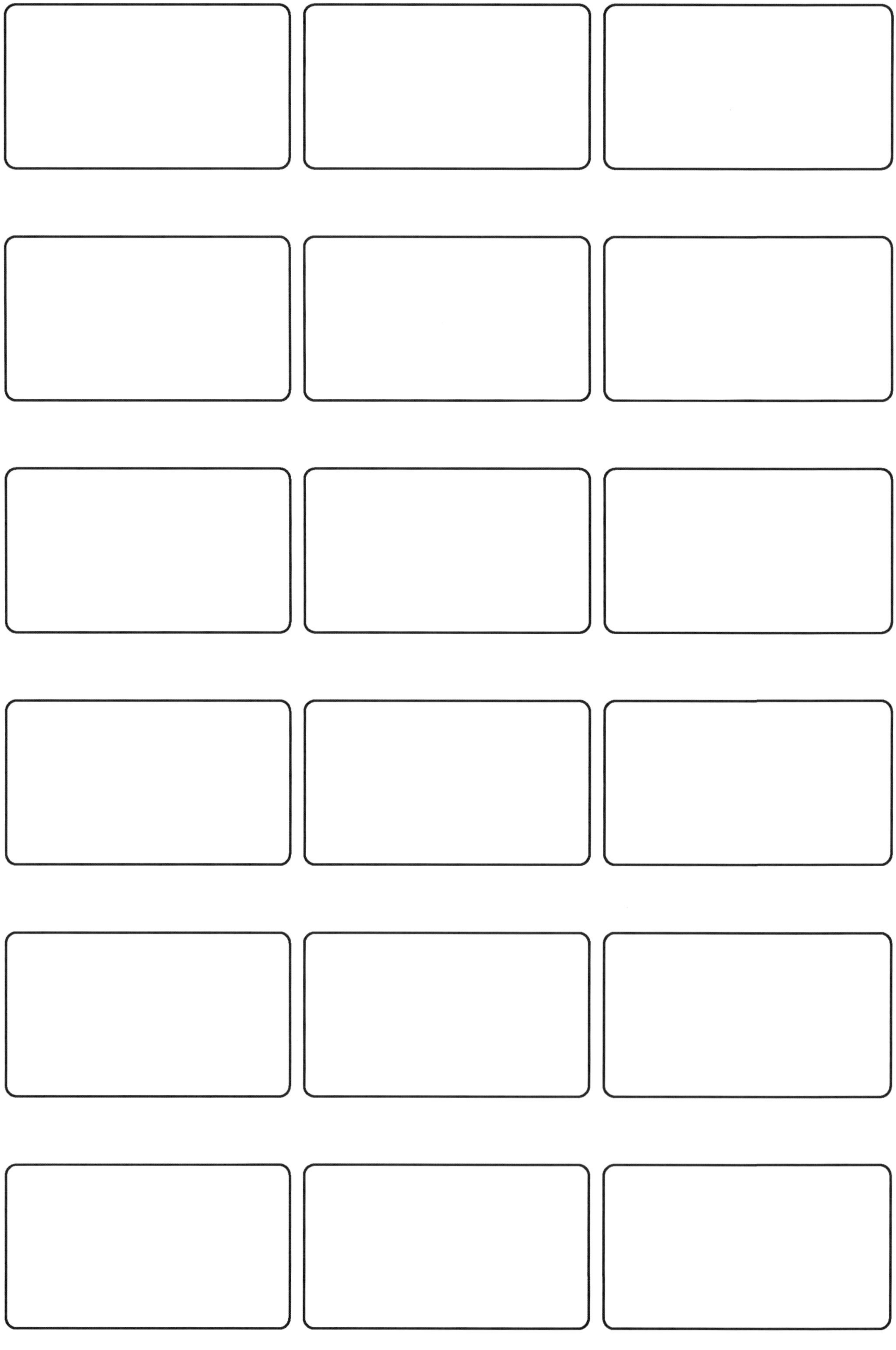

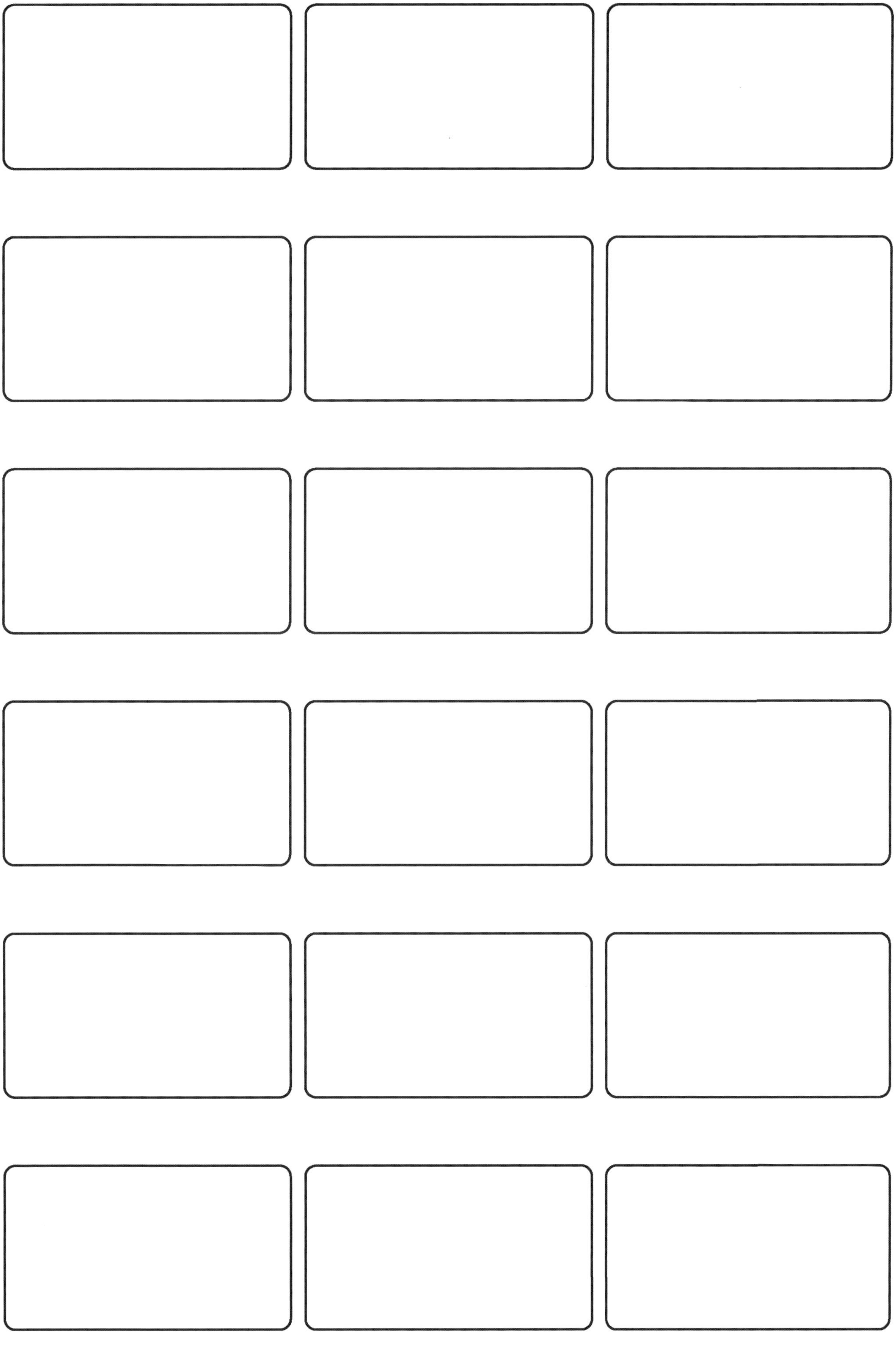

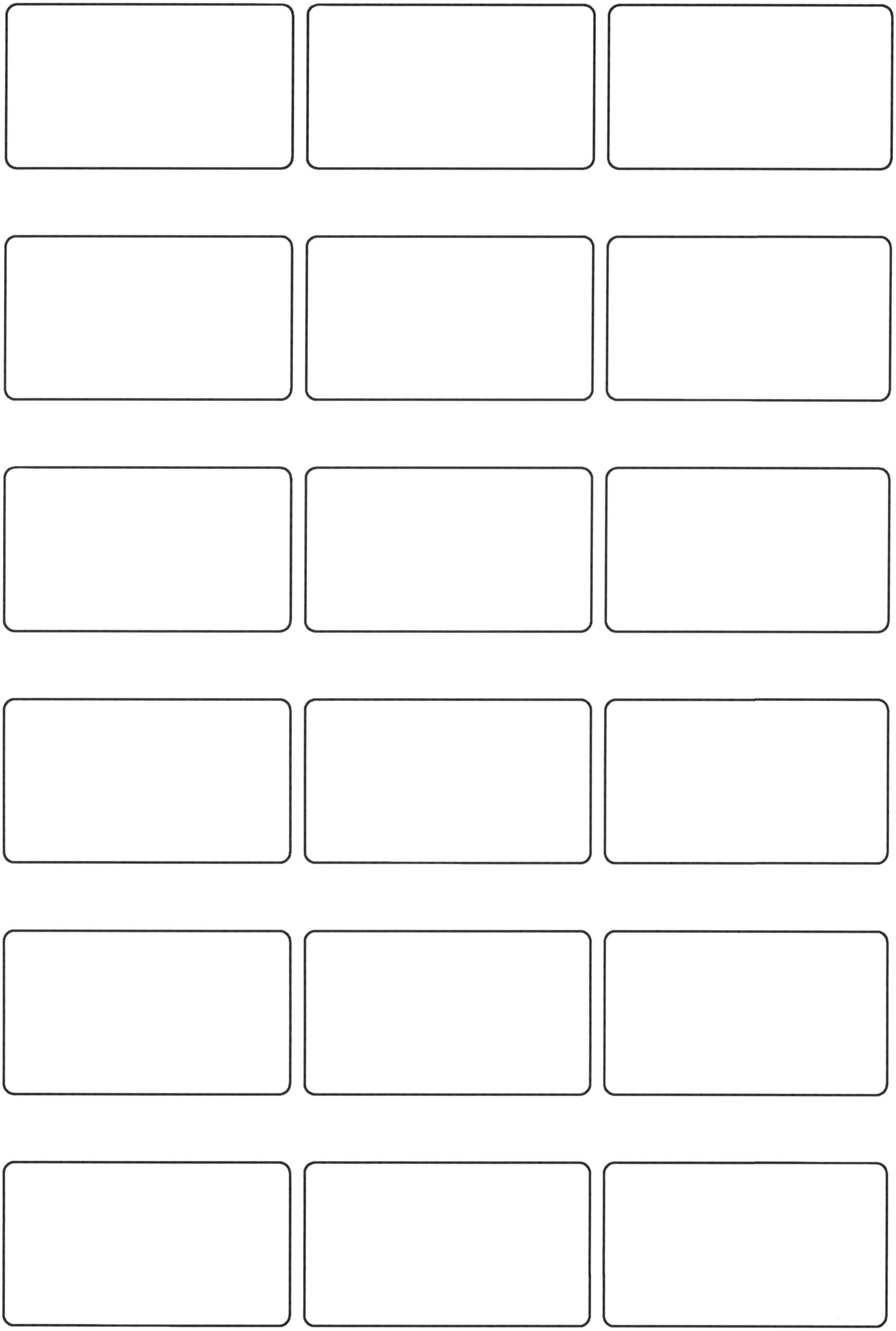

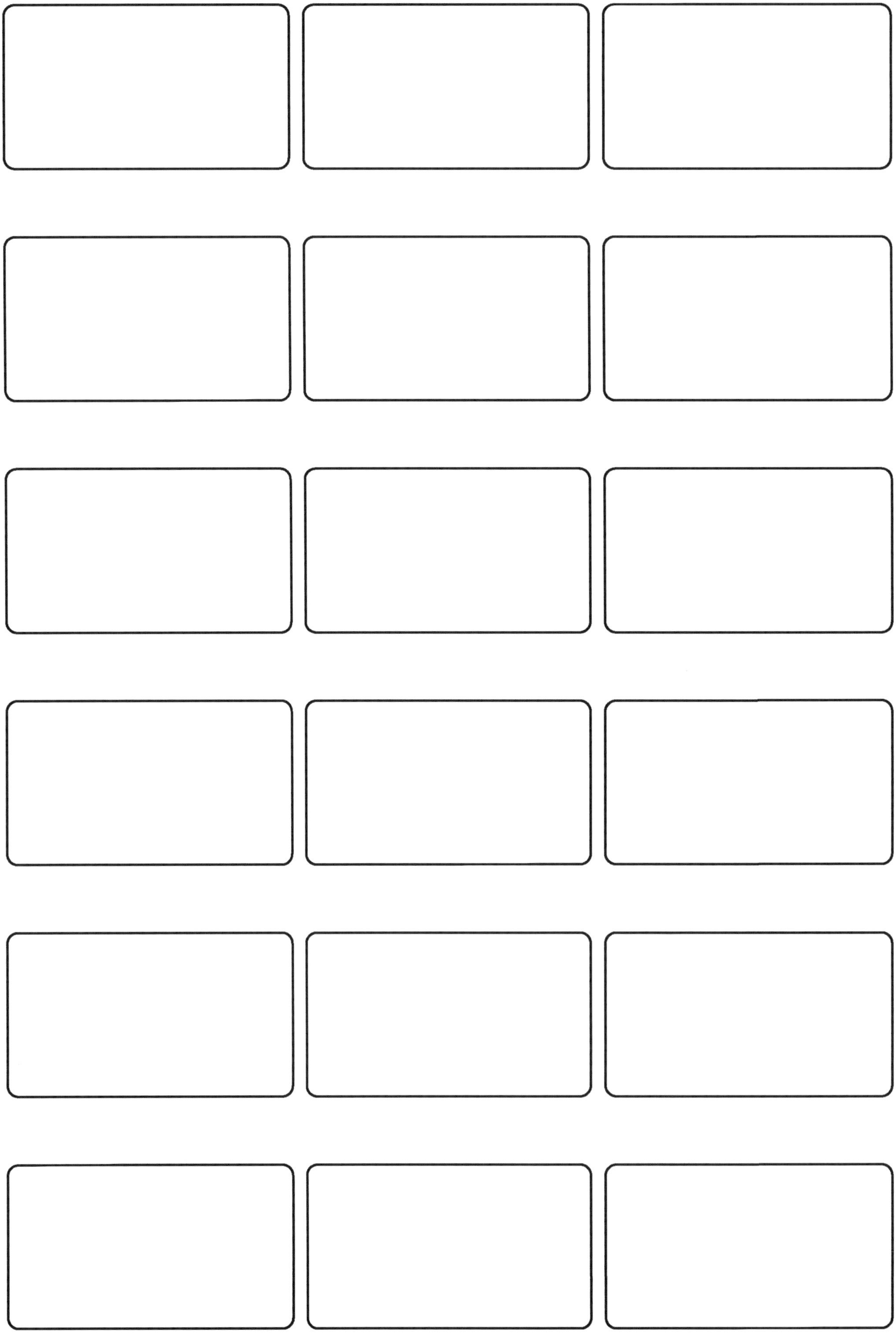

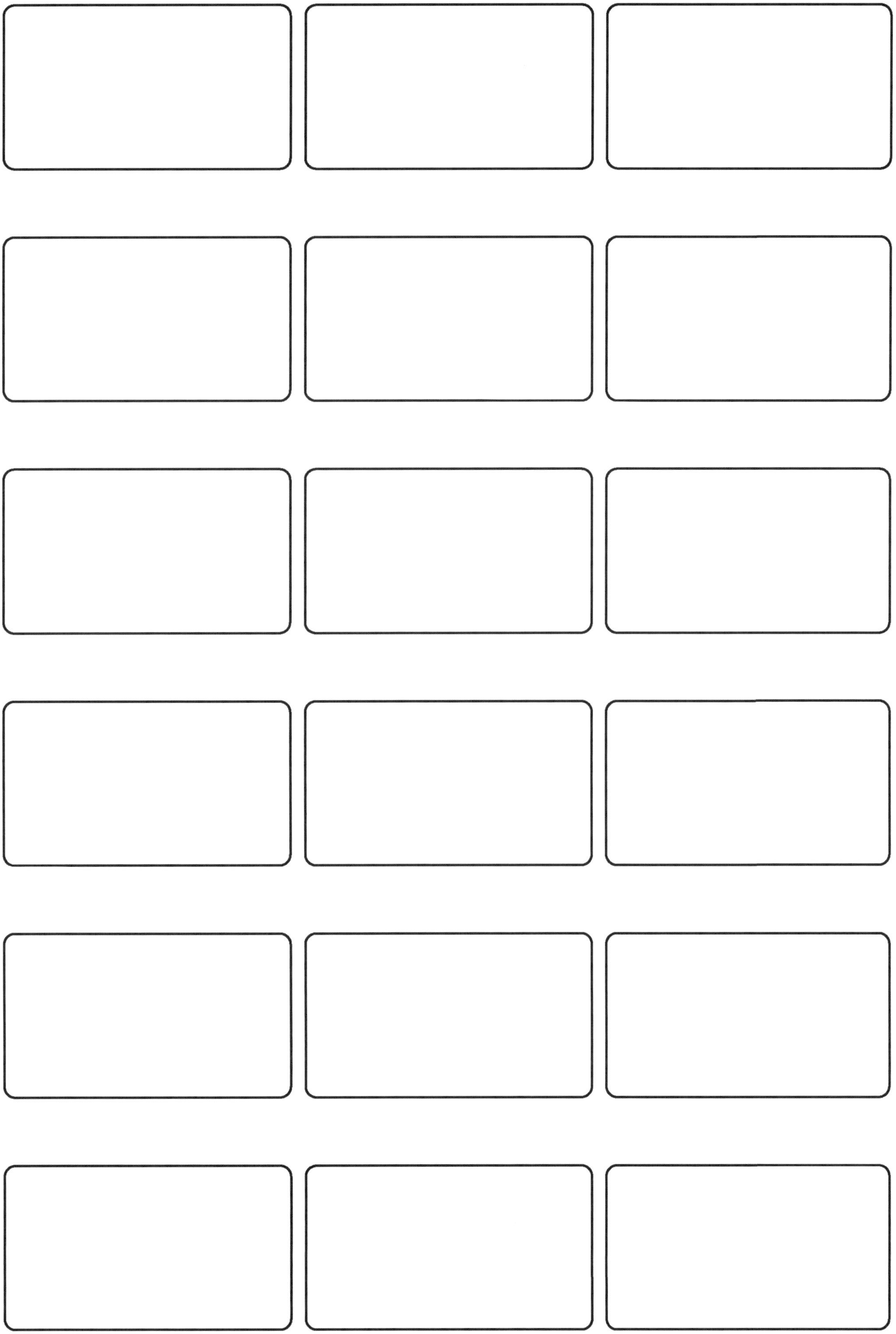

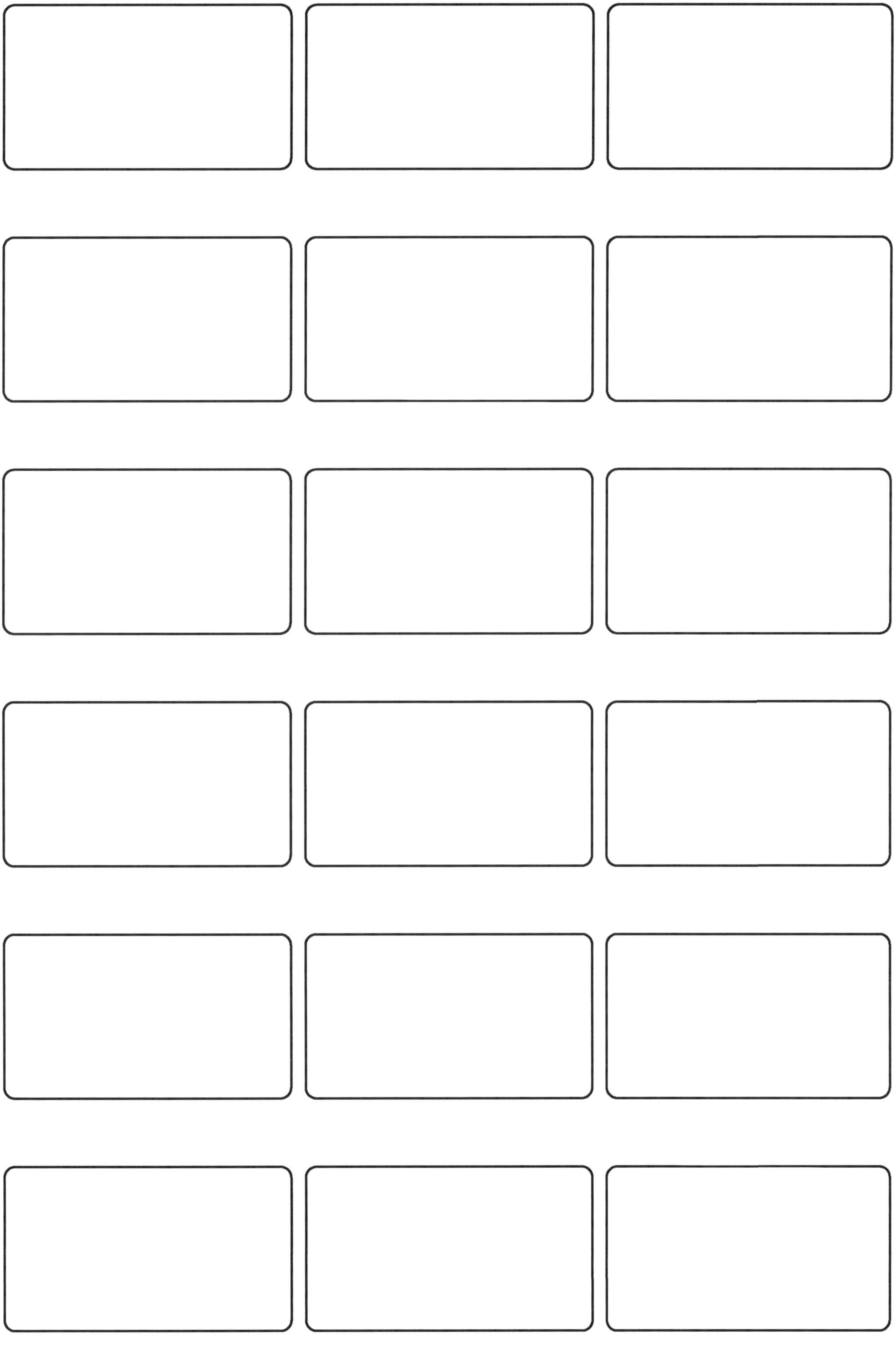

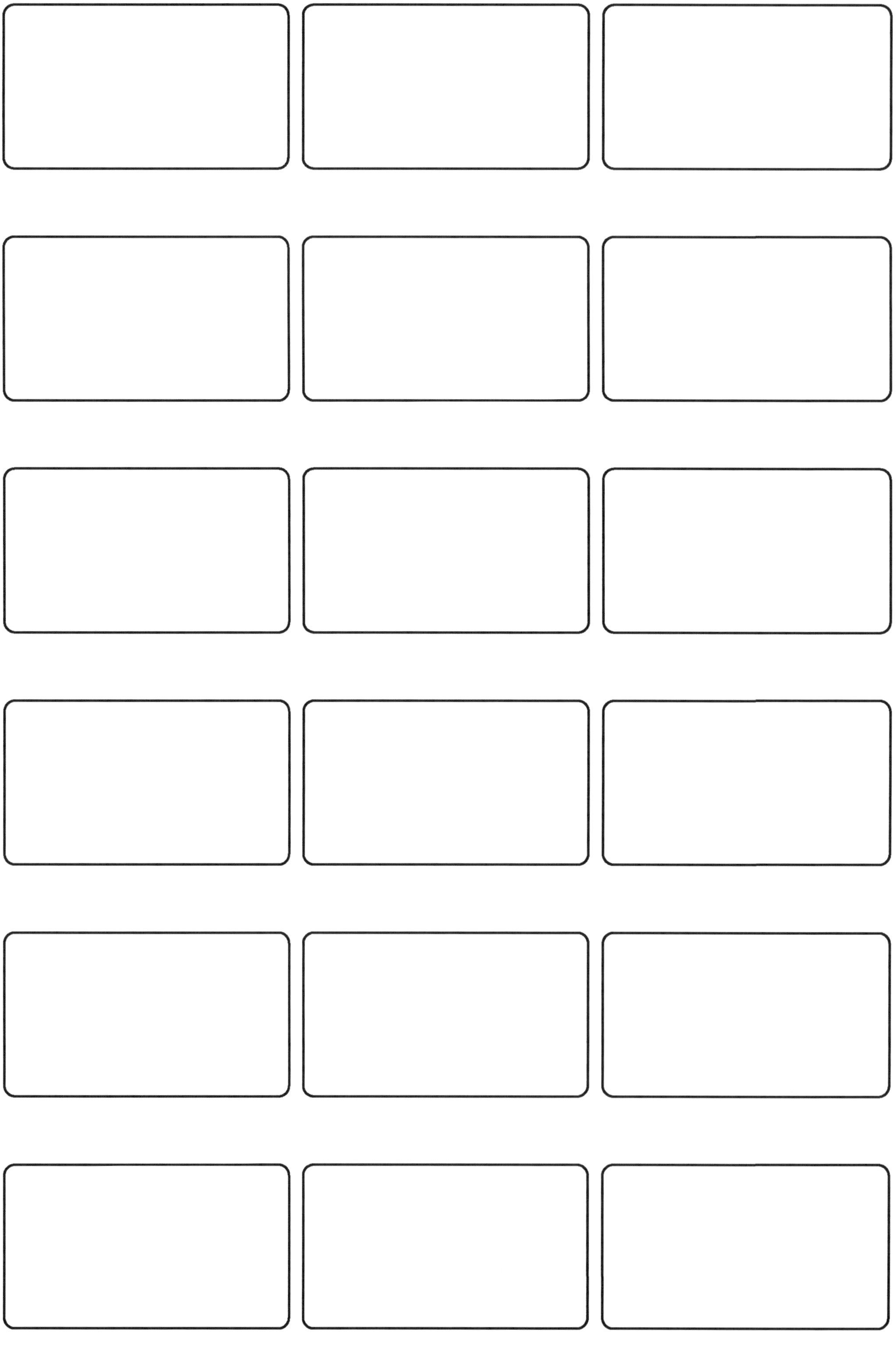

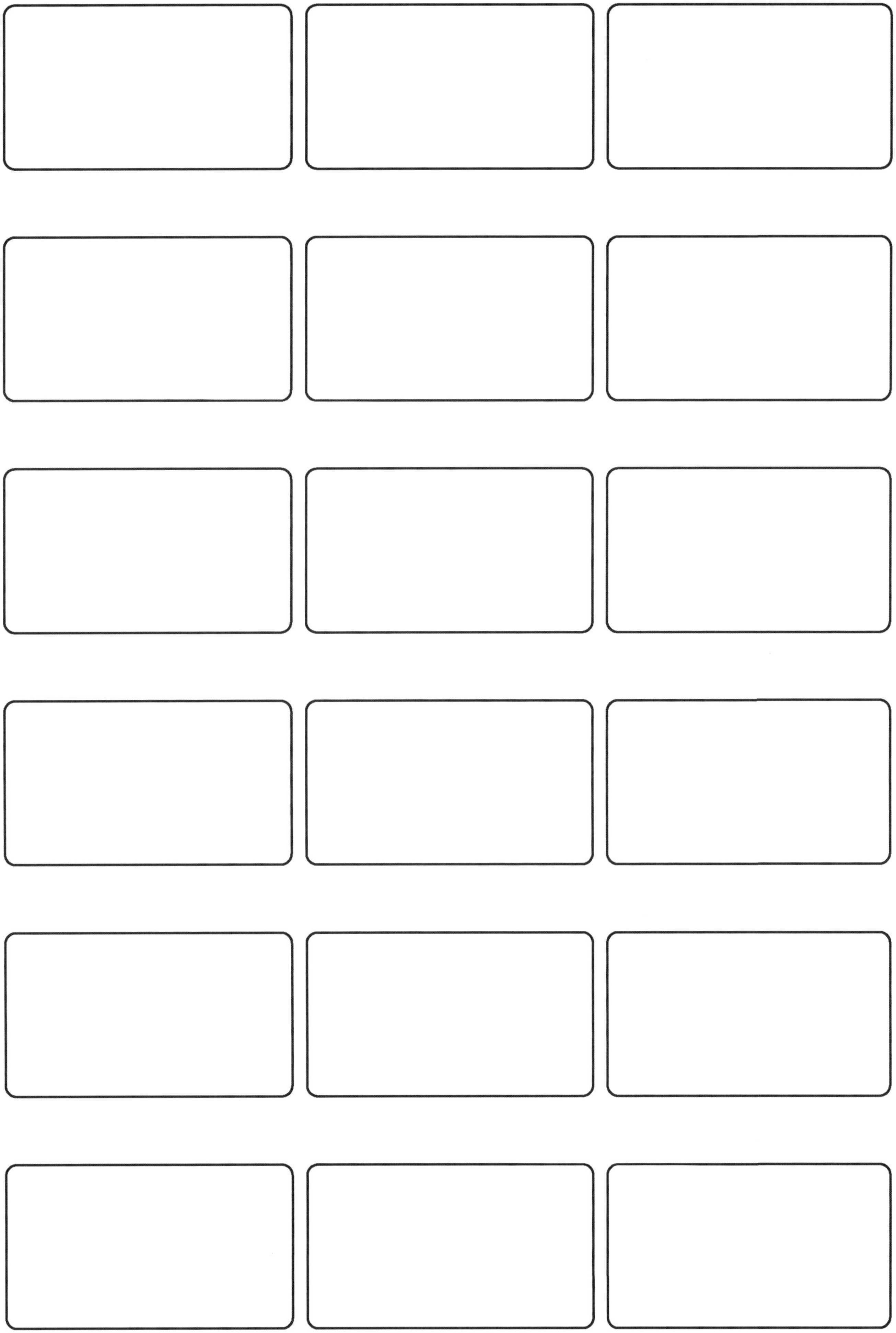

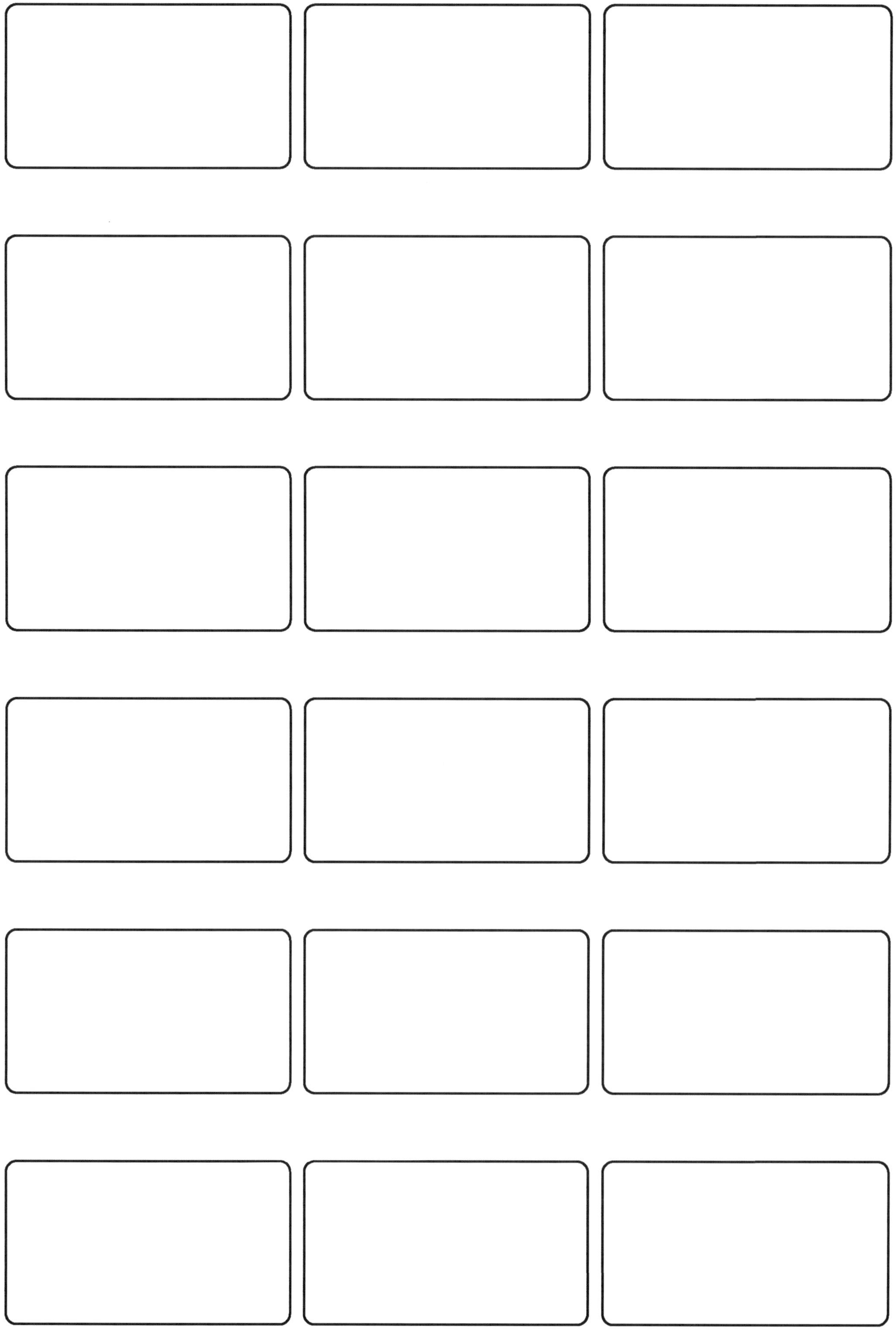

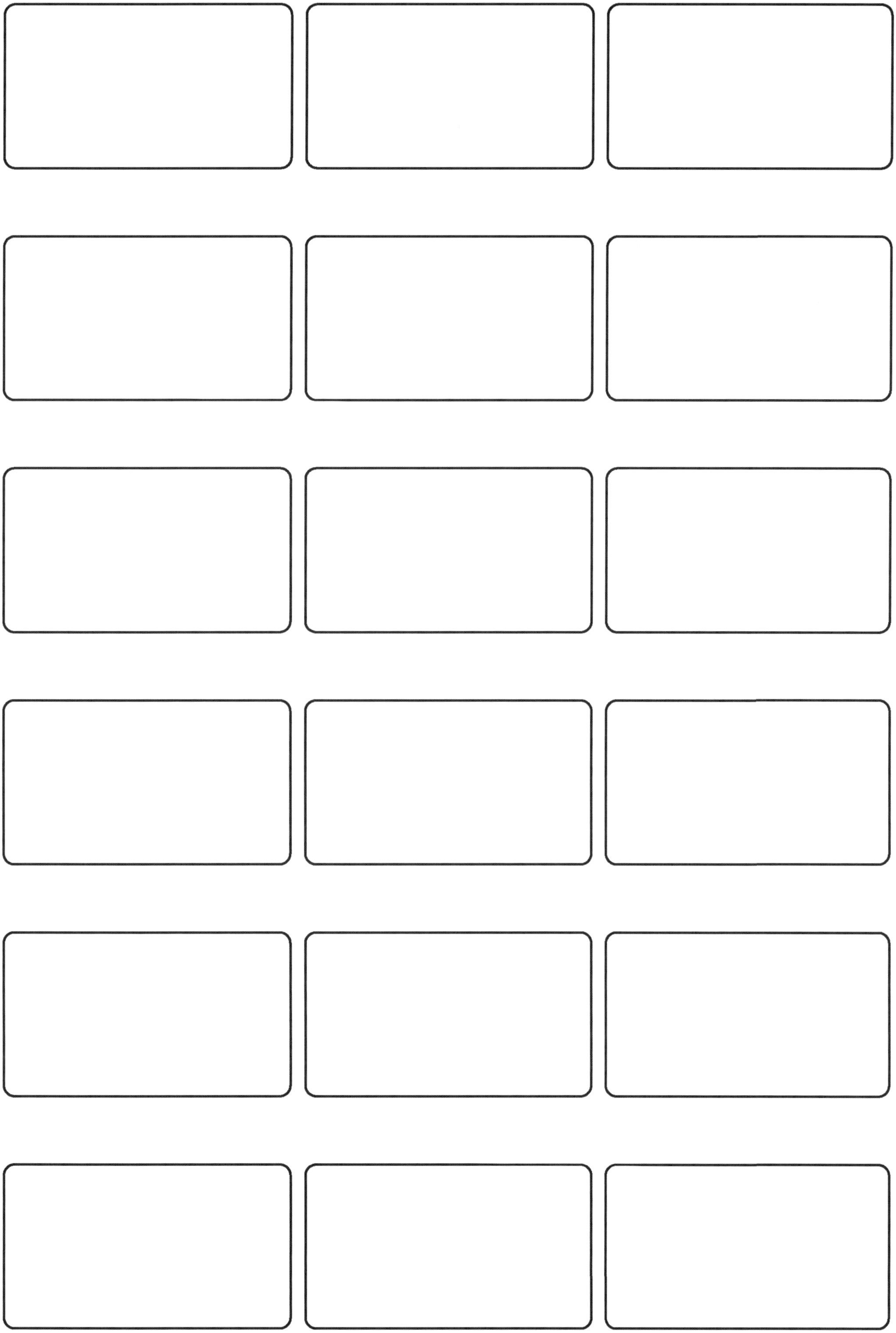

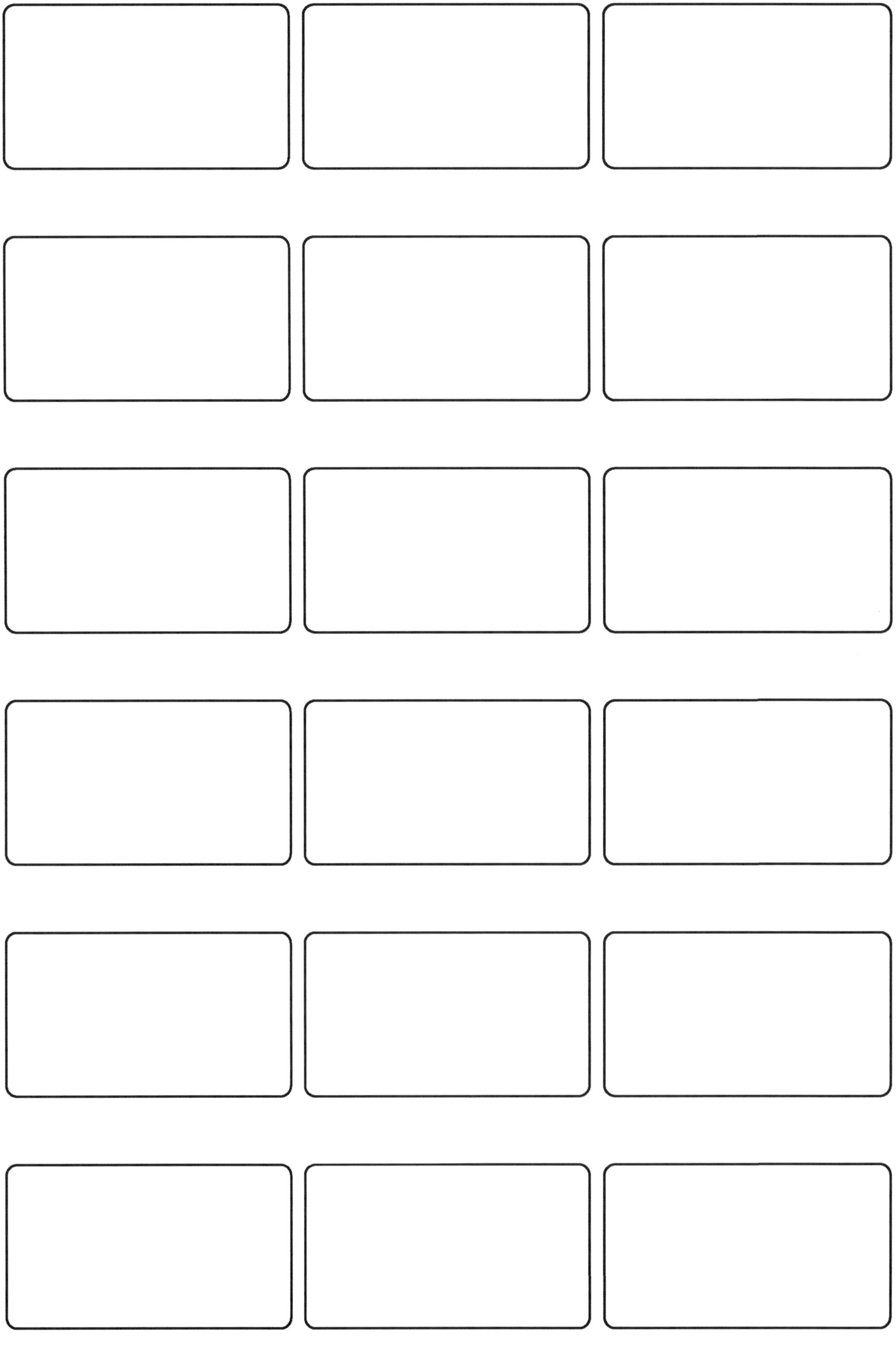

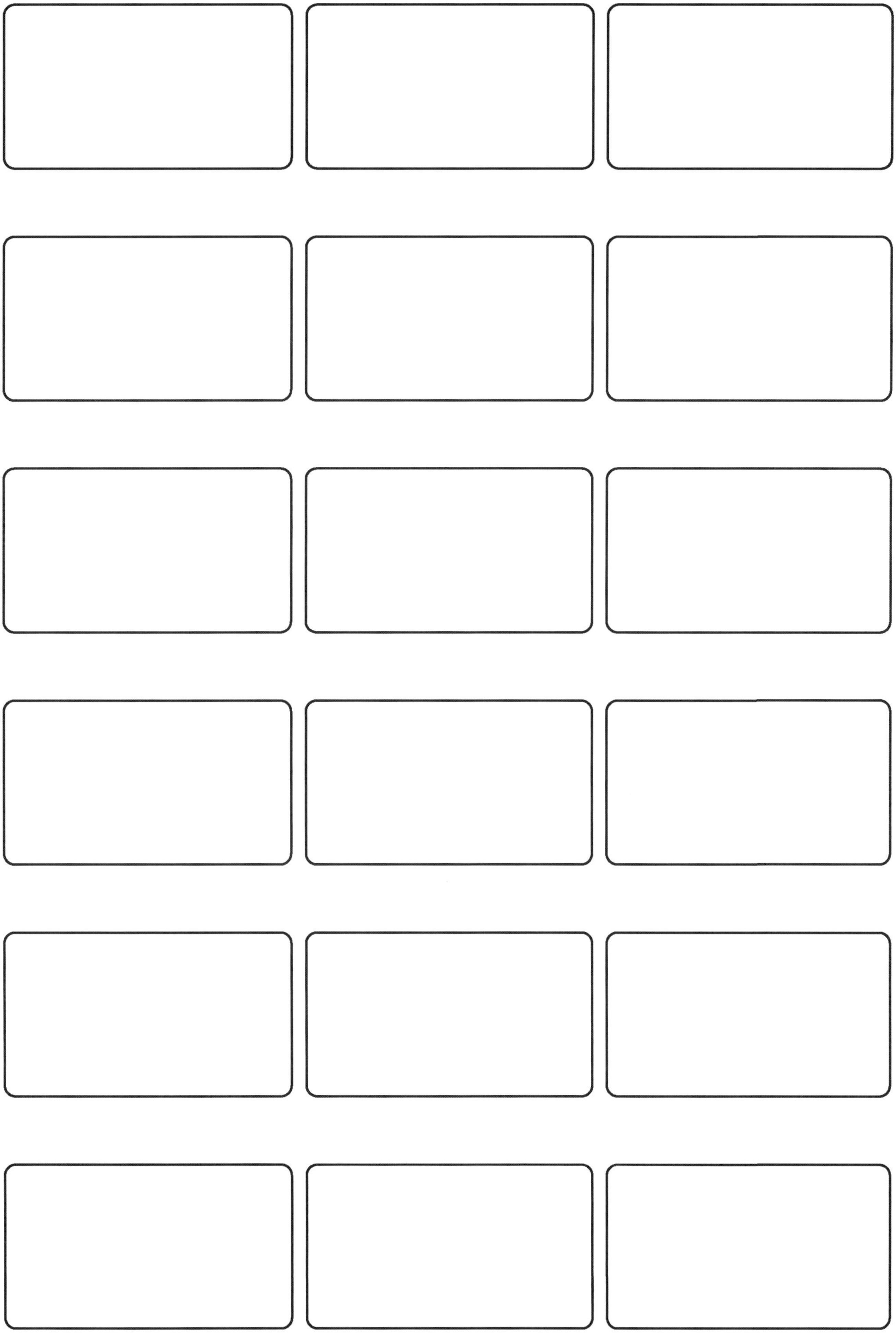

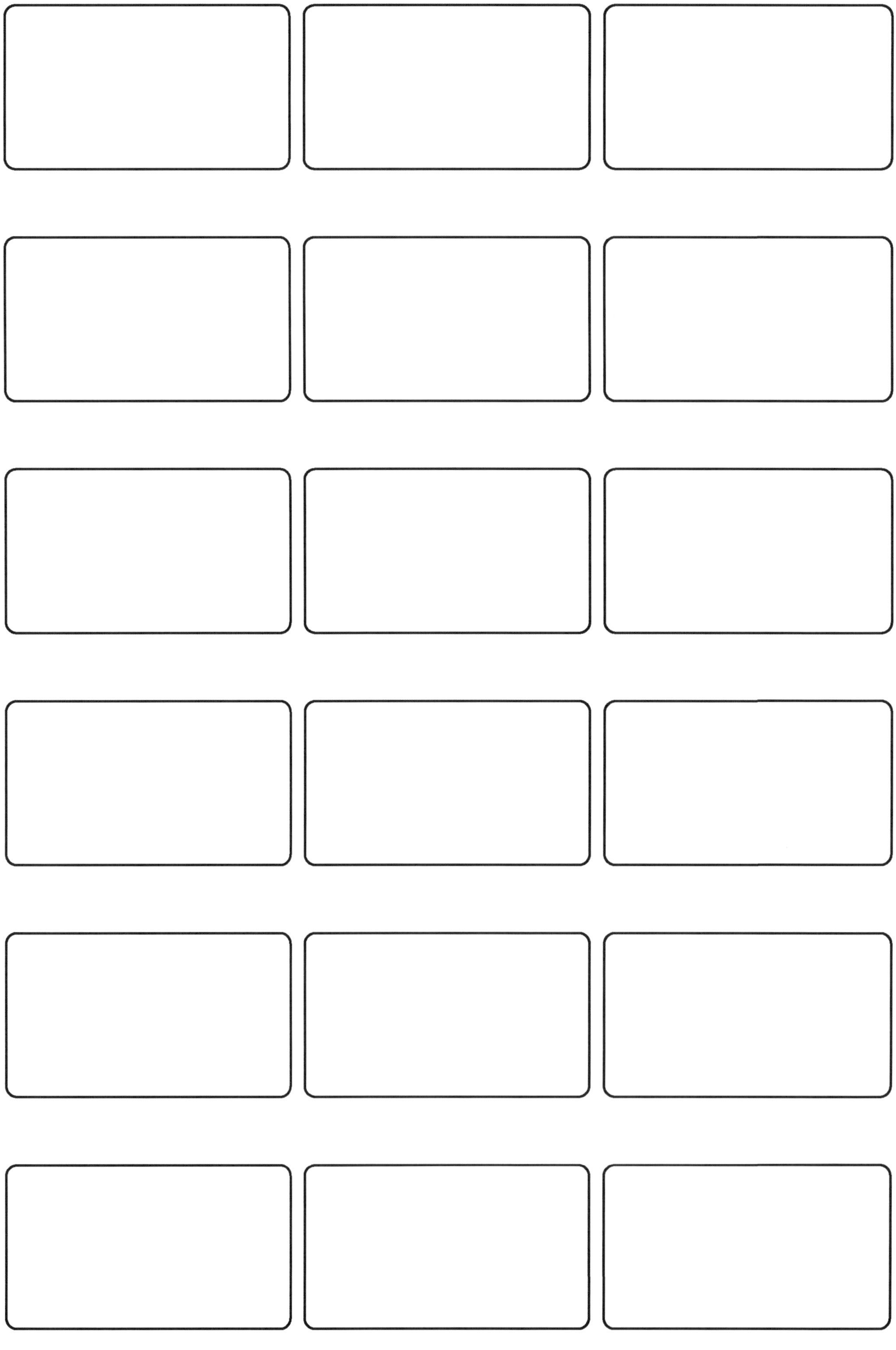

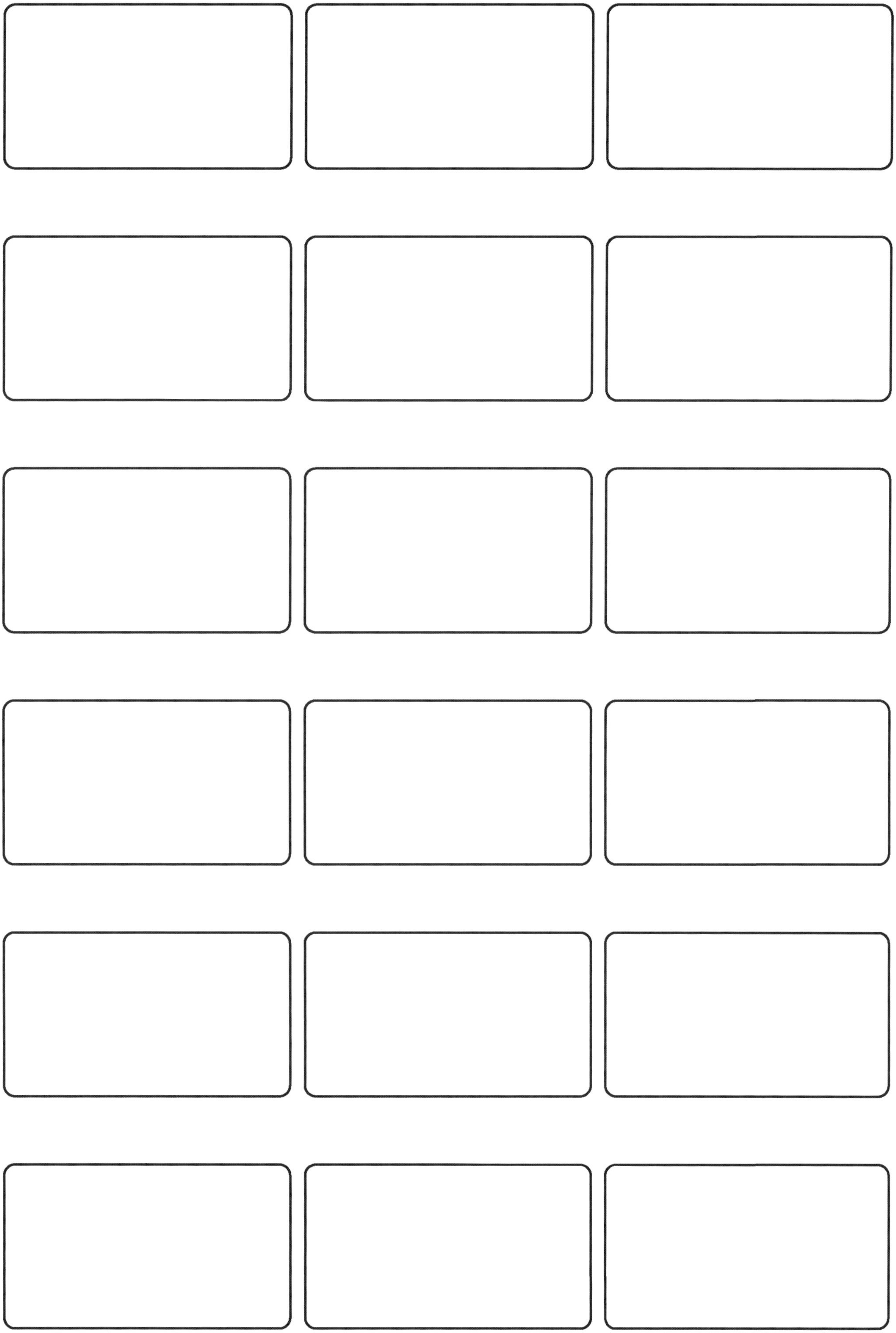

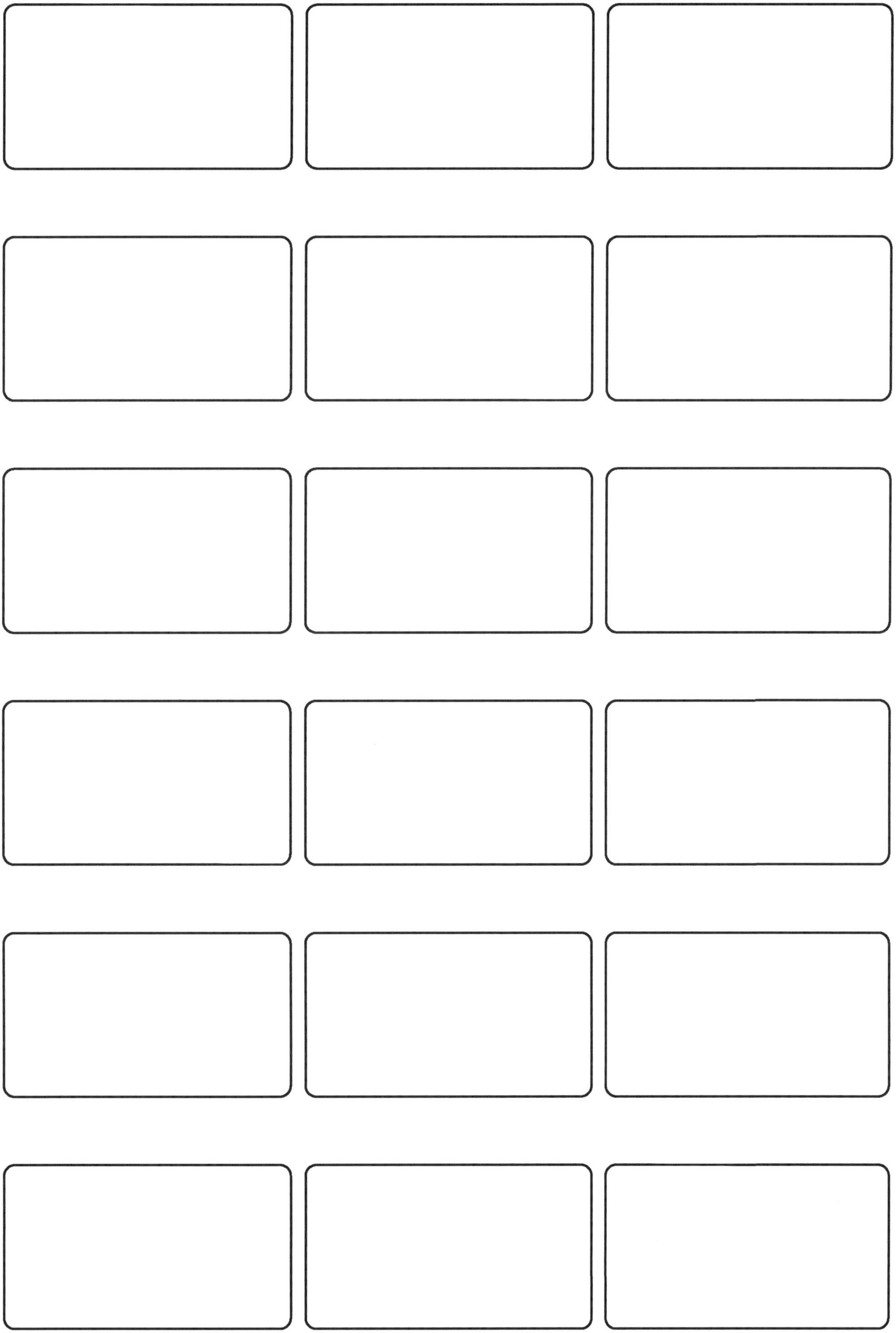

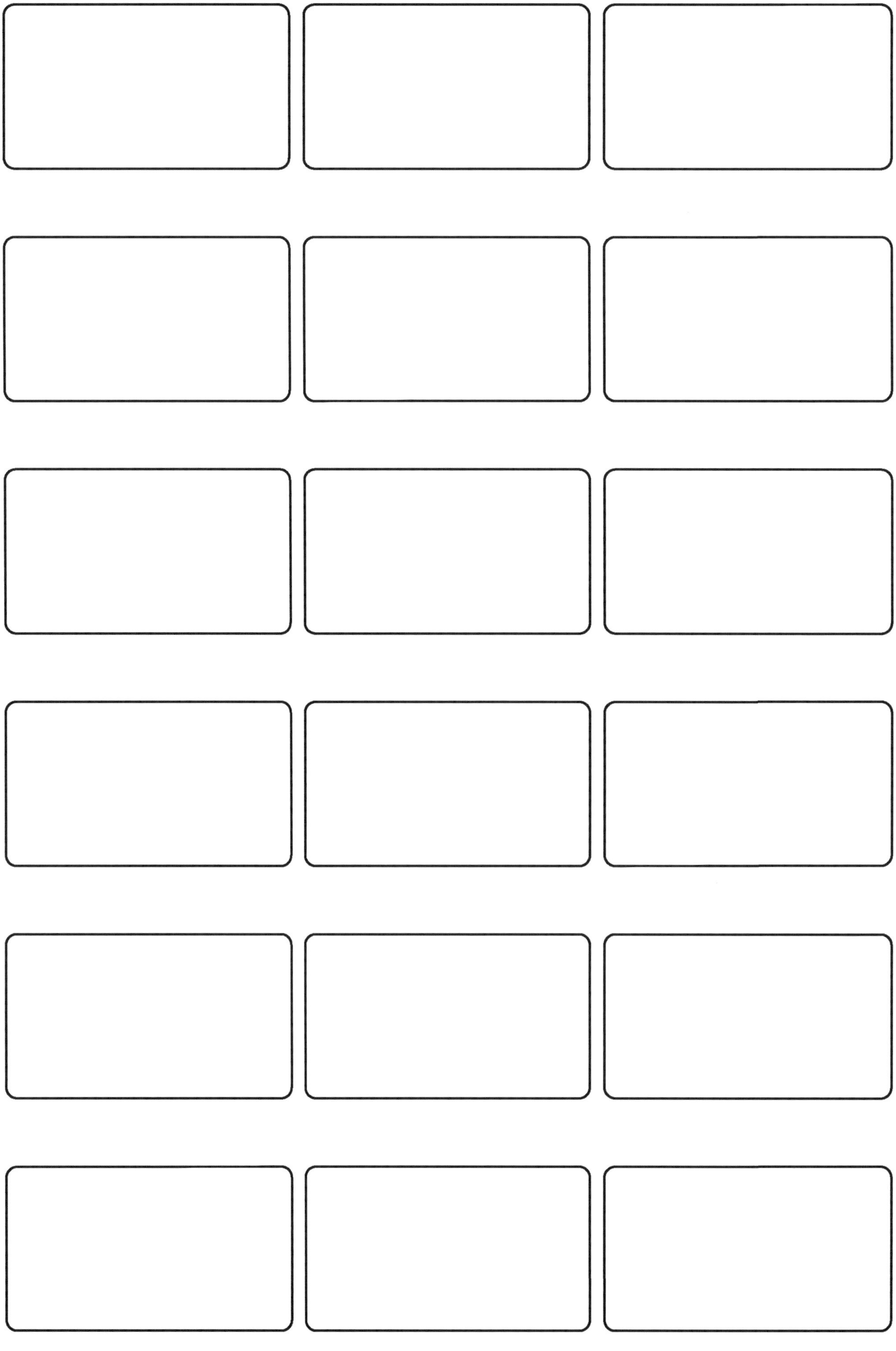

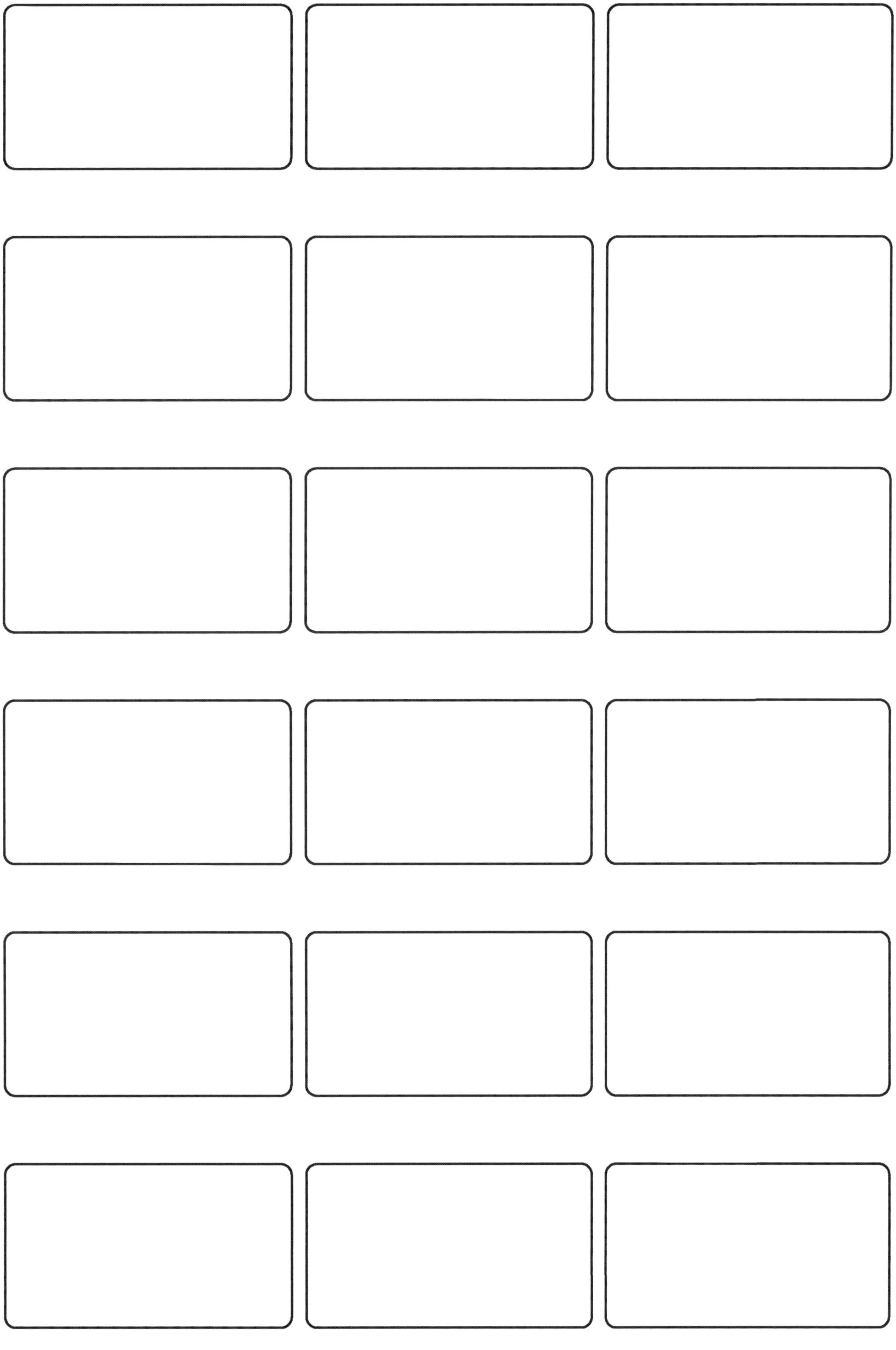

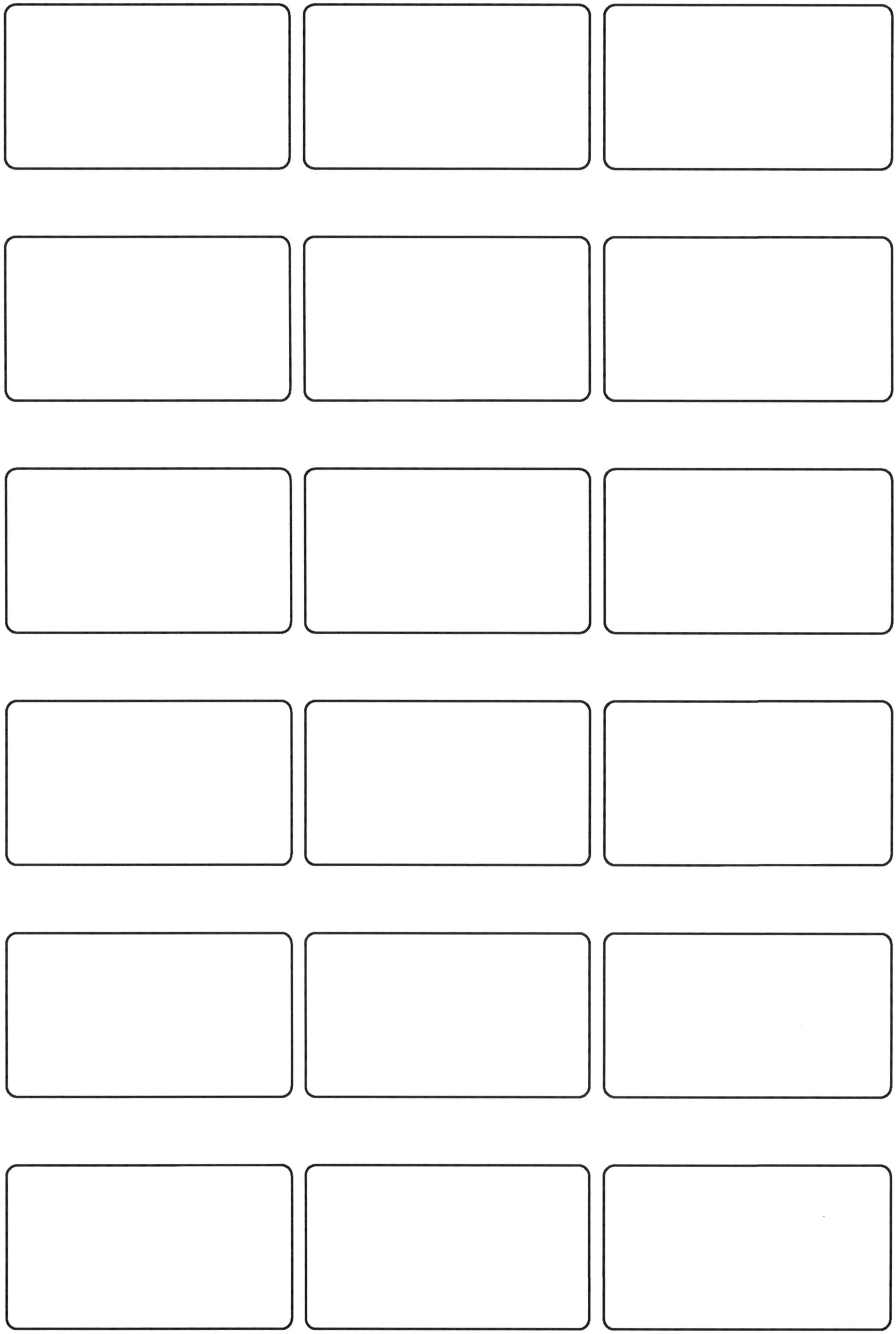

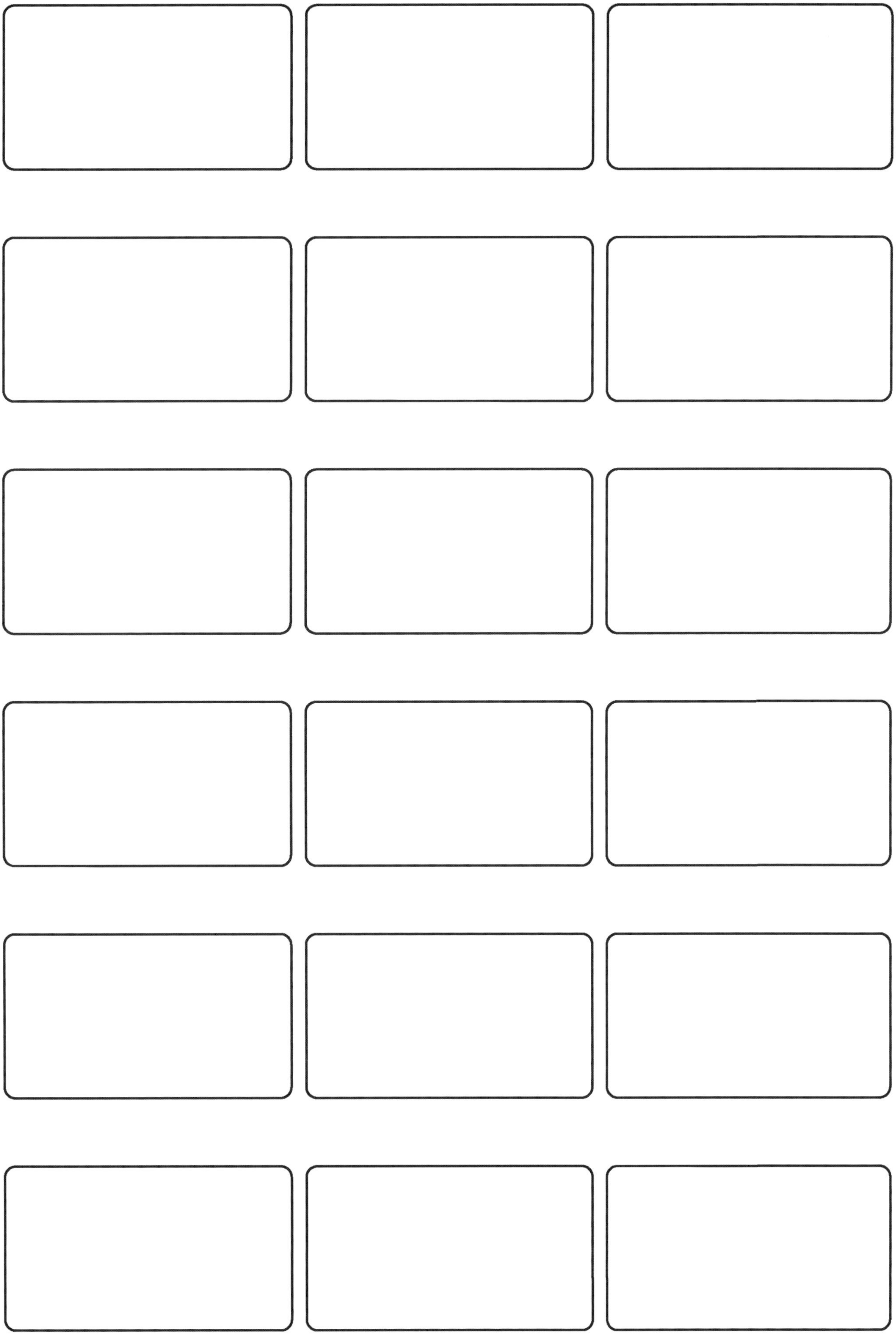

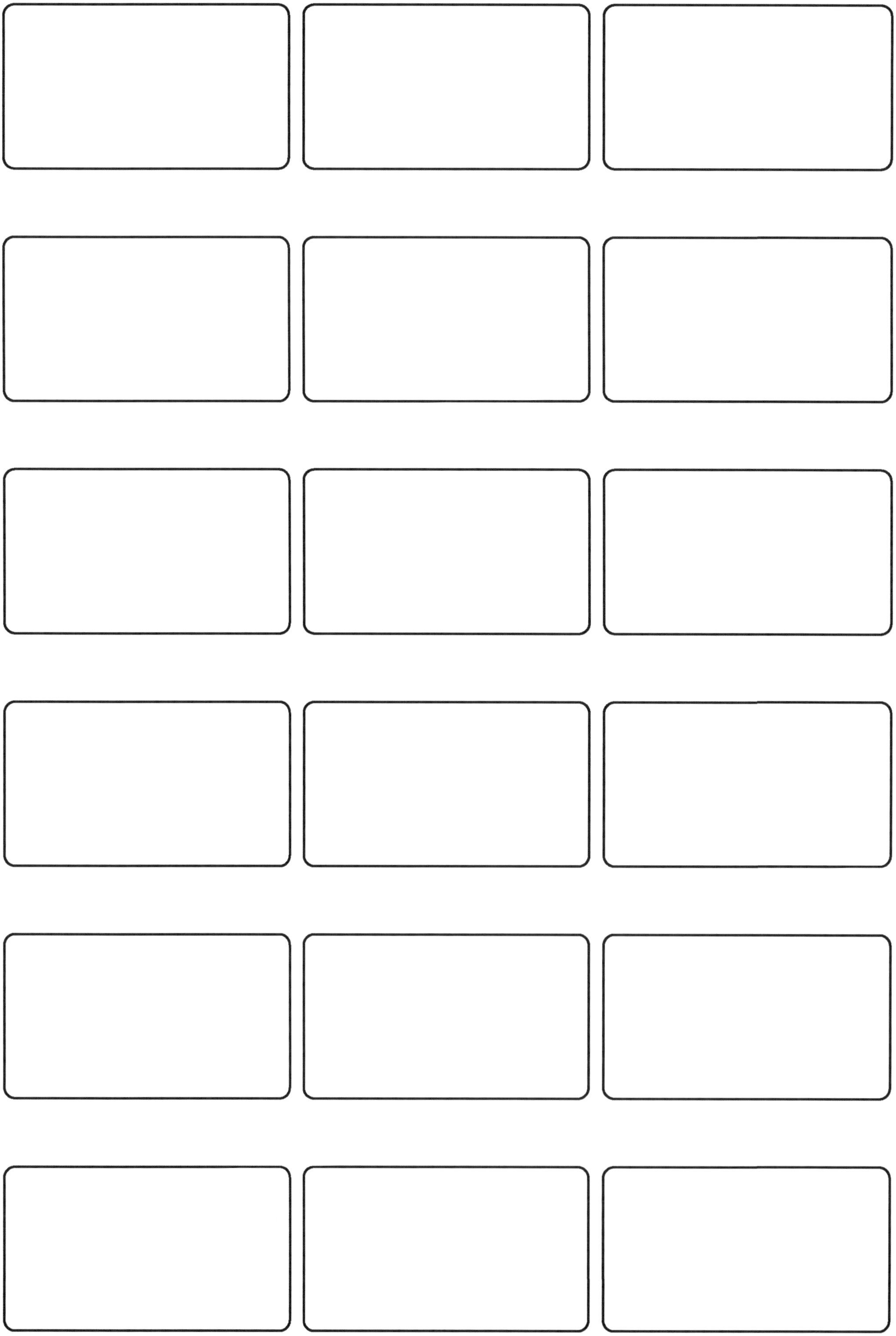

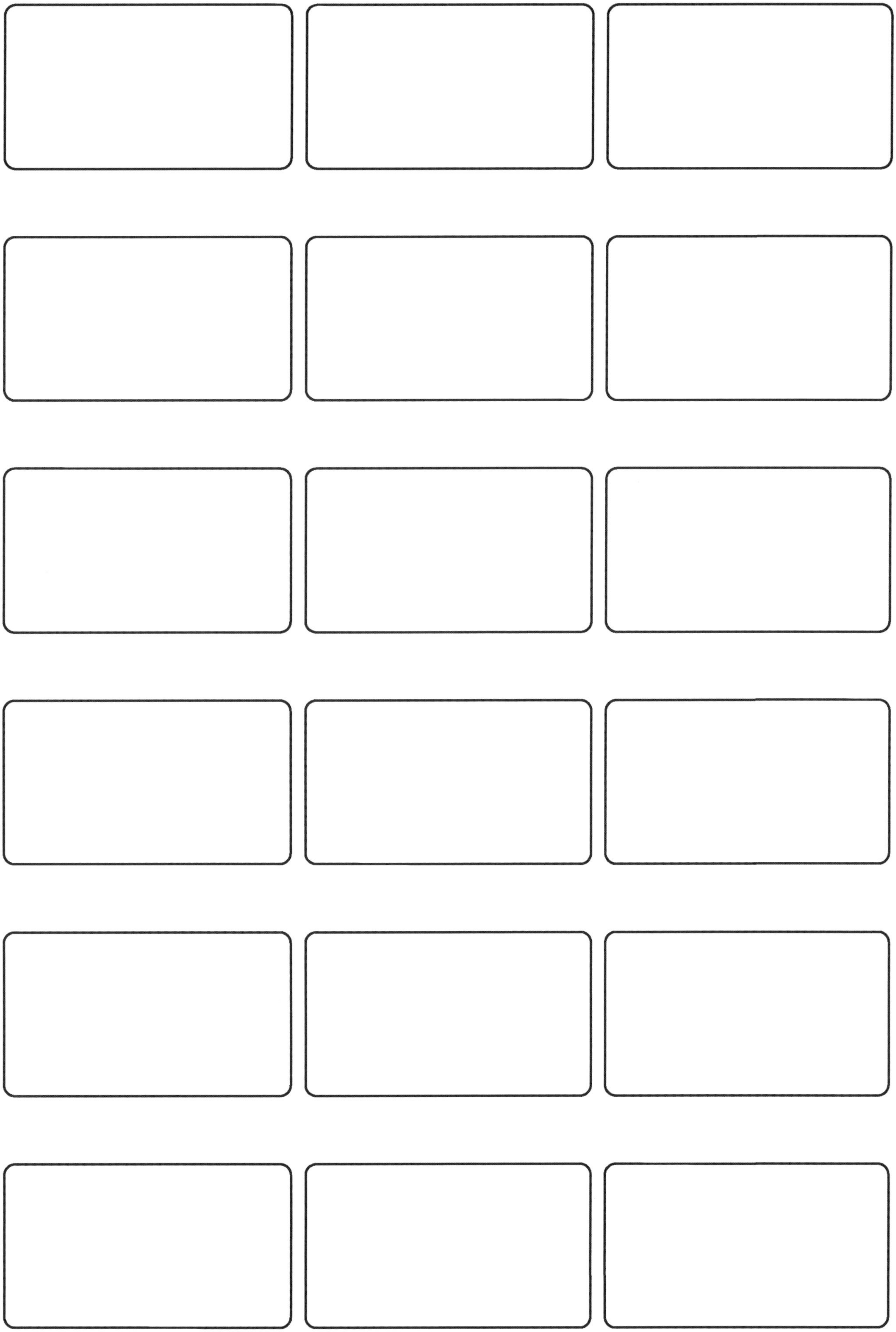

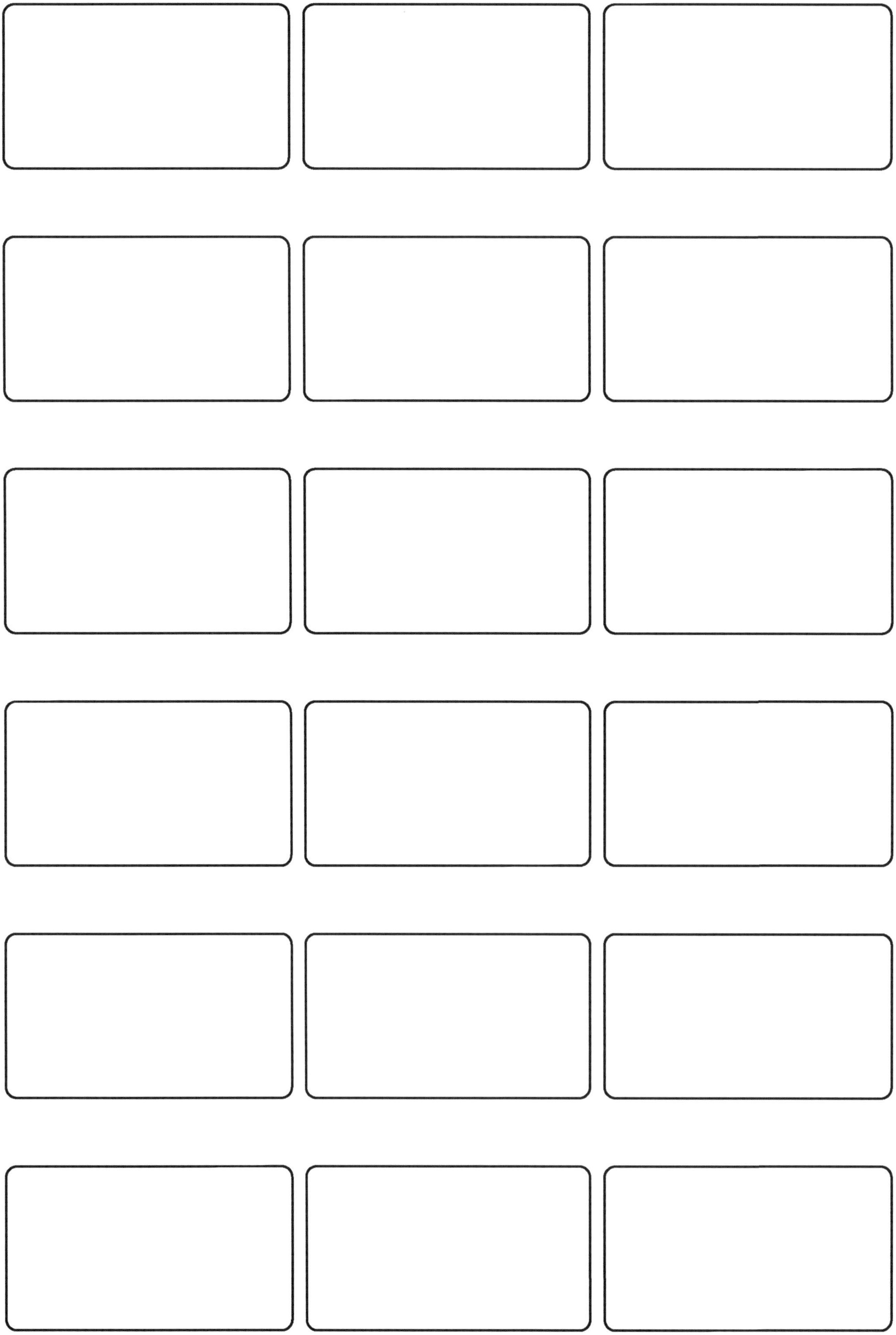

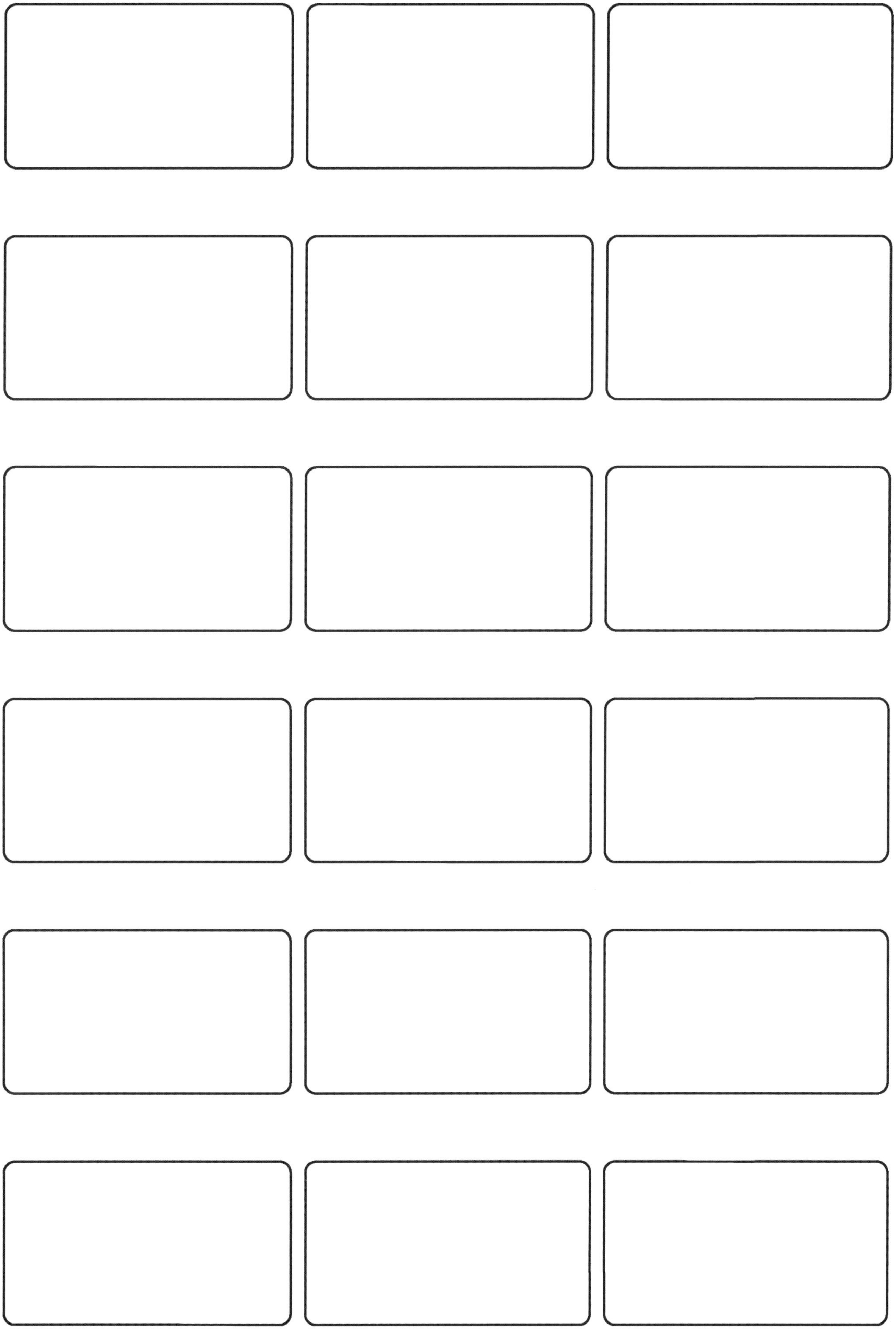

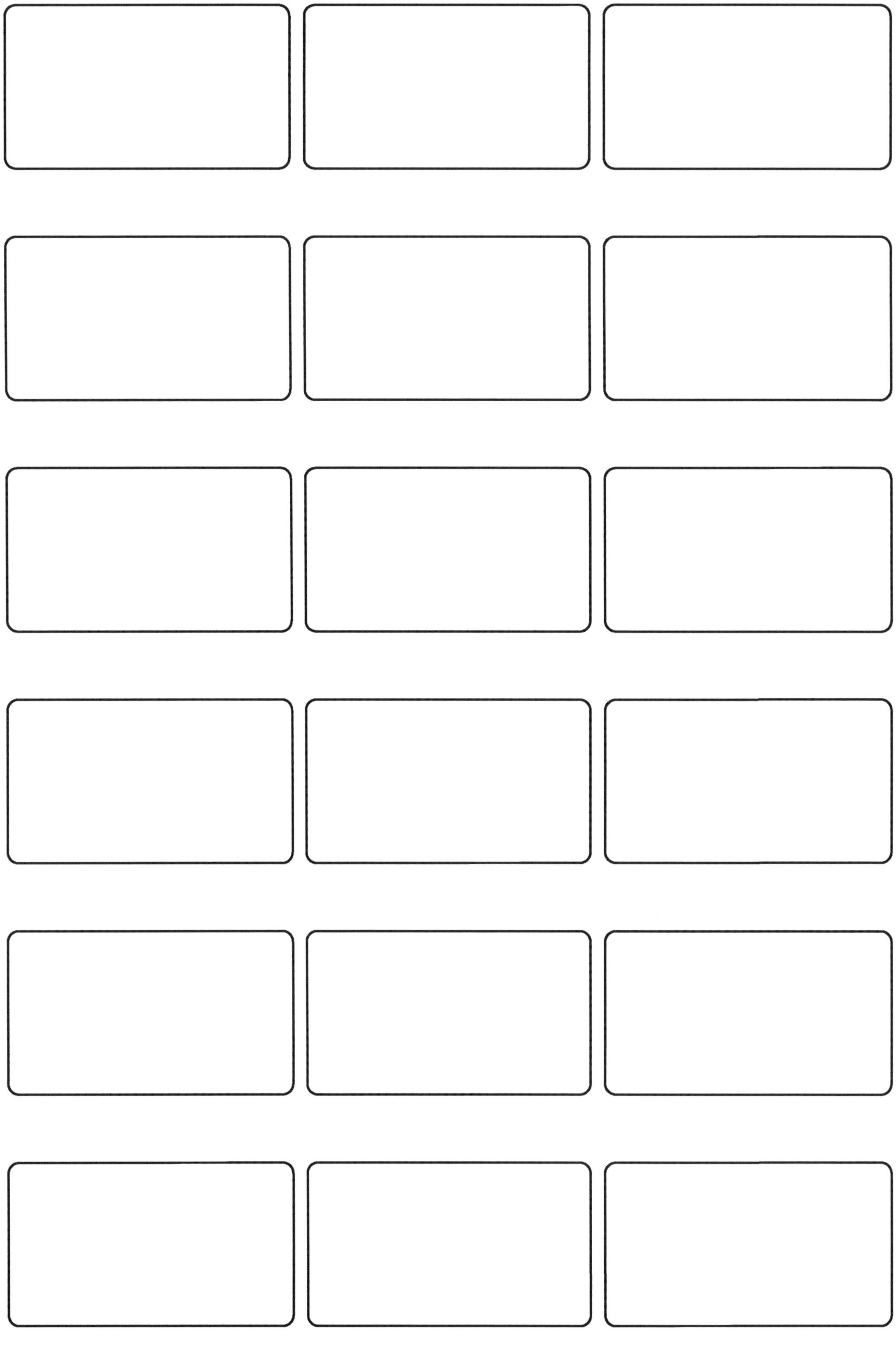

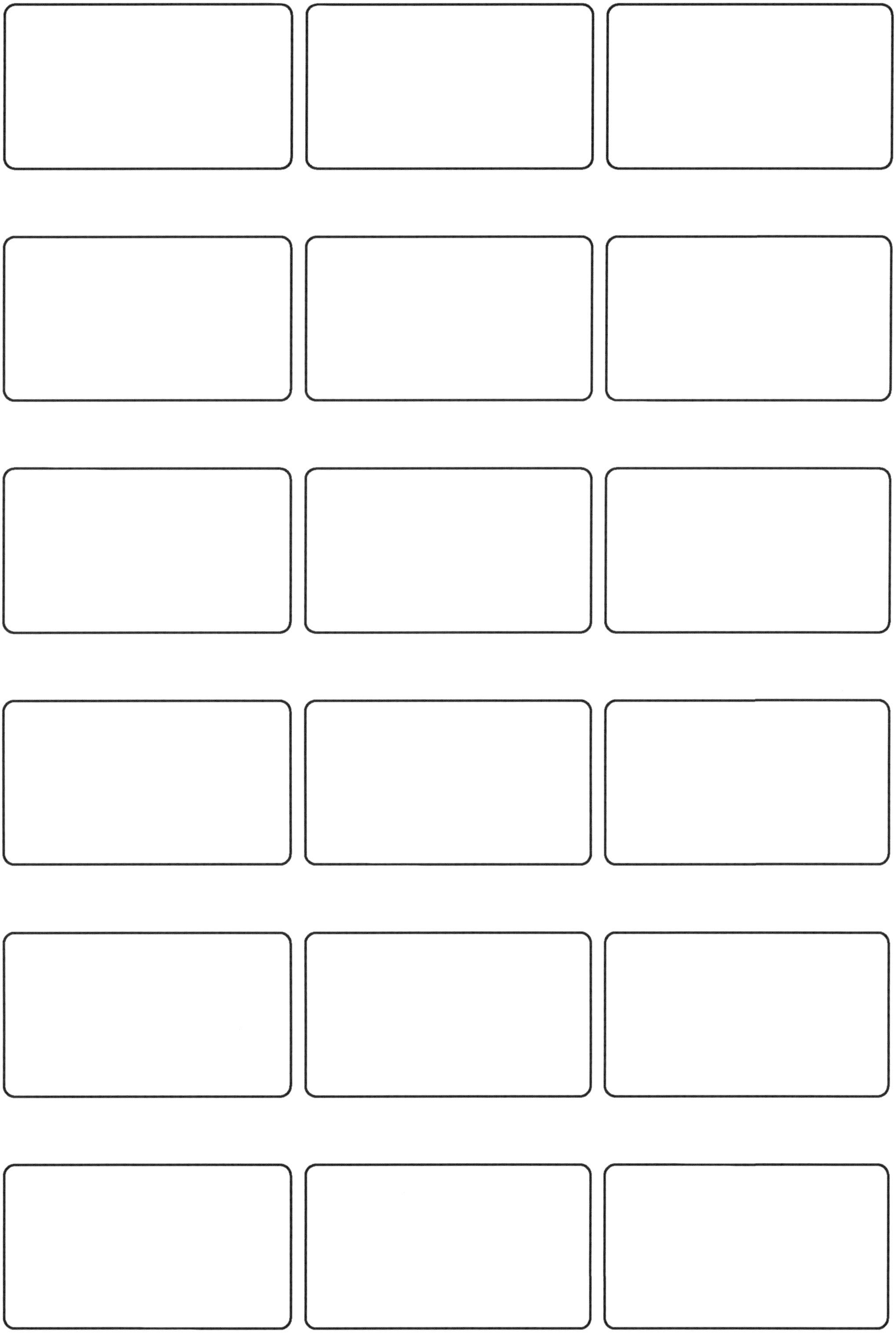

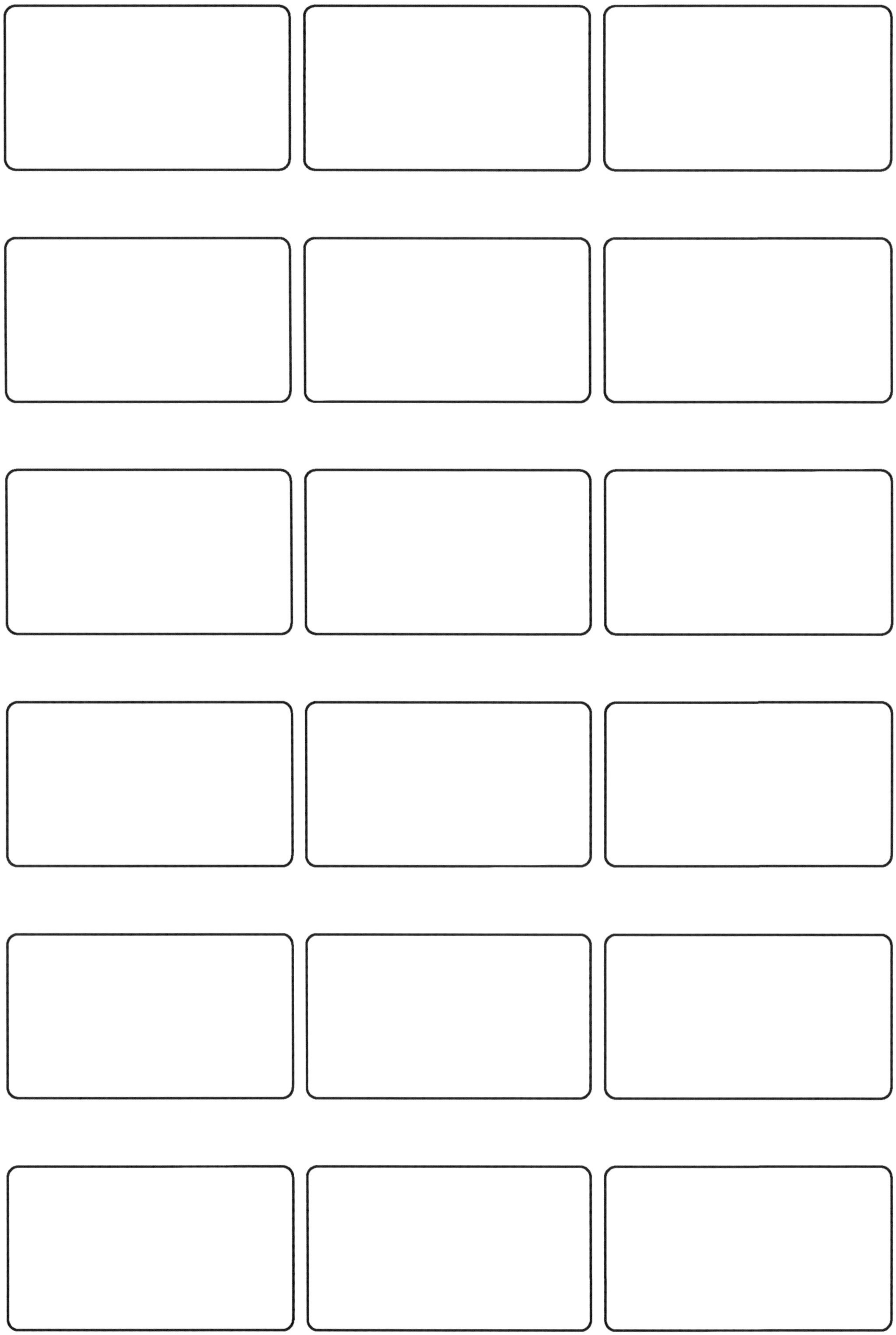

Made in United States
Orlando, FL
17 June 2022

18904914R00067